Quality in Student Financial Aid Programs

A New Approach

RONALD S. FECSO, *Editor*

Panel on Quality Improvement
in Student Financial Aid Programs

BENJAMIN F. KING, *Chair*

Committee on National Statistics
Commission on Behavioral and Social Sciences and Education
National Research Council

NATIONAL ACADEMY PRESS
Washington, D.C. 1993

NATIONAL ACADEMY PRESS • 2101 Constitution Ave., N.W. • Washington, D.C. 20418

NOTICE: The project that is the subject of this report was approved by the Governing Board of the National Research Council, whose members are drawn from the councils of the National Academy of Sciences, the National Academy of Engineering, and the Institute of Medicine. The members of the committee responsible for the report were chosen for their special competences and with regard for appropriate balance.

This report has been reviewed by a group other than the authors according to procedures approved by a Report Review Committee consisting of members of the National Academy of Sciences, the National Academy of Engineering, and the Institute of Medicine.

The National Academy of Sciences is a private, nonprofit, self-perpetuating society of distinguished scholars engaged in scientific and engineering research, dedicated to the furtherance of science and technology and to their use for the general welfare. Upon the authority of the charter granted to it by the Congress in 1863, the Academy has a mandate that requires it to advise the federal government on scientific and technical matters. Dr. Bruce M. Alberts is president of the National Academy of Sciences.

The National Academy of Engineering was established in 1964, under the charter of the National Academy of Sciences, as a parallel organization of outstanding engineers. It is autonomous in its administration and in the selection of its members, sharing with the National Academy of Sciences the responsibility for advising the federal government. The National Academy of Engineering also sponsors engineering programs aimed at meeting national needs, encourages education and research, and recognizes the superior achievements of engineers. Dr. Robert M. White is president of the National Academy of Engineering.

The Institute of Medicine was established in 1970 by the National Academy of Sciences to secure the services of eminent members of appropriate professions in the examination of policy matters pertaining to the health of the public. The Institute acts under the responsibility given to the National Academy of Sciences by its congressional charter to be an adviser to the federal government and, upon its own initiative, to identify issues of medical care, research, and education. Dr. Kenneth I. Shine is president of the Institute of Medicine.

The National Research Council was organized by the National Academy of Sciences in 1916 to associate the broad community of science and technology with the Academy's purposes of furthering knowledge and advising the federal government. Functioning in accordance with general policies determined by the Academy, the Council has become the principal operating agency of both the National Academy of Sciences and the National Academy of Engineering in providing services to the government, the public, and the scientific and engineering communities. The Council is administered jointly by both Academies and the Institute of Medicine. Dr. Bruce M. Alberts and Dr. Robert M. White are chairman and vice chairman, respectively, of the National Research Council.

The project that is the subject of this report was supported by the U.S. Department of Education under contract number LC90051001/C.

Library of Congress Catalog Card No. 93-84866
International Standard Book Number 0-309-04877-X

Additional copies of this report are available from: National Academy Press, 2101 Constitution Avenue, N.W., Box 285, Washington, D.C. 20055. Call 800-624-6242 or 202-334-3313 (in the Washington Metropolitan Area).

B133

Printed in the United States of America

PANEL ON QUALITY IMPROVEMENT IN STUDENT FINANCIAL AID PROGRAMS

BENJAMIN F. KING (*Chair*), College of Business, Florida Atlantic University
THOMAS J. BOARDMAN, Department of Statistics, Colorado State University
*JERRY S. DAVIS, Pennsylvania Higher Education Assistance Agency, Harrisburg, Pennsylvania
NATALA K. HART, Office of Scholarships and Financial Aid, Indiana University-Purdue University at Indianapolis
WILLIAM J. HILL, Allied-Signal, Inc., Buffalo, New York
GARY A. LORDEN, Office of Student Affairs, California Institute of Technology
REBECCA A. MAYNARD, Graduate School of Education, University of Pennsylvania
ROBERT E. PARILLA, Office of the President, Montgomery Community College, Rockville, Maryland
THOMAS D. PARKER, The Education Resources Institute, Boston, Massachusetts
S. JAMES PRESS, Department of Statistics, University of California, Riverside
BRIAN ROWAN, School of Education, University of Michigan
JUDITH M. TANUR, Department of Sociology, State University of New York at Stony Brook
SHARON L. THOMAS PARROTT, Governmental Relations, DeVRY, Inc., Oakbrook Terrace, Illinois

RONALD S. FECSO, Study Director
LINDA INGRAM, Research Associate
REBECCA L. HANCOCK, Project Assistant
HELEN LOPEZ, Project Assistant
MELISSA MARSDEN, Project Assistant
SUBRAMANYAM KASALA, Consultant
FREDRICA D. KRAMER, Consultant
MARGARET WEIDENHAMER, Consultant

*Served until May 1992

COMMITTEE ON NATIONAL STATISTICS
1992–1993

Preface

The Panel on Quality Improvement in Student Financial Aid Programs first convened on September 27, 1991. The U.S. Department of Education had asked the National Academy of Sciences to form a panel, under the Committee on National Statistics, to provide guidance in answering the following questions:

1. Given the nature of Title IV programs, what are realistic goals for determining whether the system is performing well or poorly?
2. Does the current system of quality control generate accurate and timely information with which to measure performance? Are all relevant aspects of certification error measured in a fair, accurate, and reliable manner?
3. Does the information generated provide management at all levels with appropriate information with which to target error reduction strategies?
4. Are the reviews, oversight, and incentives currently employed to detect errors sufficient to ensure accountability and effectiveness in program administration?
5. What changes, if any, are needed to reduce errors in program administration without detracting from basic program goals? Where is more information needed about promising alternatives, and how should this information be acquired?

The reader will see that in our response we often make recommendations that call for sweeping revisions of the present system. If this suggests the phrase *reinventing government*, although I can only speak for myself, I think that most of the panel members would be happy to be identified with that movement. While our prescriptions contain quite a heavy dose of *total quality management*, this emphasis is not the result of merely following a current fad. I would describe the individual attitudes toward TQM at our first meeting as running from *a* to *z—apathetic* to *zealous*—perhaps due to the wide diversity of the panelists' backgrounds. There are—in addition to statisticians from both university and industry—school financial aid administrators, policy analysts, college officers, and education finance experts. As the details of the postsecondary student financial aid system and issues of quality were revealed, however, the panel became unanimous in its belief that a TQM approach is appropriate because (1) customer needs were not being adequately met; (2) there should be greater focus on actions that affect fundamental problems with the system rather than overreacting to special instances that are not part of the natural process but are assignable, perhaps, only to specific circumstances; and (3) management must dedicate itself, from the top down, to continuous quality improvement in the system.

The panel met face-to-face 5 times, and those meetings spanned a period of only 13 months—an extremely efficient operation. Panel members performed a great deal of research and legwork between meetings—interviewing participants in the student financial aid process, drafting parts of the report, contributing background notes, and reviewing and editing the work of the staff. They are all to be commended for their outstanding efforts, and I hope that they received as much pleasure from this experience as I did in working with them.

On the panel's behalf, I would like to acknowledge and thank all of the people who assisted us in various ways. We were fortunate to find so many people willing to share their time and expertise. While everyone's input was appreciated, some individuals deserve identification for contributions of exceptional value to our effort.

Thanks go to the staff from financial aid offices at various institutions—Sherwood Johnson at the State University of New York at Stony Brook, David S. Levy at the California Institute of Technology, James Lockwood at Montgomery College, Patricia McWade at Georgetown University, Olga Moas at Florida Atlantic University, Michael O'Grady at George Mason University, and Robin Robinson at American University. Special thanks go to G. Kay Jacks and the staff at Colorado State University for assistance in arranging a very informative meeting with staff from Metropolitan State College, the University of Colorado at Boulder, and the Colorado Institute of Art.

The Department of Education's technical contact for this study, Daniel Goldenberg, was especially helpful. Many staff members from the department gave freely of their time to assist the panel, especially Ernest Becker, Robert Biehl, Stephen Carter, Karen Chauvin, Donald Conner, Victoria Edwards, Brian Fitzgerald, David Goodwin, John Haines, Clarence M. Hicks, Paul Hill, Molly Hockman, Gerald Malitz, Drew Malizio, Maureen A. McLaughlin, Barbara Mroz, former assistant secretary of education Carolyn Reid-Wallace,

Jack C. Reynolds, Jeanne B. Saunders, Angela Torrvella, Anne Tuccillo, Nina Winkler, and Steven Zwillinger.

Other individuals who provided valuable assistance to the panel include Paul Biemer, Maurice O. Brice, Ann Coles, Stephen Dienstfrey, Judith Fernandez, Wayne Gardner, Stanley Johnson, Graham Kalton, Walter L. Kaszuba, Arnold Kling, Anita Lancaster, Dallas Martin, Elizabeth Martin, Geri Mooney, Pedro Saavedra, Joan Sander, Richard Sigman, Monroe G. Sirken, and Jaki Stanley.

Advice from several consultants and the background papers prepared for the panel were highly valued. The panel expresses its thanks to William Adams, Urton Anderson, Mary Batcher, Daniel Carr, Subramanyan Kasala, Fredrica D. Kramer, Leda Kydoniefs, Mark Reiser, Paulette Sewell, Clifton Sutton, Marie van Melis-Wright, and Margaret Weidenhamer.

We wish to thank the members of the Committee on National Statistics whose critical and constructive comments on the draft report were invaluable to the panel. Miron Straf, director of the Committee on National Statistics, and Susanna McFarland, administrative associate, ensured the smooth functioning of our operation. Thanks are also due to Eugenia Grohman, associate director for reports of the Commission on Behavioral and Social Sciences and Education, and to her technical staff for their editorial work.

Special thanks go to the panel staff: Linda Ingram, research associate, and Rebecca Hancock, Helen Lopez, and Melissa Marsden, project assistants. Their dedication to the substantive and administrative details of the project provided a much-needed backdrop to the panel's work.

Finally, I know that the members of the panel enthusiastically join me in thanking Ronald S. Fecso, the project's study director, for his unstinting devotion to this project. Through the Intergovernmental Personnel Act, Ron was "on loan" from the National Agricultural Statistics Service of the U.S. Department of Agriculture, where, as senior research statistician, he serves as an expert on sample surveys and has contributed to the development of quality improvement efforts within that agency. This report would not have materialized if it were not for Ron's diligent efforts in background research and writing. In addition, he is to be especially commended for his ingenuity and skills of persuasion in commissioning the technical papers included in the appendix. We sincerely appreciate the support of the late Charles E. Caudill and his management team at the National Agricultural Statistics Service, who made it possible for Ron to assist us.

Benjamin King, *Chair*
Panel on Quality Improvement in
Student Financial Aid Programs

Contents

Summary of Major Conclusions and Recommendations

Since World War II, the financing of higher education has changed through the expansion of the role of need-based student aid. Scholarships for students who were both meritorious and needy have always been available. The introduction of need-tested aid in the 1950s, however, and the major federal support and regulation of student aid distribution that followed have resulted in what is today a complex aid system.

Postsecondary students can receive financial aid from the federal government, states, postsecondary institutions, other private organizations, or a combination of these sources. Direct aid to students is dominated, however, by federal aid programs (grants, loans, and work-study programs covered by Title IV of the Higher Education Act of 1965). In the academic year 1989-90, total available student aid equaled $27.3 billion, of which generally available federal aid (Title IV programs only) equaled $19.0 billion. Of the students enrolled full-time in postsecondary schools in 1989-90, 57 percent received aid from at least one source, and federal funding went to 44 percent of the students enrolled. The large expenditures and the widespread use of student aid create great uncertainty concerning the adequacy of the system for delivering federal student financial aid.

Especially troublesome for the U.S. Department of Education are the recurring questions about the accuracy with which the share of educational expenses to be borne by the family is determined and the effectiveness of the systems of accountability mandated by federal regulations. To address these questions, the U.S. Department of Education requested that the National Academy of Sciences convene a panel to study quality control in the

Title IV student financial aid programs. In particular, the panel was asked to study (1) the quality control practices employed by the Department of Education to measure the accuracy of awards provided to students and (2) the methods used by program managers, based on this information, to reduce errors. The panel's report goes beyond a simple assessment of quality control, however. It also considers possible use of this information to prevent errors through appropriate corrective actions.

This summary presents the panel's major conclusions and recommendations. Details of the analysis and other suggestions for improvement are provided in subsequent chapters.

"ERROR" IN STUDENT FINANCIAL AID PROGRAMS

Types of Error

A study of the accuracy of awards made during the 1988-89 academic year found that, of the approximately \$15.4 billion in aid distributed, almost 11 percent was awarded in error (Price Waterhouse, 1990). Although inaccuracies are possible in this and other estimates of program error, there is little doubt that the errors, whatever their exact total, are considerable. At each step of the delivery process (applying, determining eligibility, calculating awards, disbursing awards, and monitoring educational progress) errors can be made. Efforts have been focused on detecting errors in examined files and correcting them, but too little has been done to prevent error—changing the procedures that allowed the errors to occur.

Although reducing payment error (defined below) is an important aspect of quality—particularly in programs that disburse public funds—it is only one of many dimensions of quality. Its pervasiveness, however, makes an understanding of payment error prerequisite to an understanding of "quality control" as practiced by the Department of Education.

In principle, two kinds of payment error occur in student financial aid programs: (1) errors of *overpayment* and (2) errors of *underpayment*. Overpayments can be subdivided into (1) excess payments to eligible recipients and (2) all payments to ineligibles. In parallel fashion, underpayments comprise (1) insufficient payments to eligibles and (2) the lack of payments to those mistakenly classified as ineligible.

Errors can be further classified as *substantive* or *technical*. Errors in the information used to determine eligibility for student financial aid as well as errors made in the calculation of the award based on that information are called substantive errors. Technical errors occur when a legally required document is missing from a student's file. Depending on other factors, inclusion of the document may or may not have rendered the student eligible. The lack of such a document makes the student categorically ineligible for financial aid. Examples of technical errors include failure to document satisfactory educational progress, failure to indicate registration for Selective Service, failure to include a statement of educational purpose, and failure to include a financial aid transcript.

A third distinction deals with the originating source of the error—whether it is the institution, data processing contractor, or the student. The three sources of error are the primary focus of quality control efforts.

Student Error

Student error may occur because of failure to use correct data, inaccuracies in forecasting data, and/or complexities of the application and instructions. For errors that are not made deliberately, several "student errors" could not be corrected even with additional care on the part of the applicant. For example, some problems arise because, to apply for aid from some states and institutions, the application must be completed before the applicant completes his or her federal income tax form. Thus, information provided on dependency status, taxes, and adjusted gross income is generally an estimate of the data that will be reported in the tax return. Similarly, household size and the number of dependents in postsecondary school are necessarily projections for the following academic year; as circumstances change from current plans, this information will turn out to have been "in error." The panel recommends simplifying the application procedure to include fewer items subject to error.

> *Recommendation 5-1: For applicants who have filed a tax return in either of the prior two tax years, the information used to complete the application and determine the award should be based on the most recently filed of these income tax returns. When the earlier tax year is used, updated information should be required as soon as a new tax return is filed. The updated information should not be used to change the award before the next term. Further, "household size" and "number in postsecondary school" should be based on the situation as of the application date.*

Institutional Error

Institutional errors occur when institutions inaccurately process applications or do not adhere to established guidelines. The panel found that technical errors, such as a missing statement of educational purpose or financial aid transcript, have a large dollar impact on measured error, since their absence renders the entire award erroneous. Such cases may or may not otherwise be eligible for financial aid. The General Accounting Office

(GAO) requested from the Department of Education that some student files be analyzed for substantive errors only (technical errors due to missing documentation were to be ignored). The analysis found that the estimated dollar value of errors dropped by about a third, and the percentage of cases with "institutional error" dropped by half (General Accounting Office, 1985). The panel believes that there is a need to refocus the effort used to detect technical errors.

Recommendation 5-2: The Department of Education should determine which, if any, of the administrative requirements that can lead to "technical error" are useful surrogates for variables that deal directly with program goals but are difficult to measure. Administrative requirements that are useful in this sense should be retained, but others should be eliminated.

Failure to Estimate Error Leading to Nonawards

According to the Department of Education's data for the 1982-83 academic year, 42 percent of Title IV aid recipients received overawards and 21 percent received underawards. Typically, overaward has been estimated as much larger than underaward whenever such a classification is made. There is, however, a serious defect in all the major studies of error in student financial aid programs. The various surveys analyze *only cases of awards; there is no coverage of students to whom financial aid was totally denied.* It is thus not surprising that the studies find more overpayment error than underpayment error. On a more basic level, a major concern of the panel is an underemphasis by the department on measuring progress toward the program goals of access and choice in postsecondary education. Potential recipients mistakenly denied financial aid despite actual eligibility surely have restricted access and choice.

Recommendation 5-5: The Department of Education should improve estimates of "error" by including estimates of the coverage of student financial aid programs, that is, ascertaining the frequency with which eligible applicants are mistakenly denied financial aid and the underaward amounts associated therewith.

CURRENT QUALITY CONTROL PROCEDURES

The Department of Education's current quality control process is described as focusing on prevention, inspection, and oversight. *Prevention* activities include training provided by the department to data entry contractors, financial aid administrators, and other institutional officers, lenders, accrediting agencies, state scholarship and guaranty agencies, and others in the student financial aid community. Other activities that are carried out in an effort to prevent award error entail editing and verifying student data.

Inspection consists of after-the-fact monitoring activities—audits and program reviews. Such activities are often developed in the belief that they help to ensure compliance because the possibility of penalties and/or sanctions acts as a deterrent.

Oversight consists of periodic studies of various program areas within the Department of Education. The studies are conducted by the department's Office of Inspector General or the GAO and focus on review of procedures for monitoring compliance with various requirements and the management of those activities. The panel found information in the various studies to be very useful in its deliberations.

Edits and Verification of Applicant Data

Applicant-supplied data undergo several levels of editing and review. First, edits are performed by data entry contractors. During the edits, questionable data are identified and "highlighted" on the Student Aid Report (SAR) that is mailed to the student. The student is asked to review and correct all data and, if corrected, return the SAR for reprocessing.

Verification of applicant-reported data items by the institution is the Department of Education's primary tool in its efforts to control applicant error. Verification activities place a major responsibility and burden upon the schools and, as a result, are very controversial. Each school is required to verify key elements of the applicant's record for all records flagged by the department's selection methodology (in recent years, up to 30 percent of an institution's student aid applications, but the 1992 reauthorization of the Higher Education Act allows the Secretary of Education to mandate up to 100 percent verification). The department describes the current verification system as an attempt to strike a balance between error reduction and the burden imposed on institutions. Efforts to move toward 100 percent verification of applicant data have been tempered by institutional lobbying to stress the excessive burden that institutions must endure to correct errors not of their making.

Applicant records are selected for verification through a complex sequence of statistical procedures intended to target the most error-prone applicants. The verification system has been studied and modified over the years, but an extensive review by the panel yielded no evidence that major advances have been made in responding to the major criticisms of the system. The cost-benefit of the system remains a question.

Although some cases of fraud or abuse undoubtedly will arise in a program of this size, previous studies have not uncovered any widespread problems of fraud by students. The panel recognizes that the Department of

Education believes verification is necessary to fulfill its congressional mandate, yet the panel concludes that the verification process as currently used is unfairly burdensome for the overwhelming majority of well-intentioned people working within the system. In using any other technique, the emphasis should be to move from the current focus on catching mistakes to also providing information for future preventive actions.

Recommendation 4-1: A research effort should be initiated to assist the Department of Education's contractor in developing better criteria for selecting records to be verified and, more important, identifying opportunities for earlier removal of errors through instructions, form improvements, and SAR highlighting strategies. Current and future changes to the verification selection methodology should be carefully documented.

Audits and Program Reviews

The Department of Education has the responsibility to ensure that the approximately 8,000 participating postsecondary institutions administer student financial aid programs in compliance with federal law and regulations. The department executes this responsibility through two major retrospective activities: (1) requiring schools to contract for compliance audits by an independent auditor and (2) conducting program reviews through its regional offices.

The Title IV student financial assistance audit and program review processes are designed to determine the accuracy with which an institution administers its student financial aid programs. Specifically, the Title IV audit objectives are to measure the reliability of an institution's financial data, the adequacy of its internal control systems, and its compliance with program regulations. The objectives of a program review of an institution are to determine compliance with program regulations and to evaluate financial and administrative capabilities. The panel examined the operations of these retrospective activities as they relate to the problem of error in the delivery of student financial aid.

The rules and regulations governing student eligibility for financial aid are complex. The panel questioned whether and, if so, to what extent the complexities themselves are significant sources of error. The current monitoring and compliance activities and data bases do not address this issue. They are designed to assess an institution's absolute performance with respect to the accurate administration of student financial aid programs, to count the occurrences of error, and to impose sanctions on the institution based on error.

The audit and program review processes used by the Department of Education to enforce quality standards are marked by considerable duplication, ineffectiveness, and wasted effort. The independent audit of schools checks for internal controls and compliance with program regulations in a way that essentially duplicates parts of the program review process. Such checks are more effectively performed by knowledgeable reviewers and should be fully incorporated within the program review process.

Inspection is a deterrent to poor work only when it is possible to do a better job. To maximize an institution's potential, the audit and review processes must be better integrated and redesigned so as to have a sharper focus on addressing meaningful measures of quality and quality improvement rather than the current concept of measuring compliance with an unrealistic "zero defect" standard. To expend resources where risk is greatest, for example, data from past audits and reviews should be used to improve the methods for selecting institutions and the methods for sampling records at those institutions.

Audit and review activities are necessary if the Department of Education is to fulfill its responsibility to ensure that program participation is limited to those institutions that are willing and able to operate responsibly, in accordance with program goals and expectations. Since factors such as changing economic conditions and student financial aid personnel affect an institution's ability to maintain desired levels of quality, "problem" institutions will appear sporadically and must be dealt with promptly and efficiently. Audits provide reasonable promptness, especially now that they are an annual requirement. Program reviews are relatively infrequent, however, because they must be performed under departmental budgetary and personnel ceilings. Yet, the review process has the greater potential to be proactive and to provide the useful instruction and technical assistance that promote quality and help to build a sense of partnership between the institutions and the department.

Further, the match between the capabilities of the inspector and the inspection function warrants careful attention. More information is needed about the reliability of independent auditor findings. While the audit function can provide timely information, program review is the only system of institutional quality checks that is entirely in the control of the Department of Education. The panel believes that program reviews have the greatest potential for reliability and objectivity. The panel also believes that the department needs to revamp the audit and program review systems in order to support the gate-keeping function, provide technical assistance to institutions, and provide useful data to policymakers.

Recommendation 4-3: The Department of Education should redesign the current system of program reviews and independent audits. Program reviews should focus on compliance as part of an overall quality improvement program. Checks on institutional compliance and internal controls should be performed only in program reviews and audits should focus only on financial attestation.

The Department of Education should also develop, test, and implement methods to systematize and standardize the program review process. The department should not interpret the 1992 reauthorization of the Higher Education Act as a requirement to review every school according to a fixed schedule. Risk-based statistical methods should be used to identify problem schools for more frequent reviews, and other schools should be selected randomly at a nominal rate that would fulfill the necessary "gate-keeping" functions. The department must improve the evaluative feedback and technical assistance provided to institutions during reviews. At the same time, the review should be used to accumulate data that provide the department with a continuous overview of error rates, compliance levels, and other information of significance for management in making policy.

THE APPLICANT'S VIEW

As the ultimate customer of financial aid services and as the provider of the information that puts the overwhelming inspection processes into motion, the applicant's or potential applicant's experience must weigh heavily in decisions concerning process improvement. The panel focused on two areas of importance related to the applicant's need for quality: early awareness and the application process.

Early Awareness

Very few ongoing data sets are available from which to obtain information about students who have not applied for financial aid. The Department of Education maintains administrative records on only those students applying for financial aid, and studies of error have captured data on aid recipients only. Better use of the National Postsecondary Student Aid Study and coordination with the National Center for Education Statistics could help.

Recommendation 5-7: The panel commends the Department of Education for its recent efforts to improve early awareness of federal financial aid programs, such as providing financial aid software to high schools. The panel recommends increasing those efforts. Studies of the effectiveness of the efforts and users' reactions to the timeliness, accuracy, usefulness, and clarity of outreach and counseling services are needed.

Recommendation 5-8: The Department of Education should gather data on the reasons for nonutilization of student financial aid by potential recipients. Consideration should be given to ways of estimating the number of potentially qualified applicants who are discouraged for one reason or another from applying for financial aid in the first place. Further, the department should consider ways of estimating the number of potential students who do not even attempt to enter a postsecondary school because of their ignorance of available financial aid. Also, data on the knowledge of aid should be collected from students and their families before the student finishes secondary school. Such data could be obtained in a variety of ways, including ongoing national surveys. The resulting information will be important in devising a program for reaching those who are eligible but do not apply.

The Application Process

Students who wish to apply for federal student financial aid can make application in one of three ways: complete the Application for Student Financial Aid (AFSA) produced and distributed by the Department of Education; complete an application form produced by one of the multiple data entry contractors who process applications; or enter application data through the Electronic Data Exchange application process. Panel members were concerned that the current design of these application "forms" could cause confusion among applicants and financial aid officers, lead to inadvertent errors in financial aid decisions, and deter some students from applying at all. Such up-front errors could then lead the department to perceive a need for more inspection. Testimony before the panel, as well as the panel's own deliberations, suggest that the application forms for student financial aid might be difficult to complete, especially for the typical lower income applicant, and that the design of the form might complicate the work of student financial aid officers who advise students about financial aid, check the accuracy of applicants' responses on applications forms, and attempt to correct erroneous data. As a result, the panel undertook a study of the federally produced AFSA and the Electronic Data Exchange process. Based on that analysis, the panel makes two recommendations:

Recommendation 5-9: The complexity of the forms, instructions, and information booklets leads to excessive burden for applicants and is a cause of error. Thus, the Department of Education should consult experts in form and question development, such as those found at cognitive research laboratories, to aid in its efforts to improve the application materials.

Recommendation 5-10: The Department of Education should continue to improve and expand the availability of its electronic data exchanges, making sure to address the issue of appropriate balance between the potential for improved data and additional burdens that might be placed on the schools.

CONCERNS OF POSTSECONDARY INSTITUTIONS

Postsecondary institutions are increasingly burdened by the administrative complexities associated with federal student aid programs. From an original promise to administer the eligibility requirements centrally, the government has moved to an increasingly complex financial statement form, which must be verified by school personnel. The addition of information unrelated to need, such as Selective Service status, is collected through this form, which has grown from two pages to four.

The Department of Education requires institutions to collect signed statements regarding nonuse of illegal drugs and educational purpose, but the certification is not of direct use to the institution because it neither prevents drug use nor ensures that the student has a valid educational purpose. Under the current system, institutions bear a considerable amount of the burden in obtaining this type of certification. In addition, hard copies of applications and related "underwriting" materials must be physically retained by the institution for long periods of time, which creates the need for expensive warehousing in financial aid offices. There is, however, no reason why the depository cannot be changed so that the department can take on an equitable amount of responsibility.

Congress has made some progress in initiating changes along these lines. The 1992 reauthorization of the Higher Education Act calls for increased utilization of verification mechanisms in which students' reported information can be verified through record matching, by using either an automated or other system. These provisions include requiring that data base matches with the Selective Service be made and that the Social Security Number of all aid recipients be verified. With this advancement toward electronic data transfer of student financial aid information, the burden imposed by the collection of student certifications could be greatly reduced.

Recommendation 5-11: The Department of Education should increase its efforts to remove unnecessary burden from students and institutions by further development of automated data matches whenever possible.

A VISION FOR A TOTAL QUALITY APPROACH

Many industrial and service sector organizations have recognized that a system based on prevention of errors rather than inspection is necessary to achieve quality improvement and efficient operation. Such systems utilize a *total quality approach.* A total quality approach requires a commitment by the highest levels of management to lead quality improvement efforts rather than merely assigning responsibility for quality assurance to an organizational unit. It also requires a focus on the "customer" and having suppliers and customers work together to define and solve problems. It requires process simplification to reduce waste, remove redundant efforts, and eliminate time-consuming and non-value-adding steps. It requires data collection and analysis that are designed for fact-based decision making and problem solving.

These strategies are as valid in the Department of Education and other governmental agencies as they are in private industry. A total quality approach to administering student financial aid would seek not only to improve action taken at each step of the process, but also seek to continuously improve important outcomes expected of the entire process, such as accuracy of awards and accessibility of aid for eligible students. Additionally, a total quality approach seeks improvements that may eliminate mistakes before they are made and that strives to lower costs, provide faster processing, and reduce red tape. Such an approach brings greater value to all the customers and stakeholders—the Department of Education, Congress, postsecondary institutions, students, parents, and taxpayers.

A NEW STRATEGY FOR THE DEPARTMENT OF EDUCATION

The Department of Education's old strategies for ensuring quality are characterized by a centralization of authority, reliance on after-the-fact inspections to bring about quality, and burdensome sets of frequently changed regulations that focus on compliance with process requirements. Under the old strategies, the student financial aid delivery system is burdened with a multiplicity of process checkpoints that add to the cost of running the system for schools and for the government. They also contribute to a tendency for the relationship between customers and suppliers in the system to be perceived as confrontational. The deficiencies of these strategies have led some within the department to seek new strategies.

One of the difficulties in developing new strategies to improve quality is conceptual. In the absence of a statutory definition of quality, regulatory efforts fall into the trap of having no margin for error. As reported to the panel, the Department of Education has been operating with a "zero error" standard that is unattainable in practice and therefore not effective in promoting quality improvements. Departmental staff reported to the panel on efforts to develop new strategies that are characterized by delegation of authority and responsibility, the "ownership" of performance measures by those who are performing the functions of the system, and a deregulation of the aid delivery process that empowers an institution to determine how best to accomplish program objectives. The new strategies, as found in the Institutional Quality Control (IQC) Pilot Project, focus accountability on results rather than process and emphasize at participating institutions the continuous collection of data leading to quality improvement. Foregoing the usual imposition of external quotas, these strategies are intended to form proactive partnerships rather than confrontational relationships and to focus on service improvements for the end customers. At the same time, they are intended to meet the need to assess overall system performance by measuring quality on an ongoing basis. With this experiment, the Department of Education hopes to reduce the burden on educational institutions, encourage the development of innovative management approaches, improve service to students, and reduce error in the delivery of Title IV financial assistance.

Support of the IQC Project

Participation in the IQC Pilot Project is voluntary and assumes that the commitment to ensure data quality already exists in participating schools. The Department of Education has many positive activities associated with efforts to support IQC institutions, including training programs for new and continuing institutions, providing quality control software, recognition and awards processes, publishing a newsletter, state and regional meetings, and providing technical assistance from departmental and contracted personnel. The IQC staff within the department is continually updating its support mechanisms to be able to offer more help to the institutions.

The panel examined the IQC project at great length and gave much consideration to its future. The panel had many questions about the effectiveness of the project, but too little objective data to answer most of them. The IQC project offers a chance for the Department of Education to be more proactive, but it may not be making the best use of the chance.

Possibly, the IQC process is overwhelming. Perhaps the institutions need more advice on the quantitative aspects of the process. Many institutions will have someone outside the institution's aid office who is fairly knowledgeable about such quantitative methods and could learn more about the aid process as he or she goes along. Other institutions may have to ask for outside help. Statistical expertise also needs to be developed at the Department of Education to generate the appropriate statistical information from the IQC institutions and share the aggregate results with everyone.

Recommendation 8-3: Institutions in the IQC pilot program should have more at-hand statistical support, and institutions volunteering to participate in IQC activities should be required to show access to statistical expertise in sampling and data analysis as a condition of being in the program. To some extent this can be accomplished by improving the training of internal staff. Adding training material on basic statistical skills to the training program could help, but more effective strategies might include subsidizing locally obtained coursework for financial aid office staff or developing cooperative agreements with local quantitative departments to provide ongoing assistance. The Department of Education should assist the IQC institutions in these efforts by helping develop the cooperative ties and providing monetary support.

Recommendation 8-4: The IQC program should be retained and given the support of top management. However, when the common-cause regulatory burdens imposed by audits and reviews are eliminated (for details see Chapters 4 and 5), the incentives to join the pilot project will change. Thus, the following improvements should be considered:

- *Incentives for institutions to join the IQC should be reexamined with the aim of encouraging schools with known administrative difficulties to seek help from Department of Education staff.*
- *The department's measure of success in the IQC program should be reexamined with the aim of going beyond measuring retention in the IQC program to identifying ways to improve processes.*
- *More use should be made of IQC data. For example, the Department of Education should inform all institutions about the progress of the IQC program and suggest use of measurements and practices found to be successful in addressing specific concerns about quality.*

FURTHER INITIATIVES FOR IMPROVEMENT IN THE SYSTEM

In its review of the issues related to quality in the delivery of student financial aid, the panel has endorsed a customer-oriented focus that is consistent with a mission of supporting the educational needs of the student applicant while making the most efficient use possible of taxpayer dollars. A customer service philosophy must embrace all of the internal customers of the system: the students, the postsecondary educational institutions, the lenders, guaranty agencies, the various relevant units within the Department of Education, and the Congress. The 1992 reauthorization of the Higher Education Act, which occurred as the panel was engaged in its deliberations, is a step in the right direction. One of its main goals is to simplify student aid programs. As a result of the passage of the bill, some of the concerns already expressed in this report concerning the complexity of the application and its effect on student error have been reduced or even eliminated.

Part H of the reauthorization bill focuses on the strengthening of the process by which institutions of higher education are allowed to participate in federal student aid programs through state licensure, accreditation, and federal eligibility, certification, and program review processes. The panel hopes that enactment of this section will lead to the development of performance-based statutes that avoid affixing common-cause solutions to special-case events and that aim at achieving measurable and meaningful outcomes rather than additional layers of bureaucracy. Examples of meaningful outcomes would include lower default rates and higher graduation rates, employment rates, and customer satisfaction.

Toward a New Applicant Processing System

The panel strongly believes that there is a need to change the current institutional verification process, which is fundamentally redundant and inefficient. The panel suggests that the Department of Education use the knowledge it has at hand in much of the contract research that has addressed verification. Those reports have indicated that (1) large errors remain even after verification, (2) the cause of much of "student error" lies in the complicated application process, and (3) data items that must be *forecast* (e.g., estimated income, household size, and number in college) are the main contributors to student error. The reports have produced little evidence that the institutions themselves can develop procedures that will further reduce student error very much. True corrective actions lie mainly in the hands of the Department of Education and the Congress.

The Department of Education must move from a system that focuses on detecting errors after awards have been made to a system that prevents error to the extent possible. Some error could be removed by making the application materials more user friendly, but additional action is needed. A combination of changes to some data requirements and changes in the activities associated with the SAR and verification could result in large reductions in errors. For example, the panel believes that the department should develop a front-end match of applicant data with Internal Revenue Service (IRS) data tapes. Such matches are being performed at several agencies and are reportedly very successful. (The panel recognizes that the department will likely need the help of Congress to pass legislation directing IRS to allow these matches and to make some changes in data requirements.) The department must take actions that affect the system in order to reduce "student error" appreciably and not impose further requirements on the institution in the verification and compliance-review procedures.

Recommendation 9-1: The Department of Education and the Congress should work together to effectuate changes in data requirements that should simplify award determination and increase accuracy. Development of a system that requires applicant data to be matched with IRS data should receive top priority.

Centralized Verification

The panel believes that a system based on centralized verification will, in the long run, simplify the verification process and increase accuracy. Institutional burden will be removed if the signed statements of educational purpose, Selective Service compliance, and the like, are required as part of the initial application. This change would also remove considerable burden from the institution and from the Department of Education's audit and review activities. Similarly, data base matching with other agencies as directed by Congress in Title IV legislation should be used to the fullest extent possible. Federal concerns internal to the department, such as loan repayment problems and prior aid received, as measured by the financial aid transcript, should be identified from the department's own records. Here too, Congress has instructed the department through Title IV legislation to improve its internal data bases.

The remaining major sources of institutional error (cost of attendance computation, enrollment monitoring, special situation exception determinations, bachelor's degree determination, and aid packaging) are associated with information and actions most easily found at the school. With the reduction of other unnecessary activities, the Department of Education and the schools could concentrate on developing effective methods to reduce errors in these activities. Freed of trivial inspection activities, the institutions and the department should have more time to focus on important issues of quality, such as effectiveness of educational programs, institutional integrity, and the value of the service purchased by the student and taxpayer.

With data base matches and up-front certifications, many of the underlying causes of student error would be removed. Thus, the verification strategy should change. Rather than flagging the record for institutional action during verification, the SAR could request corrections or clarifying information when there are conflicts with data base information. These changes could be processed centrally, which would result in an initial award determination that would be considerably more accurate than is produced under the current procedures. It is possible that a small group of applications might require assignment to institutions for further examination to resolve special situations that might otherwise delay the determination of award.

While up-front data processing costs might increase under this proposal, the Department of Education should consider total cost and service improvement in making decisions on implementation. Repeated processing of SARs would likely decrease. Financial aid administrators would be freed of burden, allowing them to spend more time on cases requiring special attention. Awards might be determined sooner, a service improvement for applicants. Consistency of verification and documentation would also be better controlled. Finally, award error would be controlled on all applications, not just those selected for verification, as is now the case.

Recommendation 9-2: The Department of Education should begin the development of a front-end and centralized verification system in which the schools' verification burden is drastically reduced. Under a new system, the department would identify exceptional cases, far fewer than the current 30 percent, for institutional review activities.

Organizing Information About the System

The Department of Education also asked the panel to comment on the organization of available information about award error and the usefulness of such data bases for making program decisions. In a similar investigation, the General Accounting Office (1985) found the department's approach to issues regarding the quality of awards to be unsystematic. That study found that decisions that might affect improvement were hindered by a lack of goals and analyses that were hurried due to operational demands. The study cited problems in coordinating offices within the department that needed to work together and labeled the resultant reactive decision making "remedial" and "not preventive."

Recommendation 5-6: The Department of Education should not routinely embark on surveys of the type that have been used in the past to estimate total error levels in student financial aid programs. The resources are likely to be better spent on continuous monitoring—using data from audit and review activities, for example—and other approaches to quality improvement. Special studies should be done, but only when the study objectives are clearly linked to a policy evaluation or process improvement plan and steps can be taken to eliminate the methodological defects of past surveys.

The panel, after discussions with Department of Education personnel and review of earlier studies, also found no particularly well-organized use of the data that focused on improving the quality of award decisions. It is evident that operational demands continue to limit proactive thinking. Attempts to bring the parts of the department together to work on cross-organizational issues are being made, but comments to the panel indicate that there is no strong management direction in these areas.

Recommendation 6-1: The panel believes that a totally integrated applicant data base is essential for problem identification, the development of solutions, and monitoring progress—important activities if true quality improvements are to take place. The data base would compile information from all the Title IV aid programs and across years to provide, for each applicant, a complete history of participation in the financial aid system, thus facilitating a broad range of cross-sectional and longitudinal statistical analyses. The Department of Education should allocate sufficient resources and personnel to accomplish this task without further delay.

Top Management Leadership

Despite the genuine movement toward quality improvement that the 1992 reauthorization will bring about, there is much more in that direction to be accomplished. For example, a major detriment to sustaining the desired focus on quality is a lack of stability in leadership positions that influence student financial aid programs. Changing leadership may cause inconsistency in long-term vision. Frequent turnover in the position of Assistant Secretary for Postsecondary Education, a major reorganization of the Office of Postsecondary Education, and a number of shifts in line management assignments are examples of the shifting leadership at the Department of Education. While, in themselves, these changes may not be bad, and some might be necessary, the panel sensed that the long-term vision for quality in student financial aid programs often suffered as a result of frequent turnover.

The panel found that while the Department of Education required schools to invest heavily in quality *inspection* activities, it allocated limited resources for its own quality *improvement* activities. Further, the panel noted either inadequacies in the information technology available to the Department of Education or the lack of use of available information by the department in almost all the areas studied in this review.

Recommendation 9-3: To signal top management's commitment to a Total Quality approach at the Department of Education, the department should initiate a Total Quality training program that starts with the leadership group and rapidly includes everyone in the department. In this way the fundamentals, vocabulary, and principles of Total Quality will be integrated into the department. Corporations have found this to be a critical first step in implementing quality improvement. Such a training effort should include leadership's role in the commitment to change, process-improvement and problem-solving methods, Total Quality tools, focus on customer satisfaction and its measurement, teamwork, and quality planning/deployment.

Recommendation 9-4: In its review of survey activities, verification procedures, and management information systems, the panel was disappointed to find a paucity of statistically trained personnel available to the student financial aid programs to analyze data and to interact with contractors. The Department of Education should develop a much greater in-house statistical capability to manage contracts that demand high levels of statistical expertise, and the data developed by contractors should be thoroughly documented and made available for in-house analysis. The department should also strengthen the analytic capabilities of its entire work force, including those who will not be expected to attain the level of statistical "expert" but yet should be skilled in handling and interpreting data. Specifically, the department should perform a needs analysis of statistical and computer literacy. Then it should develop training programs to improve abilities and purchase the hardware required to carry out the necessary analytic tasks.

The panel recognizes that technical improvement cannot begin without some initial funding targeted toward efforts such as pilot projects, data base improvement, and hiring staff with appropriate skills to help in these efforts. Thus, the panel requests that Congress take action to help make this possible.

Recommendation 9-5: Congress should ensure that there is adequate funding and staffing to develop the quantitative information needed to manage and review the student financial aid programs effectively.

The panel found an absence of performance measures linked to long-term planning. Setting long-term plans that transcend leadership changes is important. To make sound decisions on necessary changes to the programs, a new top management team must gain experience and familiarity with the system and its processes. A thorough understanding of a system as complex as the student financial aid programs takes time.

Recommendation 9-6: To ensure the development of and commitment to long-term planning, the politically appointed position in charge of the student financial aid programs (the assistant secretary for postsecondary education) should have a fixed (commonly five-year) term.

PART I

Background

Every child must be encouraged to get as much education as he has the ability to take. We want this not only for his sake—but for the nation's sake. Nothing matters more to the future of our country, not military preparedness—for armed might is worthless if we lack the brain power to build a world of peace; not our productive economy—for we cannot sustain growth without trained manpower; not our democratic system of government—for freedom is fragile if citizens are ignorant.

— President Lyndon B. Johnson, when submitting legislation for the Higher Education Act of 1965.

The message is simple and fundamental to American ideals. Its truth is relevant to the past, the present, and the future.

1

Introduction

In a little more than 100 years, the Congress has moved from supporting institutions by building colleges and universities, to ensuring that geographically underserved populations have access to higher education, to supporting students by deciding "to put purchasing power in the hands of needy students and let the students make their own choices in the marketplace of postsecondary education" (Gladieux and Wolanin, 1976).

THE FEDERAL STUDENT FINANCIAL AID SYSTEM

Since World War II, the financing of higher education has changed through the expansion of the role of need-based student aid. Scholarships for students who were both meritorious and needy have always been available, but the introduction of need-tested aid in the 1950s and the major federal support and regulation of student aid that followed have resulted in what is today a complex system of aid. As McPherson and Schapiro (1991) point out, while some see the combined system of need-based aid and operating subsidies as a fundamental part of the higher education financing system, others see an ineffectual and ill-structured system that distorts the incentives of students and educational institutions.

The current system has roots dating to 1965, when the Higher Education Act enacted into law the principle that the federal government should assume an important share of the responsibility for ensuring postsecondary educational opportunities for disadvantaged students. There are many justifications for the federal role. One is that federal funds spent on training and education significantly increase the productive capacity and earning power of citizens and, therefore, tax receipts. Over the past decade, for example, earnings of college-educated males aged 24 to 34 increased by 10 percent, earnings of those with only high school diplomas declined by 9 percent, and those in the work force who did not hold high school diplomas saw their real incomes drop by 12 percent (National Center on Education and the Economy, 1990:20).

Others argue that in a democracy that demands an educated citizenry to function successfully the cost of an uneducated citizenry is greater than the cost of higher education. Some would infer that eventually expenditures on education and training will produce reductions in larger social costs, such as welfare and incarceration. For example, the average U.S. public investment (which includes subsidies for public institutions, state and federal student aid, and tax incentives) in the room, board, and tuition for every American student in higher education was over $8,000 a year in the 1980s. Such expenditures might seem small if, for example, they helped reduce the need to spend the $7,300 provided annually to a mother and two children receiving Aid to Families with Dependent Children (AFDC), housing assistance, food stamps, and energy assistance benefits at 80 percent of poverty level (Edelman, 1987:32-34).

Postsecondary students can receive financial aid from the federal government, states, postsecondary institutions, private organizations, or a combination of these sources. Direct aid to students is dominated, however, by federal aid programs (grants, loans, and employment programs). In the academic year 1989-90, total available student aid equaled $27.3 billion; generally available federal aid equaled $19.0 billion (College Board, 1992:4).[1] Of the full-time undergraduate students enrolled in postsecondary schools in 1989-90, 57 percent received aid from at least one source and 44 percent received federal funding. As indicated in Table 1-1, state, institutional, and other funding went to 20 percent, 23 percent, and 14 percent of enrolled students, respectively.

A fundamental principle guiding federal participation in student aid programs is that the primary responsibility for meeting the postsecondary educational expenses of a student lies with the "family"—the student and, when applicable, his or her spouse or parents should contribute to the student's educational expenses to the degree that they are able. To achieve this objective, the family's financial circumstances should be evaluated in a consistent and fair manner, recognizing that special circumstances may affect a family's ability to contribute to educational expenses.

---

[1] *Total available student aid* includes *specially directed* federal aid, such as Social Security; *generally available* federal aid through Title IV of the Higher Education Act (the programs studied in this report); and institutional and state aid.

TABLE 1-1 Percent of full-time undergraduate students receiving aid by sources of aid and by type and control of institution: 1989-90

Student/Institution Type	Any[a] aid	Federal aid	State aid	Institution aid	Other aid
	Undergraduate Students				
Total	57.2	43.5	19.8	22.5	13.5
All Public	47.8	34.5	18.3	15.3	11.7
Public, less than 2-year	51.2	33.3	9.9	7.9	17.0
Public, 2- to 3-year	44.3	31.8	17.0	12.6	12.8
Public, 4-year	49.5	35.9	19.2	17.0	10.9
All Private (not for-profit)	70.4	50.4	29.9	46.2	16.0
Private, less than 2-year	74.4	52.5	25.5	10.4	14.7
Private, 2- to 3-year	66.2	50.1	23.0	28.9	18.2
Private, 4-year	70.6	50.3	30.5	48.6	15.9
All Proprietary	85.7	81.1	10.0	19.6	19.6
Private for-profit, less than 2-year	86.4	82.0	6.9	21.9	21.5
Private for profit, 2-year and above	84.3	79.3	16.4	15.1	15.6
	Standard Errors				
Total	0.9	0.9	0.7	0.6	0.4
All Public	1.0	0.9	0.9	0.6	0.5
Public, less than 2-year	5.3	5.6	2.5	2.0	4.1
Public, 2- to 3-year	2.1	1.9	1.8	1.3	1.1
Public, 4-year	1.1	1.0	1.1	0.7	0.5
All Private	1.2	1.3	1.4	1.4	0.7
Private, less than 2-year	4.2	7.0	6.5	6.0	4.9
Private, 2- to 3-year	4.0	4.1	3.7	3.5	2.5
Private, 4-year	1.3	1.4	1.5	1.5	0.7

NOTE: Due to design changes in NPSAS:90, estimates in this table are not comparable to published estimates from the 1987 NPSAS.

[a]Sources of aid do not add to "any aid" percentage since students often receive aid from more than one source.

SOURCE. National Center for Education Statistics NPSAS:90 Undergraduate Table Generation System

Questions have persisted concerning the adequacy of the delivery system for federal student financial aid. Especially troublesome for the U.S. Department of Education have been the recurring questions about the accuracy of determining the share of educational expenses to be borne by the family and the effectiveness of the systems of accountability mandated by federal regulations.

PURPOSE AND SCOPE OF STUDY

The U.S. Department of Education requested that a panel of experts be convened at the National Academy of Sciences to study the quality control of federal student financial aid programs covered by Title IV of the Higher Education Act of 1965. Specifically, the department was motivated by concerns about the accuracy of payments, both overpayments and underpayments, to students under the various Title IV financial aid programs. A recent study (Price Waterhouse, 1991) found that errors in the determination of financial aid awards were the third most important compliance problem related to the regulation of postsecondary institutions. Payment inaccuracies, if they are widespread or systematic, raise questions about the equity with which federal student aid is distributed and could foster public misconceptions about waste, fraud, and abuse.

In particular, the panel was asked to study (1) the quality control practices employed by the Department of Education to measure the accuracy of awards to students and (2) the methods used by program managers, based on this information, to reduce errors. Thus, the panel's report is about the possible use of quality control information to prevent errors through appropriate corrective actions.

While addressing its charge of examining current quality control methods and procedures, the panel has kept in mind the broader educational objectives of the Higher Education Act. Although the panel found useful suggestions in many of the research reports that it studied, most of the suggestions in those reports are based on the paradigm that major aspects of the delivery and control systems (e.g., school-based verification) would remain essentially unchanged. The panel reviewed the existing systems and proposes several shifts in the paradigm. In reaching its conclusions, the panel was influenced by the recurring nature of several problems in previous studies. The major recurrent themes are the following:

- Making the educational institution responsible for identifying and correcting errors in student-supplied information creates inefficiencies and adversarial relationships.
- Clear evidence is lacking that schools can be regulated into achieving significant reductions in the national rate of payment error.
- The Department of Education's use of regulations that require actions by all participants to solve problems found in only a few is inefficient and unfair.
- Research to guide management of the programs lacks adequate technical guidance.

ORGANIZATION OF THE REPORT

The remainder of Part I describes the new philosophy of continuous improvement, which provides an organizational framework for dealing with such cross-cutting problems as those described above. It also describes Title IV student financial aid programs and the system for distributing the awards.

Part II discusses the outcome of Department of Education activities to control, improve, and monitor the "quality of the award" in the current system. The panel reviews and comments on the controversial processes of verification, audit, and program review, and it makes recommendations for their improvement if the current system is to be maintained. Among the special topics addressed by the panel in Part II are the methodological and statistical integrity of current quality control studies, including the accuracy of estimates of national error rates; a review of the application forms and their instructions; and the potential for risk-based management of audit and review processes.

Part III looks at the larger picture and recommends changes in the system that should more efficiently reduce the recurring problems identified in Part II. The topics addressed include knowledge and experience gained from quality control practices in other federal assistance programs and in service industries; the relationship between information collected and effective strategies to reduce errors; and institutional pilot study activities.

2

Continuous Improvement: The New Quality Management Philosophy

Many industrial and service organizations have recognized that a system based on prevention of errors rather than inspection is necessary to improve quality and operate efficiently. This approach focuses on quality improvement rather than inspection. Corporations in the U.S. (e.g., Motorola, Xerox, and Ritz Carlton) and abroad, notably in Japan, have shown that when a management system correctly implements a quality improvement approach, the results are noteworthy. In some cases, Motorola, for example, the businesses were saved. The value of this approach is exemplified in industry by the Baldridge National Quality Award, given for outstanding achievements in quality improvement. The federal government recognizes the applicability of the approach with the Federal Quality Institute's Quality Improvement Prototype Award and with the Presidential Award for Quality.

Whether the operational term is total quality management, total quality, or continuous improvement, a new philosophy of striving for continuous quality improvement in all aspects of the enterprise pervades the thinking of theorists and practitioners of quality management. Although approaches to implementation vary in the literature, the basic "philosophy" is the same—a set of commonsense actions that should be part of good management. The need to elevate these guidelines to a philosophy has arisen because, although they are rooted in common sense and management theory, they are not fully practiced in most organizations. Key elements include the following:

- Focus on improving quality rather than only measuring it.
- Identify and focus on the customers' needs for a product or service now and in the future.
- Emphasize thinking about the entire system rather than individual operations in the system.
- Make decisions based on data.
- Anticipate and accept change.
- Emphasize nonhierarchical teamwork for decision making and implementation.
- Understand variation in measurements of the process and make a commitment to reduce it.
- Identify and clearly communicate the aims and purpose of the enterprise.
- Foster the above activities through commitment and leadership of top management.

The last of these key elements is crucial. A total quality approach requires a commitment by the highest levels of management to lead quality improvement efforts rather than just assigning responsibility for quality assurance to an organizational unit. Each of the elements of continuous improvement relates to the others. Above all, the philosophy stresses an understanding of the organization and its product as a system of people and components working together toward common purposes. It requires having suppliers and customers work together to define and solve problems. It requires process simplification to reduce waste, remove redundant efforts, and eliminate time-consuming and non-value-adding steps. Further, the philosophy stresses a systematic approach to management, requiring data collection and analysis that are designed for fact-based decision making and problem solving.

These principles are as valid in the Department of Education and other governmental agencies as they are in private industry. The student financial aid delivery system, for example, constitutes a process with suppliers and customers at each step. Early in the process the student is the supplier of information to the department. Later, the department is the supplier of funds to the student. A total quality approach to administering student financial aid seeks continuous improvement in important outcomes of the process, such as the accuracy of the award, customer satisfaction, and accessibility of aid for eligible students. Additionally, a total quality approach seeks improvements that may eliminate mistakes before they are made and strives to lower costs, provide faster processing, and reduce red tape. Such an approach brings greater value to all the customers and stakeholders—the Department of Education, Congress, postsecondary institutions, students, parents, and taxpayers.

This chapter briefly reviews key elements of the quality improvement process. The discussion is not intended as a tutorial on quality management in the student financial aid system, but rather as an introduction to the concepts that the panel found useful in its review of the system.

IMPROVING QUALITY

Leading experts in the movement toward total quality management practices, such as W. Edwards Deming (1986), stress that if an organization focuses on improving quality, costs should ultimately go down and productivity should increase. As quality improves, the negative activities associated with controlling poor quality, such as inspections of work or verification of documents, are less necessary, and that in turn results in less work. As quality improves further, individuals in the organization have time to work on further changes in activities and processes, which results in further improvements, and so on as the cycle of improvement continues.

A continuous improvement approach must be distinguished from a standard of zero defects, according to which any type of defect is unacceptable and every defect must be investigated to the bitter end. Indeed, organizations held to such unattainable levels must spend more of their time on detecting and correcting faulty outputs than on improving systems and processes that cause the failures in the first place. Although zero defects is an admirable goal, it may set standards that are impossible to meet, particularly in the service sector, where the product is often more fluid, complex, and variable. Thus, the process of quality improvement begins with identifying the truly important quality issues and then learning how to find and remove factors that cause poor performance.

IDENTIFYING CUSTOMER NEEDS

To identify appropriate quality issues, it is essential to create a greater focus on the customers—the consumers or users of the product or service—and to seek input from them on issues relating to quality. One task is to identify those many interests. A second is to characterize quality as it is perceived by each of those interests. There are many different ways to assess the different perceptions of quality and the program's effect on customers, from analysis of the overall program to discussions with small groups of consumers. All should be a part of efforts to improve quality.

In the case of student financial aid programs, the focus on customers must include the constituent interests of the Congress, the Department of Education, state and local authorities, the educational institutions, and the students and families that are potential recipients of aid. Those constituents determine who is to be served by the educational institutions and how the mechanics of student financial aid affect who is served, as well as how public monies are to be safeguarded in the distribution of financial aid. Some constituents are most concerned with the breadth of outreach of financial aid, others with liability and financial exposure, others with maldistribution of scarce resources, and others with the immediate mechanics of loan application that affect timeliness and ease of compliance. It would seem most appropriate, however, to focus on students as the primary customers of a student financial aid system. Appendix B provides an example of how another federal agency, the Internal Revenue Service, takes a customer focus.

EMPHASIZING SYSTEMS THINKING

Learning to focus the attention of all activities within an organization on the improvement of services is a significant element of the new philosophy of quality management. Systems are composed of many interconnected processes. Each process has materials, equipment, methods, environment, and people blended in some manner to accomplish some task. Organizations often discover that their systems have complex structures and processes. Flowcharts, a useful tool in developing systems thinking, often reveal that many subprocesses occur before the output of any one process goes on to the next. The interaction between the "supplier" and the "customer" at each subprocess cannot be analyzed in isolation from the larger system. Making changes, even to solve a problem, in one area or subprocess without taking account of how it will affect another may result in unexpected quality reduction in another part of the system and overall poor service. Only by working on changes in relation to the entire system can an organization make fundamental improvements.

Many quality experts believe that at least 85 percent of the problems that exist in systems are attributable to sources other than people—for example, methods, environment, equipment, and materials. Nonetheless, when things go wrong within a process, even if caused by something other than the individuals involved, a person is frequently blamed. Frontline workers should be encouraged to work on quality improvement in their activities, but they cannot be expected to resolve quality problems that are the result of the system. In the case of a system as complex as student financial aid, the Department of Education must take the lead to accomplish many of the system changes that could improve overall quality.

Another fundamental concept in systems thinking is *optimization*. That is, standards, goals, and processes must be established that optimize the capabilities and product of the system as a whole. Organizations often require one department or component to make improvements, cut costs, or otherwise satisfy some goal of another department. Such compliance by one component may come at the expense of fulfilling another of the organization's missions, or at least at the expense of improvements to service for the ultimate customers. In the context of student financial aid, educational institutions may be forced to allocate additional staff to the financial aid office to comply with the Department of Education's quality control requirements or face penalties for poor performance in financial aid management. This may force reductions in other functions or force other departments at the school to offer lesser degrees of service.

Poor communication among parts of the system is also a principal cause of poor service. The student financial aid system poses special problems because of the relationships among federal, state, and private institutions that must be addressed in considering efforts to reform current practices. Problems in communication are to be expected unless all parties make great efforts to solicit inputs and listen to suggestions offered. The panel heard repeatedly of problems in communication between the Department of Education and the educational institutions. As in other organizational contexts, those institutions themselves are likely to have communication problems internally. Efforts to improve communication should be at the top of the list of problems to address in any management improvement effort.

MAKING DATA-BASED DECISIONS

Often decisions in organizations are made on the basis of the strongest voice rather than the most reasoned deliberation. That is, the person with the most persuasive argument or the highest rank wins the right to impose decisions on others. Moreover, quality experts have often found that when data are gathered that might be used in decision making, they are often gathered without a plan concerning how they will be used. The basic purpose of gathering data is to enable people to make better decisions. Further, data should be gathered as part of an ongoing effort to improve management processes.

Fortunately, many organizations are learning that genuine improvements can occur when individuals work together and make decisions using sound empirical information. This approach requires more sophisticated methods of data collection, measurement, and interpretation than are typically found in long-standing management structures. Generating and using information effectively require a rigorous system of planning, testing, assessing, and replanning based on the knowledge gained. For example, Deming (1986) called these "plan," "do," "study," and "act" cycles. Such a cyclical process imposes discipline and systematic self-examination by teams in the workplace, and it bolsters confidence in those who must ultimately implement decisions generated by the process. Another effect of this cyclical process is that the data are produced and analyzed to address problems as they are perceived by a team that includes all levels directly involved in the operation under scrutiny. This also allows for small-scale studies and incremental reassessment of the data in order to determine when sufficient information has been gathered to justify action.

Finally, to gather and use the data and information so generated, statistical expertise must be available. Management at all levels needs good information on which to base decisions; thus it needs help in properly developing studies and in interpreting the data in order to make decisions. Such expertise is often not readily available in an organization, a situation that if uncorrected may limit the success of management improvement efforts.

ACCEPTING CHANGE

Improvement of quality requires acceptance of change. People are naturally resistant to change. In many organizations, individuals may be reasonably comfortable with the way things are, certainly when compared with the unknown future. If changes are to occur within an organization, substantial planning must take place and policies must be developed that encourage innovation and support change. For innovation to occur within the planning process, a culture of risk taking must be encouraged and supported by management and line workers, and the culture must include personnel policies that support and even reward risk takers.

As alluded to above, the individuals who must implement the desired changes must be directly involved in the planning and decision-making process. Small, ongoing changes are easier to effect than large, breakthrough changes. Often incremental changes can be made over many months such that the impact on the individual is reduced. Innovative projects should be tested on a pilot basis and in the spirit of partnership rather than hierarchical dictate—whether within the organization or across organizations within the total system. Changes that are effected in a "no surprises" environment in which all parties feel they have contributed and learned from the planning process become a win-win undertaking and best ensure a lasting, positive impact.

WORKING TOGETHER

In most organizations, whether in the private or public sector, no single activity, individual, or group provides the entire service to the customer. Seeing one's responsibilities as part of a larger system and generating a commitment to working in teams require training and education because team structures are not characteristic of most management designs. Creating, training, and supporting cross-functional teams with a mission to improve a particular process generally require many organizational adjustments. Yet, this approach has been successful in many organizations. Indeed, over the past several years, the winners of the Baldrige National Quality Award, the preeminent national award for meritorious quality improvement efforts, have been organizations that undertook just such restructuring and changes in managerial styles.

UNDERSTANDING VARIATION

Measurement of any attribute in a system is subject to variation. An organization may have an ideal value to which it wants all similar units processed to "measure up," but a key to quality improvement is an understanding that individual units will vary from the ideal. Two types of variation are possible: that due to *assignable* causes and that due to *random* causes (Shewhart, 1980). Deming (1986) has suggested that these be called *special* causes and *common* causes of variation, respectively. Special causes of variation occur now and then, and are not part of the process at all times or at all places, but arise because of specific circumstances. Examples include a broken part in one of many machines producing the same item and one person misinterpreting training on how to comply with an administrative requirement.

Common causes of variation are inherently part of the process, are present at all times in the process, and affect all outcomes of the process, although the degree of their contribution may vary. Common-cause variation is the unit-to-unit deviation that occurs when the system is operating according to its specifications. The type of equipment, the quality of material, and the need to interpret regulations are examples of system specifications that result in common-cause variations. Measurement of a unit from the system is expected to be within some limits, which are the result of the system's requirements. Thus, there is no way to predict whether the next measurement will be higher or lower than the previous one or to draw any conclusions about why the variation occurs, especially about who or what is at fault. Problems that many students are experiencing in filling out financial aid applications are likely examples of common causes of variation.

Too often organizations, reacting to an incidence of unacceptable or unexplained variation in some units, attempt to solve the problem by setting new goals or increasing regulations or inspections for all units. Such inappropriate actions are often referred to as *common-cause solutions to special-cause problems*. When determining what problems to fix, it is first essential to be able to distinguish between special causes and common causes of variation (or error in the process). Special-cause solutions are applied to those few units having trouble performing to a level that other units meet. Common-cause solutions, on the other hand, are actions taken to address a system limitation that is affecting all units doing some task. The appropriate time to make the type of fundamental changes needed to fix common problems affecting all units is when measured variation exceeds desirable limits.

Failure to distinguish between common and special causes of variation may result in inappropriate actions taken to correct sources of error or variation. For example, if the Department of Education imposed new regulations on everyone in response to problems only a few were experiencing, the regulations would create systemic change and potentially add an unnecessary burden for everyone. This approach is referred to as tampering—imposing inappropriate actions on everyone when something special, not common to the system, has been observed. Similarly, punishing organizations when measured errors rise and rewarding them when the measurement drops—irrespective of any distinction between common and special causes of the errors—often does no good and indeed may make matters worse. Chasing the numbers, as it is sometimes referred to, usually results in time-wasting activities and leaves little energy for anything more productive. Congress also must be careful not to create legislation in reaction to special causes.

Defining standards is an important part of quality management, as is the method used to ensure that the standards are met. Many organizations have found that compliance inspection systems are apt to create adversarial relationships and a far more effective approach is to teach the organizations how to recognize special causes of variation and how to analyze common causes of variation. Then, individuals and groups within the organization can monitor their own processes, thereby engaging the organization in an overall effort of continuous improvement. Data gathered on an operating process should be studied to determine the distribution of possible outcomes. Understanding what is normal variation and what is not will enable the investigators to distinguish when the process is operating effectively as currently designed and when systemic redesign is required. Only with that knowledge will individuals be able to tell the difference between improvement and tampering.

Finally, when systemic changes are determined to be necessary and a new goal or target is set, it is equally essential that the organizational members assigned the responsibility to implement the change have available to it the resources and methodology needed to bring about change and that the system to be changed be under their authority.

UNDERSTANDING THE ORGANIZATION'S AIMS AND PURPOSES

An organization must identify its mission, values, and guiding principles in ways that are clear and easy to communicate to everyone in the organization. Each division within an organization should prepare its own mission statement so that everyone can clearly see the role of each organizational entity. A clear statement of aims and purposes of the organization is essential to continuous improvement efforts.

A vision statement should also be developed that expressly states where the organization is headed and makes clear the relevance and appropriateness of individual projects in the context of the overall purpose of the organization. The vision statement sets the goals for the future and enables those in the organization to "see" the picture of the desired future, at least in the best of all possible worlds. Adjustments may be needed, but the general vision and the roadmap to the goal must be understood.

The mission statement and the vision statement should be revised from time to time. However, constancy of purpose requires that the changes not merely reflect changes in administration and leadership.

FOSTERING TOP MANAGEMENT LEADERSHIP

Organizations that have been successful in implementing strategies for continuous improvement have done so with leadership from the top management in the organization. Successful leaders provide clear direction in an environment or culture that nurtures individuals and nurtures change. Leaders work with people to create the vision and direction for change, develop the plans, strategies, and methods, and then guide the organization through the process of change. Further, leaders help by coaching, empowering, and counseling their subordinates, not by directing them. And leaders understand that there are frequently no easy solutions or quick fixes. Leadership requires the perspective that fundamental change must be achieved over the long term. In the context of federal student aid programs, top management leadership in the Department of Education will be more difficult to achieve, perhaps because of the history of frequent changes of senior appointees. Nevertheless, leadership is essential and must be ongoing, even if changes are made. Otherwise, the continuous improvement efforts will wither away.

3

Overview of Student Financial Aid Programs

TYPES AND SOURCES OF STUDENT AID

Student financial aid may be described by a number of different terms and categories. A useful method of presentation is to characterize three types of aid and the four sources from which each type might come.[1]

The three types of aid are:

- gift aid—grants and scholarships, which need not be repaid;
- employment—part-time jobs, which enable the student to earn part of his or her educational expenses; and
- loans—funds that have to be repaid, almost always with interest, but usually not until the borrower is no longer attending school.

Student aid programs originate from one of four sources:

- postsecondary institutions
- state government
- federal government
- private foundations or organizations outside the school

Figure 3-1 shows the amount of financial aid awarded from these sources for academic year 1991-92.

[1] This section is adapted from *FACTS - Financial Aid Concepts for Training Staff*, National Association of Student Financial Aid Administrators (1990).

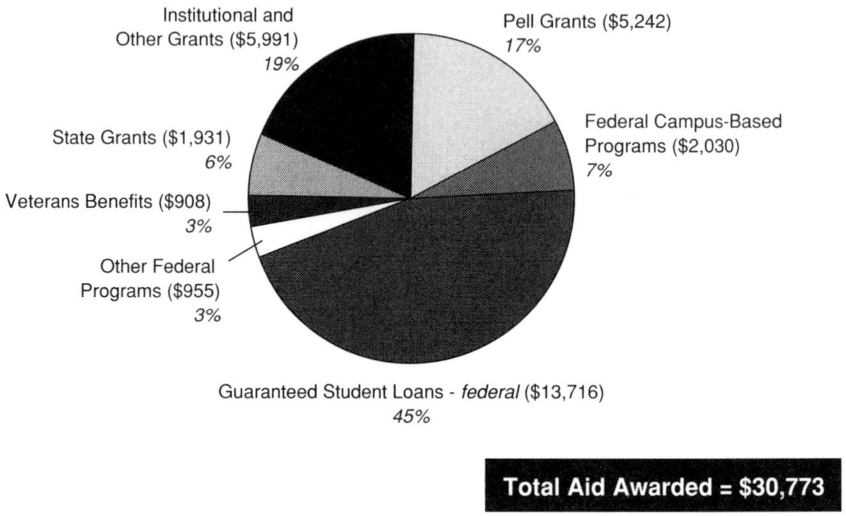

FIGURE 3-1 Estimated student aid by source, academic year 1991-92 (current dollars in millions). SOURCE: The College Board (1992). Reprinted by permission.

Institutional Programs

Most postsecondary institutions have their own scholarship and grant programs to assist students. Such institutional programs, however, are much more prevalent at private institutions than at public ones. Scholarship programs typically have specific academic or talent requirements that must be met by the recipients; grant programs are usually based on demonstrated need. In addition, many schools use their own financial resources to administer part-time employment programs, as well as short- and long-term loan programs. Since federal money is not involved in these programs, institutions are free to establish eligibility criteria without regard to federal regulations. For administrative ease, however, some institutions choose to follow federal rules in awarding their own funds.

State Aid Programs

Many of the grant programs administered by states were initiated or encouraged under the federal State Student Incentive Grant Program, which provides matching funds for state financial aid programs. Some states have relatively limited amounts and types of student financial aid, whereas others provide substantial funds through a full range of grants, loans, and employment.

The terms and conditions of state aid programs vary widely by state. For example, there are differences in whether private institutions are eligible for state aid. Also, some states restrict eligibility to state residents attending postsecondary institutions within the state. Others have reciprocity agreements with other (usually neighboring) states whereby residents from each state included in the agreement may use aid funds from their home state at institutions within the other states included in the agreement. In addition to funding student aid programs, states also subsidize tuitions in that they are by far the largest source of funds to support the operating and capital budgets of public colleges and universities.

Federal Title IV Programs

Federally funded student financial aid is made available largely through Title IV of the Higher Education Act. Title IV programs comprise Federal Pell Grants, Federal Campus-Based Programs, and Federal Family Education Loan Programs.[2]

Federal Pell Grant Program

Pell grants provide aid to undergraduates, which does not have to be repaid. A Pell grant is the underpinning of the federal financial aid program, and it is designed to help the neediest students. For this program, need is measured by a statutory methodology, which is based on a calculation of the expected family contribution to the student's education. (This methodology was called the Pell Grant Index prior to reauthorization.) Funded by Congress, Pell grants are not dependent on the availability of funds at a particular school, and qualified students who receive Pell grants may use the money for study in any approved program at any eligible postsecondary institution in the United States.

Federal Campus-Based Programs

These programs include the Federal Work-Study, Federal Supplemental Educational Opportunity Grant, and Federal Perkins Loan programs. Schools must apply annually for funding and are then responsible for awarding the monies to eligible students, based on need. For this reason, if a student receives outside funding (such as private scholarships), his or her award of

---

[2]Prior to the 1992 reauthorization, these programs were called the Pell Grant program, Campus-Based Programs, and Guaranteed Student Loans. The reauthorization was passed late in the deliberations of the panel. Discussion of the impact of the reauthorization on the quality improvement areas considered by the panel is in Chapter 9.

Federal Campus-Based program funds (and loans described in the next section) is subject to change if the sum of all sources of aid exceeds calculated need. The change may occur even after the student has begun attending the school, because total aid cannot exceed the cost of attendance minus the expected family contribution, described later in this chapter.

Federal Work-Study Programs This type of aid provides jobs for students, paid for jointly by the federal government (which pays the major portion of the student worker's wages) and the school or other employer. Undergraduate and graduate students are eligible for this assistance. Schools must pay undergraduates on an hourly basis, but they may pay graduate students based on hours or salary.

Federal Work-Study employees must be paid at least minimum wage, as determined by the Fair Labor Standards Act, but the actual wage rate will vary. Some schools pay only the minimum wage for all Federal Work-Study jobs; others vary the rate according to the job. The jobs may be located on or off campus; the employer is often the school itself, a nonprofit community agency, or a for-profit organization. While many schools try to relate all jobs to the student's academic major, only jobs in the private, for-profit sector are required to be academically relevant.

Federal Supplemental Educational Opportunity Grants These grants are a need-based gift available only to undergraduates who have not yet earned a baccalaureate or first professional degree. Pell grant recipients must be given priority for these funds, which tend to be the smallest source of student aid funds at an institution.

Federal Perkins Loans This program is available to undergraduate and graduate or professional students; priority is given to those who demonstrate exceptional financial need. Basic student eligibility for this program is determined by federal law, but each school participating in the program may distribute funds to those eligible as it sees fit. Because a school's definition of exceptional need will relate to its mission and goals as well as the unique characteristics of its student population, a student may meet one school's definition of exceptional need, but not that of another school.

Federal Family Education Loans

The Federal Family Education Loan Program, formerly Guaranteed Student Loans, encompasses three programs: Stafford loans, Supplemental Loans for Students, and Parent Loans for Undergraduate Students. These loans provide the largest amount of student aid funds administered by the federal government and are classified as guaranteed because the lender is assured of payment (by the federal government) should the borrower default, die, or declare bankruptcy.

Stafford Loans These loans provide more dollars of student aid than any other single source. Banks or savings and loan associations lend money to students, and a state or national guaranty agency insures the loans, which are offered at a below-market rate. While a student is in school, the federal government subsidizes the interest on the loan, paying the student's share of the interest to the lender plus an additional percentage, which brings the total interest paid up to market rates. Once out of school, the student becomes responsible for repayment of the loan amount as well as interest that has started to accrue.

Recent changes in the Higher Education Act added an unsubsidized component to the Stafford Loan Program, for which financial need is not a criterion. The loans are limited to Stafford limits and cannot exceed the cost of attendance minus other aid. All Stafford eligibility criteria, except financial need, apply. However, for this part of the student's Stafford borrowing, there is no interest subsidy, and repayment of principal and interest begin while the student is in school unless capitalized to be paid later.

Supplemental Loans for Students These loans are primarily available to graduate and professional students and to undergraduate students who are independent of their parents. The amount that a student may borrow is limited to the smaller of (1) the difference between the cost of attending the school and any other aid that the student is to receive, and (2) limits set by legislation. These loans come from lending institutions and banks, and they are insured by guaranty agencies in the event that the loan is not repaid due to default, death, or permanent disability. There are, however, no interest subsidies in this program, and repayment of principal and interest begins 60 days after the loan is disbursed, unless the borrower capitalizes interest for later repayment.

Parent Loans for Undergraduate Students This program is similar to the supplemental loan program above, but it is designed for parents rather than students. The loan can be used to substitute for part or all of the family contribution. The amount that may be borrowed is limited only to the difference between the cost of attendance and the other financial aid the student is expected to receive.

Brief Background on the Programs

These "generally available" types of student aid programs (excluding student aid for veterans and Social Security recipients) are administered by the Department of Education. Because the Federal Campus-Based Programs have not grown much in real terms since their inception in the mid-1960s, the Federal Family Education Loans and the Federal Pell grant program have gradually become the main sources of federal student aid. Since

1985, the Pell program has grown by 12 percent and Family Education Loans by 20 percent in real terms, leading to the latter becoming the major federal higher education financing mechanism (McPherson and Schapiro, 1991:27).

One factor related to the change in major financing mechanisms is that, except for Federal Family Education Loans, these programs are not entitlements (uncapped funds). Under an entitlement program, if a student meets requirements and wants support, it *will* be provided. Under a nonentitlement program, however, a student may meet eligibility criteria but may not receive the amount of funds he or she is "entitled" to because of the amount allocated to the program and the number of students applying.

Federal Family Education Loans are funded so that all who apply and are eligible may receive the full amount of aid allowed by law. Maximum awards for other programs may be less than the law allows, as has usually been the case with Pell grants. Also, in the Federal Campus-Based Programs, students who apply early have the best chance of receiving funds before the monies allocated are exhausted.

In instances in which students with similar characteristics apply for aid, the amount of the Pell grant awarded will be the same. With Campus-Based funds, students with similar characteristics may be awarded different amounts, as decided by the institution.

FEDERAL STUDENT FINANCIAL AID RECIPIENTS

Initially, the federal student aid programs were designed solely to provide funds for postsecondary education to students who could not otherwise attend because of their parents' financial circumstances. Over the years, programs and funding were expanded to broaden the goal to include choice among the institutions offering the student's intended course of study. Thus, students can select an institution based on the quality of the program offered rather than their family's financial circumstances. In addition, students should be provided reasonable assurance that if they reapply each year in a timely manner and continue to meet program eligibility requirements, they will be provided the funds they need to complete their program of study.

The targeting of federal student aid programs, across students and institutions, has varied considerably. When the programs were begun, most aid recipients were full-time students in traditional colleges and universities who were financially dependent on their parents. In recent years, however, there has been rapidly increasing use by financially independent students, many of them adults, who now make up the majority of applicants (Figure 3-2). In the 1988-89 academic year, for example, there were 3.4 million independent and 3.1 million dependent recipients of federal student aid.

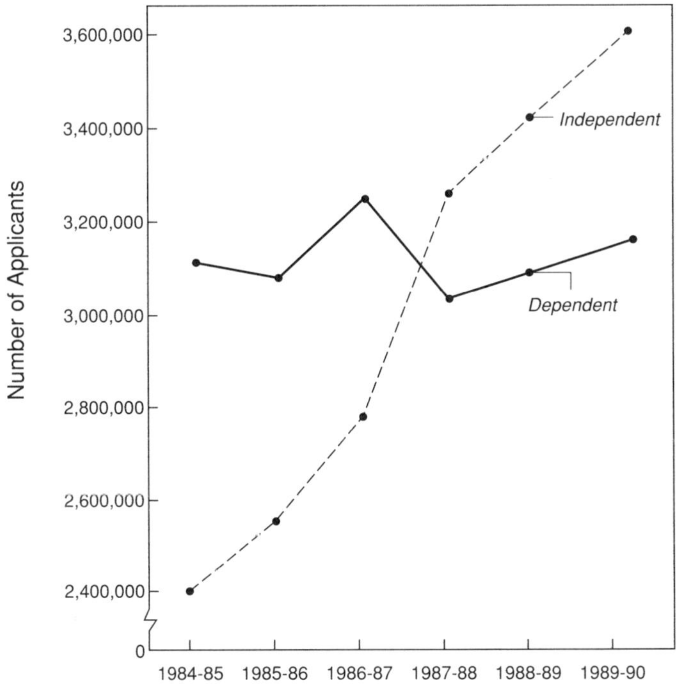

FIGURE 3-2 Applicants by dependency status. SOURCE: National Computer Systems (1988-89, 1989-90).

The applicant changes are also linked to changes in financial aid patterns among various types of institutions. Currently, students at proprietary vocational and technical institutions, most of which offer nondegree programs of less than two years and which enroll fewer than 7 percent of undergraduate students, receive more than a quarter of all Pell grant funds. That figure is up from only 11 percent in 1979-80 (McPherson and Schapiro, 1991:28). For a similar time period, the percentage of Stafford loans going to proprietary schools increased fivefold, to about 30 percent (U.S. Department of Education, 1990b:19).

ELIGIBILITY

In student financial aid programs, *eligibility* has a number of meanings, depending on who or what is being considered. The most common use of the word concerns student eligibility. Even if an individual meets the student eligibility criteria, however, he or she must be enrolled in an eligible program of study at an eligible institution in order to receive federal student financial aid. An institution's eligibility is certified by the Department of Education. But the fact that an institution is eligible does not mean that all of its academic programs are eligible. When the Department of Education confirms an institution's eligibility, it also specifies which programs of the institution are eligible. The institution's president or chief executive and the Department of Education then sign a Program Participation Agreement, which specifies the financial aid programs in which the institution may participate.

Enrollment in an eligible program does not in and of itself mean that a student may receive federal student aid. To receive student financial aid administered by the Department of Education, a student must meet all of the following criteria:

- be a U.S. citizen or eligible noncitizen
- be enrolled or accepted for enrollment on at least a half-time basis[3] at an eligible institution in an eligible program of study
- if required, register with the Selective Service and file a statement indicating Selective Service registration status
- file a Statement of Educational Purpose stating that all funds received will be used solely for educational purposes
- maintain satisfactory academic progress in the program
- not be simultaneously enrolled in elementary or secondary school
- not have had federal benefits suspended or terminated as a result of a conviction for a drug offense
- not be in default on a previous federal educational loan or owe a repayment on a previous federal educational grant
- not have borrowed in excess of federal loan limits

Some federal aid programs have additional eligibility criteria that are specific to the particular program.

THE AID FORMULA

The awarding of Title IV aid, prior to the 1992 reauthorization of the Higher Education Act, has been based on two formulas, one for Pell grant awards (the Pell Grant Index), which go to lower income students, and one (the Congressional Methodology) for other programs. With reauthorization, only one formula, the Congressional Methodology, will be used. Basically, using this formula, family resources available for educational costs are determined, and student need is then calculated by subtracting the amount the

[3] Recent changes in the Higher Education Act will permit undergraduate students to receive Pell grants if eligible and attending less than half-time beginning in academic year 1993-94.

student and family are expected to pay from the student's cost of attending school.

Cost of attendance is an estimate of how much money the student will need to cover tuition and fees, room and board, and miscellaneous expenses, such as books, supplies, and transportation to and from home. Key student choices must be made before financial aid administrators can determine the cost of attendance, including what institution to attend, whether to live on campus or off, and for students living off campus, whether to live with parents.

The *expected family contribution*, based on the family's ability to pay, is driven by the premise that the student and parents have primary responsibility for paying for the education. The family contribution is determined by making allowances for family size and the number of family members in college, in addition to considering the amount of federal, state, and local taxes paid. A student's dependency status is also considered to determine whether the family contribution should consist of a parental contribution and a separately calculated student contribution.

Under the Congressional Methodology, the expected parental contribution is calculated based on the parents' income and assets above specified amounts. In what is called the simplified formula or application, assets are not considered for applicants with income below specified levels ($15,000 pre-reauthorization and $50,000 subsequently). As income increases, so does the expected parental contribution. To arrive at the expected parental contribution, available income is calculated by subtracting allowances (including such things as basic living expenses, taxes, and so on) from total income, and then income supplements from assets are estimated to get an adjusted available income, which is used to determine the proportion available for the parental contribution.

The Title IV legislation is a major factor in determining who gets what amount of student aid. Based on established guidelines, financial aid administrators must consider all sources of aid and determine a suitable and accurate aid package for each student. The Pell grant award amount is the first item considered. Any need beyond the Pell grant can be satisfied by a combination of non-need-based aid obtained from outside organizations, state grants, loans, federally funded campus-based aid, and institutional aid, as determined by the school. At this point, some students still require aid, and they often resort to higher interest loans.

THE AWARD PROCESS

As an introduction to the student financial aid process, the panel reviewed a flowchart of the Federal Family Education Loan Program. The process diagram stretched from fingertip to fingertip of the outstretched

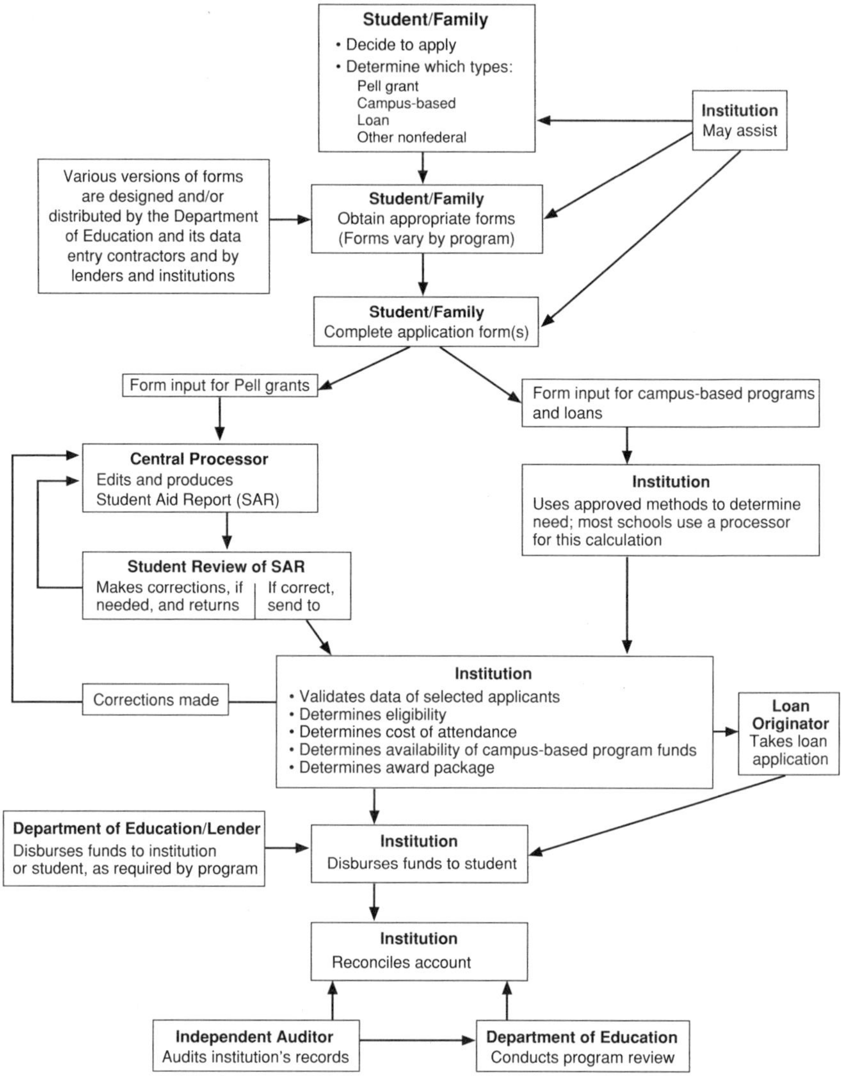

FIGURE 3-3 Basics of the Title IV award system

arms of the presenter. The presenter made the point, which the panel heard many times from players in the system, that the system was very complex. Although the detailed flowcharts for the Pell and Campus-Based programs were less complex, the major and the subtle differences among the programs in determining program eligibility and in administrative policies and practices posed a challenge for the panel in determining how to report on the quality of these activities. (It seems to be a problem for the Department of Education too; the panel was cautioned that the charts, which were produced for the Department of Education by contractors, are outdated.) The panel had two problems to overcome. First, reporting on all the detailed differences would make the report tiresome to read. Second, correctly incorporating regulatory changes due to reauthorization that were being made during the drafting of this report would be impossible. Thus, throughout this report we discuss the system that awards financial aid according to its basic form, which involves the activities of (a) applicants as they learn about and complete appropriate forms and correspondence; (b) the Department of Education's processing contractors as they input data, edit data, request corrections from applicants, and try to predict applications that are prone to error; (c) institutions as they labor to help students under tight time frames and a myriad of activities; (d) lenders as they work with an additional application process; and (e) the Department of Education as it tries to regulate activities. Figure 3-3 provides a greatly simplified view of the process.

PART II

"Quality" in the Student Financial Aid Programs

In Chapters 4 through 6, the panel reviews the concept of *quality* as it is perceived in student financial aid programs and the approaches used to control and measure quality. There is little disagreement over the need to consider quality in a program that distributes some $18 billion in direct funds or guarantees, but many issues concerning the approaches currently used are open to discussion. The issues arise from the complex web of federal and institutional relationships that complicate administration and create conflicting interests and views.

The panel examined several indicators of quality in student financial aid as defined and measured by the Department of Education. The most detailed indicators include measures of the incidence of various types of errors in awards. However, we also assembled evidence of inefficiencies and/or suboptimal performance in the system, as well as possible causes of unproductive burden on the administering institutions and shortcomings in meeting the needs of students.

This review of current "quality" begins with Chapter 4, in which we review the Department of Education's quality control strategy. In Chapter 5, we consider the views of three of the major players in the aid system: the Department of Education, the academic institution, and, most important, the applicant. While others, such as the taxpayer, banks, and guaranty agencies, also have an investment in the quality of the system, we concentrated on the interaction among the department, students, and the institutions, the three players most directly involved with determining awards. Finally, in Chapter 6, we discuss recent developments concerning the department's data bases.

In discussing the adequacy of the Department of Education's quality control information, we point out system activities found to be most in need of quality improvement. In Part III, we look beyond local optimization attempts to find more global strategies to improve quality.

4

Current Quality Control Procedures

In this chapter, the panel reviews current efforts by the Department of Education to control and monitor the quality of the award and payment processes, the types of error that are uncovered and the importance of detecting them, and the burden quality control places on those in the system. For the purpose of this chapter, and in many respects in the Department of Education's historical view and its charge to the panel, "quality of the award and payment processes" is synonymous with the concept of accuracy in the award and payment to recipients of student financial aid. This narrow, "payment error" view forms the rationale for the department's current control and monitoring activities. We examine the views of other participants in the system in Chapter 5.

ERROR DEFINED

Although reducing payment error (defined below) is an important aspect of quality—particularly in programs that disburse public funds—it is only one of many dimensions of quality, as discussed in Chapter 2. Its pervasiveness, however, makes an understanding of payment error a prerequisite to an understanding of quality control, as practiced by the Department of Education. In principle, there are two kinds of payment errors in student financial aid programs, or in fact in any program designed to dispense resources to those in need of them: (1) errors of overaward or overpayment and (2) errors of underaward or underpayment. Overpayments can be subdivided into (1) excess payments to eligible recipients and (2) all payments to ineligible recipients. In parallel fashion, underpayments comprise (1) insufficient payments to eligible recipients and (2) the lack of payments to those mistakenly classified as ineligible.

Two further characterizations of error apply to overpayment and underpayment errors. One distinction is between substantive errors and technical errors. *Substantive errors* are directly associated with the provision of information that determines eligibility for student financial aid and the calculation based on that information. *Technical errors* occur when a legally necessary document has not been submitted or has been submitted but is missing from a student's file. The lack of such documents makes the student categorically ineligible for financial aid; the inclusion of the documents, however, may or may not render the student eligible, depending on other factors that could be examined if the file were further investigated. Technical errors include the failure to have on file documentation of satisfactory educational progress, an indication of registration for Selective Service, a statement of educational purpose, or a financial aid transcript (a report of federal aid given to the student by institutions previously attended). Certainly, an existing but temporarily misplaced document, while a possible indication of poor administrative work, is not as serious a technical error as noncompliance with a requirement, such as maintaining satisfactory educational progress.

A second distinction deals with the originating source of the error—whether it is the institution, data processor, or student. These three sources of error are the primary focus of the quality control efforts discussed in this chapter. Data processing errors are basically self-explanatory, but a few comments on institutional and student errors are warranted.

Institutional error may occur in the form of failure to follow Title IV regulations or the institution's own policies for Title IV aid even though failure to follow the latter may not violate Title IV regulations. (Some failures, termed *liability errors*, require reimbursing the federal government for the amount of the error.)

For their part, students may make intentional reporting errors, for which they are liable for fines or imprisonment. Alternatively, students may make unintentional errors in reporting, which if found in verification, should result in an adjustment to their award, but which do not make them liable for fines or imprisonment. Still another type of student error arises from incorrect projections or estimates (e.g., federal income tax to be paid) on the application form. These do not count as errors under Title IV regulations, but they have been tabulated as error in some studies of program quality (e.g., the Integrated Quality Control Measurement Project, discussed in Chapter 5).

The differences among the various Title IV programs also lead to different ways in which errors in the analysis of student need translate into dollars misspent. Because the Pell program involves a direct grant, the conceptualization of error in that program is the most straightforward: Error is simply defined as the difference between the payment made to a student and the amount that should have been paid according to a correct need analysis. Thus, errors in Pell grant need analyses are dollars actually misspent or erroneously not spent.

On the other hand, an error in a Campus-Based program is conceptualized as the discrepancy between calculated need and need if correctly calculated with accurate data. Because funding is limited, however, actual awards are often less than the calculated need. Hence an error, as a concept, is not equivalent to actual dollars misspent or erroneously not spent.

Similarly, in the Stafford Loan Program, error is conceptualized as any mismatch between appropriate and actual certification amounts. A student, however, may choose not to borrow the full amount, so again, errors do not necessarily represent actual dollars misspent or erroneously not spent. In addition, the student may repay the loan, which limits the cost of the error to any subsidies or allowances provided by the federal government on the erroneous part of the loan.

As a final note on these errors, the errors addressed in this chapter involve, for the most part, applicants who were found eligible for an award. Recently, the Department of Education has made an effort to inspect the cases of unsuccessful applicants as well. Eligible individuals who do not apply are also a source of underpayment not addressed by current quality control activities. This is a major issue of quality in the system rather than a source of error and is discussed in Chapter 5.

THE QUALITY CONTROL PROCESS

The questions concerning the quality control process that were posed by the Department of Education in requesting this study included the following:

- How much information should be obtained from applicants and how intensively should its accuracy be reviewed?
- What are appropriate or realistic levels of performance to be expected from participants in the financial aid system?
- What are reasonable trade-offs between performance and the burden imposed on those in the system?

Materials provided to the panel by the Department of Education's Division of Quality Assurance describe the current quality control process as a three-part effort consisting of prevention, inspection, and oversight. The department has another activity related to quality control—special sample-survey studies—that are discussed in the next chapter.

Prevention consists of activities aimed at avoiding errors. The Department of Education identifies two such activities:

- training, which is provided by the department to data entry contractors, financial aid administrators and other institutional officers, lenders, accrediting agencies, state scholarship and guaranty agencies, and others in the financial aid community; and
- verification of student data, which entails institutional review of student-submitted information and, if necessary, correction of errors.

Inspection consists of after-the-fact monitoring activities during audits and program reviews designed to determine the accuracy of program administration by the schools. Such activities are often developed in the belief that they help to ensure compliance because the possibility of penalties and/or sanctions acts as a deterrent. There are two types of inspection activities:

- Audits. Audits are typically conducted by a certified public accountant and are submitted to the Department of Education for review and approval. Audits focus on determining the reliability of institutional financial data, management controls, and compliance with requirements of participants in the federal student financial aid programs. Until the 1992 reauthorization of the Higher Education Act, participation in federal Title IV programs required that all institutions undergo at least a biannual audit of the Title IV financial aid programs in which they participated. The reauthorization requires annual audits.
- Program reviews. The Department of Education's regional and central office staff conduct program reviews to determine compliance with federal rules and regulations governing the student aid programs. The reviews are conducted at educational and lending institutions and guaranty agencies. (The department also requires guaranty agencies to review their largest institutions and lenders. The reviews, which are not discussed in this report, focus on compliance with the rules and regulations for guaranteed student loan, or GSL, programs. The reports must be submitted to the department for review and approval.)

Oversight consists of periodic studies of various program areas within the Department of Education. The studies are conducted by the department's Office of Inspector General (OIG) or the General Accounting Office (GAO) and focus on procedures for monitoring compliance with various requirements and the management of those activities.

The panel reviewed the award determination system and related quality control efforts using an approach that looks for potential to improve the accuracy of awards. In viewing the study this way, we identified several activities related to quality control and process improvement that were not part of the prevention, inspection, and oversight strategy defined by the

TABLE 4-1 Current Activities Related to Quality Control and Improvement in the Process of Awarding Student Financial Aid

Stage in the Process	Current Activities
Learning about the programs	— Outreach activities — Financial aid administrator help
Filling out forms	— area code 800 telephone information lines — Feedback from involved organizations — Electronic application — Financial aid administrator help — Renewal applications
Data entry	— Inspection sampling and reporting by data entry contractors
Data editing	— Computer flagging — Student Aid Reports generated with highlights from edits and applicant corrections
Verification	— Verification of data from a selected percentage of applicants
Retrospective activities	— Audits — Reviews — Oversight — Special sample-survey studies

Department of Education. Using the simplified process diagram presented in Figure 3-3, we identified six distinct but interconnected activities related to control, improvement, or consequence of poor performance (see Table 4-1). In the remainder of this chapter, we review inspection activities after the student submits an application for aid. The inspection activities include the processing activities of data entry, editing, and verification and the retrospective activities of audit and review. In Chapter 5, we review the measured outcomes of the financial aid process and relate the findings to the inspection activities and to problems the applicant faces in understanding and completing the application for aid. The issue of where the burden for ensuring effective performance of the system should be placed is addressed in Chapters 5 and 9.

PROCESSING ACTIVITIES

Data Entry

Data entry is done under contract. A central processor handles the federal application form, and several data entry contractors (called multiple data entry contractors, or MDEs) each handle a separate version of the application form, which includes federal application information and state-required data.[1] Entry of the application data and subsequent corrections of the data involve opening and handling mail and entering and processing data. (We also include printing and mailing the Student Aid Report, or SAR, in this category.) The amount of work during peak application periods and the turnaround time required increase the risk of errors. Error in processing is a concern because applicants might be incorrectly informed of their eligibility status, which could affect their decisions about whether to attend school and, if so, where.

The panel examined specifications, developed by the Department of Education and/or the contractors, that would indicate that extraordinary care is taken to ensure that data entry operations are accurately and efficiently accomplished from the time applications and corrections are received to the time that the SAR is produced. At every step of the process, traditional quality control inspection procedures are specified. At the receipt and review stage, for example, documents must successfully pass an initial completeness check and then a further review. A random sample of batches of applications is also selected and checked for key entry errors. At the output stage, quality of print and integrity of data are checked in a sample from each stack of printed SARs.

In its efforts to improve data processing activities, the Department of Education encourages contractors to obtain ongoing feedback from employees at different levels, such as data entry, operations, systems, and project management staff. In addition, the department requires all MDEs to submit an annual requirements analysis, a comprehensive review of all major aspects of the system, comments from applicants and institutions, and recommendations for any changes that are necessary.

To assess ongoing work performance and product quality, the MDEs have developed feedback systems. One MDE, for example, utilizes Corrective Action/Error Cause Removal Sheets, on which employees indicate and describe the existence of a problem. The MDE's quality assurance department then works with management to implement corrective action. Additionally, units specifically assigned to address quality issues collect and maintain detailed statistics on data entry quality and conduct ongoing review and evaluation of processing functions and requested changes.

The panel did not attempt to verify the contractors' strict adherence to, or the success of, the defined quality control activities. However, a General Accounting Office (1985:9) study reported that "a small-scale review that was part of the 1980-1981 error study suggested that keystroke error in entering data from application forms to the computer terminal was low."

[1]As explained in more detail in Chapter 5, application forms can be obtained from the Department of Education, lenders, schools, or from one of the MDEs.

This still appears to be true; management reports consistently indicate error rates well below 1 percent for keystroke and other data handling activities. Given the extensive quality control efforts employed over the years, the panel concludes that the handling of applications and data entry are well under control. The quality control methods at data entry may be somewhat excessive, but the total cost of data entry with those quality control activities is low, especially compared with the more controversial areas of controlling student and institutional error.

Data Editing

When an application or correction arrives at the processing facility, data are edited on a very rudimentary level (e.g., completeness of key fields, such as a signature, and decisions on poor handwriting). After the data pass data entry quality control inspections, the processor transmits the data file to the central processor for more extensive computer editing. There, the Central Processing System (CPS) performs checks for consistency with data in several federal data bases (e.g., Selective Service, Immigration and Naturalization, Drug Enforcement, and defaulted federal student loan data bases) and performs edits similar to those used in many survey operations (e.g., assume and impute values for missing or illogical data of a noncritical nature, consistency checks among data elements, and range checks of data elements). Processing of applications failing the most critical aspects of these edits is suspended. For other edits, incorrect or "suspect" data elements are "highlighted," and an award index is computed. The data as entered from the application, highlighted data elements, and award index information are mailed to the applicant as part of the Student Aid Report.

For applications originating with the central processor, SARs are mailed directly by the central processor. For applications originating with an MDE, the information needed to produce a SAR (highlighted and eligibility information) are transmitted back to the MDE. The MDE then prints the SAR and mails it to the student. There was some objection to this process in the past. For example, an MDE complained to the Department of Education about rigid rules on overly specified formats and the wastefulness of having each of the MDE organizations develop programs to print the SAR forms.

The student, whether subject to highlights of possible errors or not, is asked to review all the data on the SAR and, if corrections are needed, return the corrected SAR to the processor. The corrected data are re-edited and a new SAR is produced. Almost one third of applicants must "recycle" their SAR, which delays their award determination (see Table 4-2). Following the completion of the correction cycle, the student provides the SAR to each institution to which he or she has applied for aid (recall Figure 3-3).

Data from the Department of Education's Management Information System

TABLE 4-2 Frequency of Valid Applications, by the Number of Transactions, 1990-91 Academic Year

Number of Transactions	Count of Applications	Percent of Applications
1	4,827,615	68.4
2	1,555,070	22.0
3	443,479	6.3
4	146,134	2.1
5	49,739	0.7
6	18,819	0.3
7	7,469	0.1
8-55	6,086	0.1
Total	7,054,411	100.0

NOTE: Number of transactions is the sum of the number of times the Student Aid Report is returned plus one for the initial application. SOURCE: National Computer Systems (1990-91a:5-1).

(MIS) are used to produce tables of aggregate correction rates for each data item, but use of other statistical analyses might be instructive. For example, a cross-tabulation of error items by the number of SAR cycles might indicate the items that are responsible for most of the repeated SAR cycling. Taking actions to reduce the need for SAR recycling could reduce program costs.

There is evidence that the SAR itself is an effective quality control device. On applications for the 1990-91 academic year, for example, more than half of the corrections of data critical to computing the award formula were made without the corrected field having been highlighted. For "federal income tax paid," a field that is influential in the award formula, the proportion of unsolicited corrections was over 80 percent (National Computer Systems, 1990-91a:4-11 to 4-14). Some of these changes may occur as a result of verification initiated by institutions (some schools do 100 percent verification anyway). Thus, further information on why the changes were needed would be useful for planning strategies to get the correct information the first time.

The central processor performs a second edit function—flagging applications for institutional verification. Verification activities are discussed next.

Verification

Verification, formerly called validation, by the institution of applicants' reported data items is the Department of Education's primary tool in its efforts to control applicant error. Each school is required to verify key elements of the student record for all records flagged by the central processor (or by the school's own error-prone profile in the case of the limited number of institutions participating in the quality control project discussed in Chapter 8). Additionally, whether the student's file is selected for verification or not, the institution is responsible for resolving any conflicting data it may contain (e.g., between an unsolicited tax return and the federal record). Corrections, if made, must be reported to the central processor (either through the mailed SAR process or electronically at the institution).

Adding to the complexity of the verification process is the structure that requires the process to occur at each institution to which the student applied for aid. The panel was informed that an institution initiating data corrections based on information from its file frequently finds that the data are then changed by the student or another institution, and the resultant central processing data do not match the institution's record.

One of the burdens of this prolonged SAR process is that with each change the student's Pell award may have to be recalculated, and if adjusted, the interdependencies among the various aid programs may cause changes to any Campus-Based or loan determinations that are part of the student's aid package. For example, for each dollar of Pell correction in the case of a fully awarded student, a Stafford loan dollar often must be changed and the Stafford loan certification process begun again. Data on the Stafford loan must then be revised by the school, the lender, and the guaranty agency.

There is little year-to-year comparison of an applicant's information in the student financial aid system unless instituted by the school, in which case it also becomes liable for errors in reconciliation when using the prior data. The need to make quick decisions concerning the award, changing family and student incomes, and the increasing degree to which students move among institutions of higher education are likely barriers to year-to-year data comparisons, which might otherwise lead to increased veracity. Although the verification design, at one time, reportedly called for some applicant records to be purposely reselected for verification in successive years, no formal reports on studies of the data were made available to the panel. Also, since only about 50 percent of applicants reapply for aid the next year, the ability to make good verification decisions on first-time applicants is important.

Verification activities follow a basic cycle for each program year, which includes the following steps:

• The Department of Education develops strategies for selecting applications thought to be more likely than others to be in error.

• The central processor compares each application with the verification selection criteria at the time the application first enters into the system (recall that some initial edits lead to the application being rejected).

• Institutions verify applicant data for the selected applications. (Rules concerning the maximum percentage of applicants an institution must verify, the data items that must be verified, and acceptable documentation for data item verification have varied over the years. By federal rules issued prior to reauthorization, the institution need not verify more than 30 percent of applications. Reauthorization, however, allows the Secretary of Education to mandate verification of all applications.)

• Institutions report data changed in the verification process to the central processor for recalculation of the award formula and for creation of the analytic data sets used in the Management Information System. (The data are used in the analysis to create the selection strategy for the following year.)

In essence, verification is reapplication for financial aid with supporting documentation.

The institutional verification process has been the subject of considerable research expenditure by the Department of Education since 1980. From the earliest reports through the most recent, the approach has been criticized. (A list of the reports is provided in the next chapter, where the panel summarizes data from the reports.) Major criticisms include the following:

- The cost-benefit of the approach is questionable.
- Unfair burdens are placed on the academic institutions.
- The timing of and changes to awards create difficulties.
- The approach may possibly unfairly target certain groups.
- The verification data are also prone to error.

Although not a focus of the reports, the panel considers the impact of reapplying on the applicant an additional criticism.

The Department of Education describes the current verification system as an attempt to balance error reduction and the burden imposed on institutions. Efforts to move toward verification of all applicants have been tempered by institutional lobbying that sought to limit the burden that institutions must endure to correct errors not of their making. As a result, the 30 percent of valid applicant records that are selected for verification are chosen through a complex sequence of statistical procedures (see the next section) intended to target the most error-prone applicants.

The verification system has been studied and modified over the years, but the panel could not find evidence that major advances have been made in responding to the major criticisms of the system. For example, the cost-benefit of the system remains a question. While the MIS estimates the additional error removed by each selection criterion, there are no current estimates of the overall cost of the system, including resources used by the Department of Education and the institutions and the applicant's time. The General Accounting Office (1985) estimated the 1982-83 cost to institutions as slightly more than the dollars of award error eliminated by the verification process. The GAO study did not measure the potential deterrent effect that verification may have on student or institutional error, nor did any other studies reviewed by the panel. But, a recent quality control study (Price Waterhouse, 1991) shows little difference in the amount of final award error (based on a "verification" conducted during the study) among applications selected by the Department of Education's verification strategy, those selected for verification by institutions, and those not verified. Thus, the SAR process may provide most of the deterrents, and what appear to be marginal gains at best may result from verification activities. (Besides, 50 percent of applicants are first-time entrants to the process and would likely be much less aware of the verification possibility than a taxpayer is of an Internal Revenue Service, or IRS, audit.)

Going further, several studies suggest a return to the original concept that verification be done centrally and not at the institutions. Verification requires an enormous effort from most everyone involved. The institutions must perform this unwanted task, often duplicating efforts for students applying to several institutions. The Department of Education has to use a contractor to help develop efficient selection criteria and conduct studies of verification efforts, and it must monitor the criteria for fairness and react to audits and conduct reviews of the institutions to determine compliance.

The panel, recognizing the costly consequences of verification activities, devoted considerable attention to verification. Panel members, staff, and consultants visited with Department of Education staff and contractors involved in verification and reviewed several contracted analyses and analysis plans. The panel focused its initial activities on assessing the efficiency of the verification selection methodology and the burdens verification imposes.

Selection Methodology

The panel was interested in the statistical underpinnings of the verification selection strategy and observed the following. The analysis that leads to the criteria for selecting applications and the creation of computer programs that select the applicants are carried out under contract. The contractor provides detailed plans for conducting the activities in accordance with a very comprehensive, long-term analysis plan that was developed in 1986. That plan recognized the importance of such issues as timing, the need to account for student corrections and actual payments, biases in using data from past years to develop current selection criteria, and the need for information on ineligible applicants. Commendable progress in many of these areas is evident in the system. However, the panel's evaluation was hampered by a lack of complete documentation of the statistical procedures used to create selection criteria, which forced the panel to rely on verbal descriptions provided by the Department of Education and its contractors. Some detail on the methodology was presented in a report prepared for the panel by Carr and Sutton (1992), but limited quantitative information was available to assess the admittedly ad hoc procedures.

The approach to determining the criteria can be considered a three-part model, as follows:

1. "Suspect" groups of applicants are defined based on selected responses in categorical data and ranges in other data supplied by the applicant on the initially accepted form. Each group generally constitutes less than 2 percent of the total applicant population. The groups are created (that is, the categories and ranges are selected) on the assumption that they are more error prone than the applicant population in general. Several methods are used to define groups. Groups examined in the past and found to have relatively high error rates, logical groups based on program changes or other consistent ideas, and any other groups identified using statistical methods, such as discriminant analysis, are all considered candidates for use. The ranges and categories that statistically define or characterize a group, say income above a certain value and independent status, form what is called a *criterion*.

2. A measure of effectiveness is computed for each criterion. The effectiveness of a criterion is measured using data from two control groups that were randomly selected from the prior year—a "verified" and a "not to be verified" control group. As the names imply, these groups contain records that were specifically chosen to be verified or excluded from verification, respectively. Using the verified control group, an estimate is made of the "error" found by verification within the records that meet each criterion. This estimate is the difference in the computation of the award formula using original data and the verified data. Using the "not to be verified" group, an estimate is made of the self-corrections during SAR transactions by computing the difference in the award formula using original data and the final SAR transaction data. A differencing between the estimates of the two control groups for each criterion removes the effect of self-correction by the applicant in SAR processing, which provides a measure of verification-induced corrections.[2]

[2]Note that this is not an exact measure of error removed because verification data are subject to measurement error, but it is a reasonable proxy.

3. The criteria are then rank ordered based on the effectiveness measure. The criteria selected for use in the current year are selected from the rank ordering beginning with the criterion with the highest ranking and ending when the percentage of the total population to be verified by the criteria reaches a preset cutoff (currently 30 percent).

Any applicant with initial data meeting the definition of a criterion selected for use is flagged for verification, and the applicant is so informed on the returned SAR.

At first glance, this ad hoc approach would appear to be better replaced by logistic regression or other techniques that would directly identify individual applicants at high risk of error. But two factors affect the methodology to be used to identify error-prone applicants. First, records to be verified must be selected based on the data in the initial application. This is necessary because the first SAR is often the SAR sent to the school, and the SAR indicates to the school which applicants are to be verified. Logistic regression could certainly do this, but it is the second factor that led to the ad hoc approach. The second factor is that applicants often correct much of their initial error by returning a corrected SAR. This self-correction must be considered; otherwise, the selection technique could inefficiently pick cases that would self-correct anyway. Records selected early do not allow analysts to distinguish between self-corrections and verification-driven changes. The system developers are to be commended for their creativity in setting up the control group of applicants held immune from selection for verification, thus allowing measures of applicant self-correction (returned SARs). Still, logistic regression might provide an efficient and more straightforward methodology if some items that are often corrected in the SAR process were excluded from the analysis (e.g., income items reported before the tax form is filed). The point is that the relevant measures of error corrected in verification are those remaining after the SAR corrections. To the extent that precorrection errors and post-correction errors differ in magnitude and source, a methodology that measures error based on pre- rather than post-SAR data is flawed. Also, a major shortcoming of the logistic regression method is that it identifies applicants with a larger probability of error, not those with a larger magnitude of error.

Reports produced by the MIS provide indications about the interaction and performance of verification and SAR processes. The data made available to the panel, however, provided little direct information on the distribution of errors "found" using the criterion and control groups. Additional analysis of the data indicated that only about 14 percent of applicants correct data that result in a change to the award calculation, which implies that a few large errors and not many average-sized errors dominate the average. The similarity of averages among the control groups suggests that many applicants self-correct to an almost error-free state during SAR processes. That is, the SAR process may have corrected most of the errors in the initial application data, and it may be a very effective quality control tool. The control groups could be used as an "embedded experimental design" to assess the value of highlighting strategies. If such experiments lead to improvements in the data, the SAR process could be even more effective. The 1986 MIS management plan indicated that highlighting and criterion methods were to be studied for their influence on correction behaviors and their ability to detect errors. It was not obvious to the panel, however, that the Department of Education supported an extensive effort on those activities by its contractors. Similar criticisms about the lack of knowledge about the effectiveness of those activities were expressed by the General Accounting Office (1985).

Tabulations produced by the MIS indicated that from 1986 to 1989 verification of randomly selected applicants would "find" more than half of the error "found" in the applications selected by criteria. The additional error removed was, on average, only about 70 points (roughly dollars) in the computation of the award index across all records studied during those years. Another MIS output gave evidence that large verification-induced changes were difficult to isolate. Only a few criterion groups had average verification changes that altered the award computation by more than 30 percent and, combined, those groups contained only 2 percent of the applicants.

Some methodological improvements might be possible in defining the criterion groups. For example, are there more efficient groupings of applicants that would jointly maximize the post-SAR error found and minimize the selection of correct applications? The contractor suggested that incorporating more sophisticated research on tax code relationships would be worth investigating. Other methods mentioned, such as discriminant analysis and procedures like those used by the IRS (Hiniker, 1987), may not perform well when used with mixtures of categorical and nonnormally distributed data like these. Looking for multivariate outliers within categorical data cells might be worth study, as well as nonparametric methods such as classification and regression trees (CART), as proposed by Carr and Sutton (1992). Finally, an alternative prediction hierarchy might be used to classify records into groups that would self-correct versus those that would not. Predicting records in need of verification within each of those groups might then be more accurate.

Although some cases of fraud or abuse undoubtedly will arise in a program of this size, none of the studies the panel reviewed indicated any widespread problems of fraud by students. The panel recognizes that the Department of Education believes verification is necessary to fulfill its congressional mandate, yet the panel concludes that the verification process as currently used is unfairly burdensome for the overwhelming majority of well-intentioned people working within the system. In using any other technique, the emphasis should be to move from the current focus on catching mistakes to also providing information for future preventive actions.

Recommendation 4-1: A research effort should be initiated to assist the Department of Education's contractor in developing better criteria for selecting records to be verified and, more important, identifying opportunities for earlier removal of errors through instructions, form improvements, and SAR highlighting strategies. Current and future changes to the verification selection methodology should be carefully documented.

A final comment on existing verification methods is needed. The 1992 reauthorization made several important changes to the data structure. Several items associated with wealth that were error prone in the past have been removed from the award formula and the application either entirely or by raising the income boundary for the "simplified" needs test from $15,000 to $50,000. Unlike IRS audit-scoring methods, which make use of external data such as employer- and bank-transmitted records, or federal benefit programs that require up-front verification of critical data items (see discussion in Chapter 7), the Department of Education's verification selection methods rely on the internal consistency of the applicant's reported data. With fewer data items being collected, the criteria development procedures will most likely be less effective in finding error in the remaining data items. Regardless of the reauthorization changes, the panel believes that the current verification approach is inefficient, and it builds a case for redesign of the verification approach in Chapter 9.

A Further Role of the Financial Aid Administrator

To this point the quality control activities described have been mechanical in nature. At times, circumstances can be expected that are rare or that occur after the application process has started. In such cases, the institution's financial aid administrator must, for certain circumstances and may for other circumstances, by federal law, exercise professional judgment in determining and documenting when the circumstances for an individual student warrant variation from the law or regulations. Most typical are nondiscretionary, recent changes in a family's financial circumstances or structure, such as death of a parent, loss of job, or legal action to sever the family's relationship with the student. Additional documentation of such changes is required for the Central Processing System and for the institution's own files. The exercise of professional judgment occurs in a small percentage of cases, but it is highly labor intensive and subject to human error and varying interpretation.

Thus, the financial aid administrator stands in the middle of the processes, attempting to serve as the student's advocate to ensure the maximum legitimate award while appearing to the student to be a barrier. The penalty for error when making these decisions is seen by the administrator not only as a financial liability for the aid pool of that cohort of students but also as a potential mortgage against the aid of future cohorts of students. The capacity of financial aid administrators to make such subjectively determined changes has been strongly and increasingly endorsed in each recent reauthorization of the Higher Education Act. Yet, this activity may increase the potential for error (as discussed below) and the liabilities assessed during audit and review.

AUDITS AND PROGRAM REVIEWS

The Department of Education has responsibility for ensuring that the approximately 8,000 participating postsecondary institutions administer student financial assistance programs in compliance with law and regulations. The department executes this responsibility through two major retrospective activities:

- requiring compliance audits by an independent auditor; and
- conducting program reviews through its 10 regional offices.

The Title IV student financial assistance audit and program review processes are designed to determine the accuracy of the administration of student financial aid programs by an institution. Specifically, the Title IV audit objectives are to measure the reliability of an institution's financial data, the adequacy of internal control systems, and compliance with program regulations. The objectives of a program review of an institution are to determine compliance with program regulations and to evaluate financial and administrative capabilities. Until recently, program reviewers also attempted to provide technical assistance. The operations of these retrospective activities as they relate to the problem of error in the delivery of student financial aid are described below.

Audits

The objectives of an audit are to provide the Department of Education with information to determine whether an institution has

- provided financial data and reports that can be relied upon;
- internal controls, structure, policies, and procedures in place to provide reasonable assurance that it is managing student financial assistance programs in compliance with applicable laws and regulations; and

- complied with the terms and conditions of federal awards and, thus, has made expenditures of federal funds that are proper and supportable.

Institutions identify eligible audit firms and contract for their services. The *Audit Guide* prepared by the U.S. Department of Education (1990a) describes the audit and provides procedural guidance.[3]

Prior to the 1992 reauthorization, audits were required at least every two years (annual compliance and financial audits are now required). Audits must be conducted by an auditor who meets standards of independence specified by the GAO. The GAO's audit standards also require that auditors engaged in auditing Title IV programs have sufficient understanding of the institution's internal controls structure and federal compliance requirements to fulfill the task adequately.

The *Audit Guide* specifies mandatory audit areas and the minimum number of cases to be tested for each area. For example, the auditor is generally required to select at random and test a minimum of 50 cases (25 percent if the total population is less than 200) from appropriate populations to determine procedural correctness in the following areas:

- determining student eligibility,
- coordinating student aid programs,
- calculating and disbursing awards,
- maintaining student files,
- certifying and disbursing loans, and
- calculating refunds.

The auditor must select sufficient samples during an on-site visit to render the required opinions on each program even if that necessitates selecting larger samples than the specified minimums. The auditor must report as "findings" all instances of noncompliance, regardless of their materiality. The audit process also requires a review of prior audit findings. At the conclusion of the visit, the auditor prepares a report that details every finding and renders opinions on the institution's overall internal control program and compliance with federal law and regulations. The auditor discusses the report with school officials, and the report is then sent to the Department of Education.

---

[3]Authority for audit of the Title IV student financial assistance programs is contained in Section 487(c)(1) of the Higher Education Act of 1965, as amended by Public Law 94-482, Part D, 133. Anderson (Appendix F) describes several forms of audit that apply, depending on the type of institution. For ease of presentation, we focus on the audits contracted for by the schools.

Audit Results

In response to the panel's request, the Department of Education supplied the following list of the areas in which audit findings most frequently occur:

- ability-to-benefit determination
- missing financial aid transcript
- entrance/exit counseling
- late refunds
- student not making satisfactory academic progress
- verification of student-supplied data
- excess cash
- improper Pell disbursements
- excessive loan default rate
- missing certification statements
  - — Selective Service registration
  - — drug abuse
  - — nondefault
  - — affidavits
  - — educational purpose
- dropout/withdrawal rate excessive
- late lender notification
- Perkins loan notes unsigned/missing/improper

As a result of the audit findings, institutions may be liable for the amount of erroneous awards and for administrative penalties, such as fines, limitations on Title IV programs, suspensions, or termination of their participation in Title IV programs. Each institution must submit to the Department of Education a corrective action plan detailing the process by which it will correct any deficiencies or findings uncovered in the audit. Material findings or nonsubmission of the audit may result in further inspection activities, such as a program review by the Department of Education student financial aid staff or an audit by the Department of Education's Office of the Inspector General, and punitive actions, such as limitations on, suspension of, or elimination from participation.

According to the Department of Education, in recent years slightly over 3,000 institutional audits have been completed each year. Typically, 40 to 50 percent of the audits yield significant findings. Penalty assessments in the period 1984 to 1990 averaged nearly $11,000 per audit (as best estimated from various data provided to the panel). The department also reported that very little of the penalty assessed is actually collected by the time all appeals and negotiations for informal fines (see below) have been concluded and indicated that this is due to an insufficient number of staff.

A recent OIG internal report (U.S. Department of Education, 1992) found widespread problems with the effectiveness of audit programs, including the following:

- Almost half of the schools did not submit the required audit reports during the period 1981-88. (Some departmental staff consider this finding to be inaccurate and believe the rate was lower. Also, there has been more effort during the past two years to identify schools that are late in filing reports.)
- While there is a process for informal agreement between the department and the school on fines for significant program violations, recurring audit deficiencies, or overdue audits, in some instances, the fines were not proposed or were for such nominal amounts that they would not deter further violation. Moreover, the department was lax in collecting informal fines.
- The department accepted unaudited documentation provided by the auditee in violation of Office of Management and Budget (OMB) rules. (Departmental staff indicated that they often request that the documentation be verified in the "prior audit" section of the next required nonfederal audit.)
- Error rates and amounts found in the audit sample should have been expanded to obtain an estimate of error in all cases, using the appropriate sampling fraction. (Note that total file reviews are required when evidence indicates excessive problems. Departmental staff indicated that a 10 percent or greater error rate in the sample would trigger a full-file inspection.)

The OIG report attributed these weaknesses to "multiple causes including the lack of a reliable database to monitor compliance with the audit requirements, a lack of reconciliation procedures, and inadequate guidance to the staff" (p. 6).

The panel also noted that assessments made for errors found in the auditor's sample were not expanded by the sampling fraction used in selecting the sample. This favors institutions with nontrivial compliance problems, such as poor academic progress by aid recipients or inappropriate handling of funds. On the other hand, some of the items examined do not lead to serious administrative problems (e.g., misplaced certification statements), which would make the department's strict intolerance of any error, a zero defect standard, especially unfair if findings were expanded to reflect all cases.

A fair solution to assessments based on audit findings might parallel the actions recommended by the NAS panel that reviewed quality control in welfare systems (Kramer, 1988). Such a solution would require obtaining data from the audits to estimate the distribution of institutional error rates.[4] This estimated distribution, reflecting the current capabilities of the institu-

[4]The distribution could be estimated using an iterative process of density estimation that identifies and adjusts outliers during each iteration.

tions, becomes the basis for determining the cutoff points for unusually low or unusually high error rates. Institutions found to have unusually high error rates would be subject to penalties. Further, rewards might be considered for those institutions exhibiting exceptionally low error rates. The panel has similar concerns with program reviews (discussed later in this chapter).

> *Recommendation 4-2: The Department of Education should review the use of sample findings in audits. Adequate expansions of sample findings are needed, but their use must also reflect the seriousness of the error and make allowance for tolerance of reasonable error levels. While the panel will not directly suggest an acceptable error level, the choice of level should be based on the distribution of errors by all or similar types of institutions.*

Risk-Based and Internally Based Audits

The panel heard many reports of problems with audit activities during its open meetings and in private discussions with departmental staff and financial aid administrators. Those reports led it to commission a study by Urton Anderson, an expert in the field of audits (see paper included as Appendix F). Anderson reinforced the panel's concerns about the ineffectiveness of the audit programs and made a number of suggestions for improvement. For example, he suggested that the Department of Education be encouraged to follow the current movement by the auditing community toward a risk-based approach to auditing compliance.

Risk-based auditing refers to the practice of systematically distinguishing audit areas/locations by factors that predict the likelihood that the area/location has problems and then allocating auditing resources across audit areas/locations based on those predictions (i.e., more audit resources are devoted to places determined to have the higher likelihood of problems). *Problems* may be variously defined depending on the objective of the audit (e.g., material error in the financial statements or material compliance).

Risk-based auditing should be applied to the selection of institutions for audit and to the allocation of audit resources across areas within the audit of each institution. Progress in the latter has already been made with the use in some independent audits of the compliance risk model presented in Statement of Auditing Standards (SAS) No. 68 (American Institute of Certified Public Accountants, 1992). However, such an approach is inconsistent with the current approach sanctioned by the Department of Education and OMB guidelines and by the 1992 reauthorization legislation, which requires annual audits. Congress and the oversight authorities at the Department of Education and OMB should revise those guidelines and legislation to be consistent with a risk-based approach.

The SAS 68 compliance risk model, however, retains a focus on attestation of compliance (measurement of the level of compliance) rather than on the use of audit resources to improve compliance. Risk models that more effectively identify potential problem areas directly and promote compliance could be developed using techniques such as those employed in internal audit functions to allocate audit resources (Siers and Blyskal, 1987). Indeed, the Department of Education is currently using a direct risk approach based on logical risk assessments to allocate program review resources (discussed in the next section). However, the department has used it only to identify problem areas and has not taken full advantage of its potential to promote compliance by including a strategic component (Anderson and Young, 1988a, b). A direct risk approach could also be used in independent audits that cover multiple administrative units, as is frequently the case for public institutions (e.g., a single audit covers all the public institutions within a state).

Anderson also indicated that other models for ensuring compliance have recently been developed. One such model that has shown promise is the "certification" model, an approach that has been applied in the European Economic Community's "Eco-audit" scheme and by internal auditors in organizations implementing total quality management programs. The approach consists of relying on those people actually involved in the process to take more responsibility for assuring the quality of the process. Critical points in the process are "audited," or certified, by people who are independent of the process but not necessarily independent of the organization. For example, in the European Eco-audit scheme, management at each site participating in the scheme prepares an environmental statement. The statement includes a description of significant environmental issues, a summary of the data on pollutant emissions and the like, a presentation of the organization's environmental policies and specific objectives for the particular site, and an evaluation of the environmental performance of the protection system implemented at the site. The statement is then verified by an accredited environmental auditor (i.e., one who meets specifically outlined standards of training). This auditor can be an employee of the organization (if the organization has set up an appropriate system to provide independence from the activity audited, such as an internal audit function) or an external auditor.

The important modification in this approach is that the emphasis regarding the "auditor" is on being qualified to conduct the audit rather than on organizational independence. One of the frequent and very troubling problems encountered with the independent audit of student financial aid programs has been that independent auditors do not understand program compliance requirements or financial aid operations. Requiring more specific accreditation of the auditor improves the quality of the auditing process. Allowing the audit to be conducted by direct employees of the organization who are independent of the activity can provide for further expertise of the auditor through the auditor's knowledge of the institution and the industry. Appropriate actions would have to be taken when institutions or auditors violate the independence or objectivity that is expected of these audits.

In Chapter 8, the panel discusses the Department of Education's Institutional Quality Control Pilot Project, an example of applying the certification approach to student financial aid programs. In the project's "sample certification" requirement, a third party, such as an institutional auditor external to the financial aid office, certifies that the sample has been drawn according to the required procedure. The panel views extension of this technique to other compliance areas, such as using certified auditors, as productive.

The panel is concerned about many quality-related aspects of the audit program, including the recent backlog of unresolved audits, the system of fines, the accuracy of audit findings, the burden placed on institutions, the inability to provide recommendations to schools for positive changes, and the apparent lack of information about the effectiveness of audits as a deterrent to improper program administration. Using a risk-based approach to selecting institutions for compliance audit (as is now done for program reviews) appears to offer increased efficiency in the use of audit resources, particularly if the responsibility for conducting the audits is centralized at the state or national level.

Many criticisms of audits also apply to program reviews, and the overlap of purpose and function between audits and reviews should be addressed. Thus, the panel has deferred making a recommendation until after the discussions that follow on program reviews and OIG activities.

Program Reviews

The Department of Education describes the role of program reviews as identifying and addressing, through assessed liabilities, regulatory violations. Authority for the program review function of the Title IV student financial assistance programs is contained in the Higher Education Act. Program reviews of postsecondary institutions, lenders, and guaranty agencies are generally conducted on site by Department of Education staff from one of the 10 regional Student Financial Assistance offices. Typically, a reviewer is at a school from three to five days. With the department's current emphasis on fewer but more thorough reviews, however, on-site stays are more frequently longer than one week. Generally, reviews are conducted by one reviewer, although two or more often work together. The objectives of program review are to (1) determine an institution's (postsecondary school, lender, or guaranty agency) compliance with Title IV program regu-

TABLE 4-3 Program Reviews, by Type, Fiscal Years 1985-92

Fiscal Year	School Reviews	Lender Reviews	Guaranty Agency Reviews	Total
1985	763	675	10	1,488
1986	417	463	10	890
1987	372	239	8	619
1988	677	313	10	969
1989	820	524	13	1,357
1990	1,139	802	31	1,972
1991	1,016	728	36	1,776
1992	699	500*	24*	1,124

*Estimated.

SOURCE: U.S. Department of Education, Office of Student Financial Assistance

lations and its capability to perform financial and administrative processes and (2) provide technical assistance to individual schools. As noted earlier, guaranty agencies are required to review their high-volume lenders and institutions, potentially adding another level of inspection and burden on schools. (We note that there is some effort to conduct concurrent reviews to avoid duplication.)

Frequency of Reviews and Selection Criteria

Generally, reviews of closed schools and precertification reviews are given first priority.[5] Otherwise, the department's goal is to review each institution once every four years. In the past 10 years, however, a shortage of personnel has prevented the department from meeting this objective. Table 4-3 indicates the year-to-year variability in the number of reviews completed. While approximately 8,000 postsecondary institutions participate in Title IV programs, fewer than one in eight is reviewed each year.

To balance the risk associated with the longer time between reviews, the department selects most institutions for program review based on a series of deficiency factors. For the past several years, the great majority (about 80 percent) of program reviews have been conducted based on "screening" criteria, which have been updated annually. The screening criteria (see Table 4-4) are intended to reflect concerns regarding the management of student aid programs. Each criterion is weighted by assigning it a numerical value. The criteria assign the highest review priority to schools with

[5]Certification reviews and, generally, closed-school reviews are not conducted on site.

TABLE 4-4 Program Review Selection Criteria, 1993

CRITERIA	POINTS
1. Schools with Federal Family Education Loan Program (FFELP) default rates in fiscal year 1990 of 25% and above (includes those schools with default rates that are based on 30 or more borrowers entering repayment and those schools with average default rates)	40
2. High student withdrawal rate of 33% and above	
33-39%	10
40-49%	20
50% and above	30
3. No program review in past 4 years	30
4. Schools with change of ownership/recertification since January 1, 1990	25
5. Schools new to Title IV programs since January 1, 1990	25
6. Schools being monitored for financial capability	20
7. Significant increases in FFELP loan volume (1988-89 and 1989-90) or Federal Pell Grant volume (1989-90 and 1990-91) based on percentages for most recent award years (The number of points assigned depends on the dollar range of the program and the percentage increase.)	10, 15, or 20
8. Regional assessment (e.g., student complaints, adverse publicity)	25

NOTE: Overdue audit report was removed from the criteria in 1993.

SOURCE: U.S. Department of Education (1991b).

high default rates, high student withdrawal rates, and no program review in the past four years. Overdue audits were a high-priority criterion before 1993. Within the ranking, schools are reviewed according to the resources at the disposal of each region. Since 1989, an average of 900 school reviews have been conducted each year.[6] While regional staffing appears to

[6]This number reflects reviews of all types, not necessarily those resulting from the screening process. For example, reviews of closed schools frequently do not involve a site visit and complaint-based reviews may be limited to the subject of the complaint. All are counted as school reviews.

be roughly proportional to the percentage of schools and the loan volume, staffing reportedly is not proportional to high-risk characteristics, such as schools with high default rates or the rate of schools with potential liabilities identified in reviews.

The Visit

The monitoring function of the visit is to assess the institution in terms of (a) the accuracy of its student eligibility determinations and the calculation and disbursement of awards and (b) its general administrative capability and financial responsibility. Institutions are usually informed of the pending visit and are required to provide information and materials, including student rosters and policy manuals, prior to the on-site visit. Each of the following programs is reviewed:

- Federal Pell Grant
- Federal Supplemental Educational Opportunity Grant
- Federal Perkins Loan
- Federal Work-Study
- Federal Family Education Loans

The aspects of the administration of Title IV student financial assistance programs that are subject to review include the following:

- ability to benefit
- satisfactory academic progress by students
- student eligibility
- verification of student-provided information

The reviewer also examines the disbursement of aid to student accounts and the financial accounting for Title IV program funds. At institutions with a high default rate, additional processes are required. As with audits, the program review outcomes can include corrective actions, liabilities, and administrative penalties, such as fines and limitation, suspension, or termination of Title IV programs.

The core of the program review is derived from observations based on a sample of student financial aid files selected by the reviewer. The reviewer selects 10 files from each award year being reviewed (usually two years). There is no set method for the selection. Some reviewers select random samples, others select discretionary samples, and others select a combination of the two. Reviewers are supposed to select files that represent all the Title IV programs in which the school participates. The reviewer then evaluates, through the evidence in the student and financial files, the various operations of the school to test for compliance with law and regulations. Reviewers may expand their sample if a noted deficiency indicates a problem with potentially greater frequency than indicated by its occurrence in the sample. If an instance of noncompliance is noted, the reviewer is expected to document the deficiency using worksheets provided in the department's *Program Review Guide* (U.S. Department of Education, 1991b).

The reviewer not only identifies errors, but also calculates the value of the errors and identifies necessary corrective actions. The calculations cover payments to ineligible recipients and overpayments and underpayments to eligible recipients. The extent of corrective action depends on the frequency of error based on the sample. It may involve correcting the individual case file in which the deficiency occurred, or it may involve a requirement that the school identify all such cases over a one- to five-year period that have the same characteristics and report the frequency of error noted and the value of such errors for that subuniverse.

The on-site review ends with an exit interview with administrative personnel from the school, during which the reviewer summarizes the findings, makes recommendations, and presents the required actions and any potential liabilities. A written report follows, usually within 30 days, which details findings, required actions, and recommendations for change. The institution then has 30 days to respond to the report and provide any documentation or information that rebuts the findings. The Department of Education then evaluates the institution's response and produces a letter to the institution, which includes the final determination for all findings and any assessed liabilities or proposed fines. This part of the resolution process may extend over several months and may involve many complications, such as extensive file reviews. The program review is closed when all assessed liabilities have been paid and the institution has sufficiently responded to required findings. Table 4-5 identifies the most frequent findings based on recent program reviews.

Based on the regional office's evaluation of monetary liabilities, the reviewer prepares data entry forms that show the codes for violations found during the review and the reviewer's assessment of the overall seriousness of the violations taken as a whole. Liabilities can be based on only the students in the sample or a total file review. Program review liabilities are entered into the data base after they are final (that is, the program review has been resolved and closed). Frequency of violations are not recorded, only the occurrence. However, depending on the type of violation(s), significant liabilities may result. Thus, one instance of a violation, such as inadequate student consumer information, at a large number of schools, will appear as a high-frequency error in the data base. On the other hand, an error that occurs at 10 percent of the schools but has serious implications, such as inadequate attendance records at a clock-hour school, will appear as less significant. Similarly, an error that occurs in a large number of cases at 10 percent of the schools will appear as less significant. Thus, a data base

TABLE 4-5 Top 15 Program Review Findings, by Occurrence, Fiscal Year 1991

FINDING		OCCURRENCE
Verification—procedures not followed/documented		408
Financial aid transcript missing/incomplete		371
Consumer information requirement not met		274
Satisfactory academic progress standards not adequate/developed/monitored		261
Guaranteed Student Loans—refunds not made/late		236
Guaranteed Student Loans—exit interview not documented		227
Refunds—late/not made to Title IV account		219
Ineligible student—citizenship		197
Excess cash balances maintained		167
Inconsistent information in student file		161
Ability to benefit—undocumented		145
Accounting records—inadequate/not maintained		141
Bank accounts—federal funds not identified		136
FISAP income grid not documented		135
Student budgets (Pell Grant) improper		128
	Top 15 total	3,206
	Total for all others	3,844
	Grand total	7,050

SOURCE: U.S. Department of Education, Office of Student Financial Assistance.

is maintained, but it does not serve the purpose of a management tool consistent with comments in Chapter 2. That is, it is not used to identify common and special causes of error and would be difficult to use in such a way.

The seriousness of problems uncovered in a program review determines whether the reviewer's report will be reviewed by central office personnel. The central office review is, reportedly, largely an edit for compliance with Title IV regulations, policy, and procedures to ensure that corrective actions are proper and consistent with national guidelines. Central office staff routinely consult with regional office staff to discuss any significant deviations from policy or procedure. The central office review does not include a review of workpapers or other objective information provided or requested on a routine basis, nor is there a standard process to verify the reviewer's assessment of seriousness.

Outcomes

In some cases, the actions of an institution indicate enough of a risk to the federal government that an immediate suspension of participation in

TABLE 4-6 Summary of Administrative Actions

Action	Fiscal Year 1986	1987	1988	1989	1990	1991
Terminations initiated	13	14	27	30	53	113
Terminations imposed	5	1	10	16	18	38
Disqualifications	N/A	N/A	2	6	7	13
Limitations/settlements	8	2	8	5	17	51
Emergency actions	2	2	9	1	0	38
Formal fines imposed	4	3	7	13	27	87
Informal fines imposed	43	81	106	194	215	254
Debarment/suspension	N/A	N/A	N/A	24	58	57
Put on the reimbursement system	19	13	52	126	192	277
Total school reviews	417	372	677	820	1139	1016

NOTE: N/A - not applicable

SOURCE: U.S. Department of Education, Office of Student Financial Assistance.

Title IV programs is sought. This emergency action occurs when the risk outweighs due process considerations.

Given serious violation of regulations, significant liability, or the exposure of fraud and abuse, the Department of Education may fine an institution and limit, suspend, or terminate its program participation. *Fines* can range up to $25,000 per violation for schools and may be combined with other actions. *Limitations* restrict an institution's participation and sometimes are used to settle a termination action. *Suspensions* range up to 60 days; they are rarely used, however, because they require the same process as a termination and may take up to a year to effect. *Terminations*, which are effective for up to 18 months, are sought for serious program violations, failure to pay a fine, noncompliance with a limitation agreement, or failure to solve a program review or audit finding. See Table 4-6 for a summary of administrative actions in recent years.

Data and the Targeting of Reviews

Because on-site reviews are conducted at institutions with high deficiency factors or occasionally at those going out of the program, the results may not be easily used to represent the overall problems occurring with the institutional administration of Title IV programs. Moreover, even in the institutions reviewed, the number of findings per institution is small, on average (e.g., an average of seven per institution in fiscal year 1991 (Table 4-5).

Targeting of institutions for review has improved somewhat recently.

Institutional liabilities averaged over $32,000 per review in fiscal year 1992, compared with under $15,000 in fiscal year 1991, and the number of reviews declined from about 1,100 to under 700. The department views this as progress in the right direction, that is, focusing on fewer schools with larger "returns" per school. Another interpretation is that error rates have increased, but there are no procedures for making such inferences from program review data. Further, the liabilities assessed do not equal recoveries of funds. Linking recoveries and measurement of the degree of assurance that all potential assessments were found would not be useful. Nevertheless, the panel is concerned about the targeting of the reviews. According to Department of Education staff, data management initially focused on tracking the occurrence of a review, not the findings that resulted. In more recent years, in response to requests for data on findings, data have been gathered concerning the findings of noncompliance with regulations. Yet, data continue to be anecdotal, that is, to reflect what individual reviewers said they saw at selected schools.

Although field reviews and the central office coordinating and data system are based on uncontrolled anecdotal observations, refinements in the automated system have permitted the manipulation and combination of data elements and their use to make general statements concerning the types and frequencies of errors. This has guided policy and management practices to an important extent. The panel believes that what is needed is a well-defined and well-maintained data base system that incorporates the results of program reviews in a form that management can use to guide policymaking.

From information provided by Department of Education personnel and discussions with financial aid administrators, the panel learned of the following problems with the data base associated with the program review process:

- The current design of the data base uses a cutoff sample weighted by the screening criteria. This is because neither the selection of institutions for review nor the selection of cases within an institution is based on a sampling strategy that would allow inferences about the population. While the selection methodology does help target reviews toward the most problematic institutions, the process does not result in the development of a data base from which generalizations about either institutions or cases within institutions can be made. Also, reviews do not cover all regulatory, statutory, and administrative requirements, because of time and personnel limitations. However, even if the cases and institutions were statistically sampled, the "findings" data base would be flawed because there is no control for which requirements are subject to review across regions or even within regional offices. The data base is further limited in that it contains only exceptions (violations); information about successful practices that resulted in compliance is not recorded.

• The reliability of the categorization of "error" is a cause of concern. The definitions of some errors are incomplete or unclear. Thus, the experience of the reviewers can contribute to measurement variability. There need to be more specific evidentiary requirements governing observations of error.

• No standards are in place by which to compare conclusions across regions or within regions. Reviews need not be identical in scope and process, nor in documentation. In addition, the levels of seriousness of institutional problems, by which each review is characterized, are not well defined. Although reviews with the highest problem rating go to the central office for clearance, there are no measures of the reliability of the reviewers' ratings. Nor is there assurance that reviews that were not referred to the central office were, in fact, not serious. Verification on a sample of cases would be needed.

• The reviews do not lead to a measure of the success of follow-up or oversight activities. Essentially, schools that are found to have significant problems must identify the extent of the problem through a review of all students' files and report their own error rates. (The Department of Education may require CPA certification.) As an alternative for less significant findings, at the next scheduled audit, the auditor must review the school's self-examination results and report to the Department of Education in the "prior audit" section of the audit report. Moreover, the actions taken to resolve program review findings are minimally observed by the department. The findings do not lead to a program improvement process—they just report "assessed liabilities" over and over, and future reviews are not targeted based on the findings. Most important, the focus on assessed liability may be misleading. As noted above, actual liabilities after appeals are much less than the assessed amounts. The panel did not learn of any efforts to link the denied amounts to problems in the error definitions, risk, or future oversight activities.

OIG Activities

In addition to the audits and program reviews just described, the OIG conducts and supervises audits, investigations, inspections, and other reviews of the department's programs and operations. The OIG's role is to provide leadership, coordination, and policy recommendations to promote economy, efficiency, and effectiveness; prevent fraud and abuse in the department's operations and programs; and review proposed and existing legislation and regulations governing the department's programs. The OIG has also implemented a procedure for evaluating audits performed by nonfederal auditors. This procedure includes a review of audit working papers and information sharing with some state boards of accounting.

Departmental staff indicated that for the past several years, OMB and the OIG have identified the department's student financial assistance programs as vulnerable to fraud and abuse. OIG audits, investigations, inspections, and other reviews disclose problems that involve ability to benefit and other admissions abuses; ineligible courses and course stretching; accreditation, eligibility, and certification; branch campuses and ineligible campuses; refund practices; loan due diligence; issues related to the Supplemental Loans for Students and Parent Loans for Undergraduate Students programs; and issues related to bankrupt and closed schools. In addition to recommending the recovery of funds in individual cases, the OIG makes recommendations for changes in systemic requirements and practices, which if implemented, are intended to help prevent many of the abuses from occurring in the future.

The Panel's Comments and Recommendations on Audits and Reviews

The rules and regulations governing student eligibility for financial aid are complex. The panel questioned whether and, if so, to what extent the complexities themselves are significant sources of error. The current monitoring and compliance activities and data bases do not address this issue. They are designed to assess absolute performance with respect to the accurate administration of student financial assistance programs, to impose sanctions based on error, and to count the occurrences of error.

Audit and review activities are necessary if the Department of Education is to fulfill its responsibility to ensure that program participation is limited to those institutions that are willing and able to operate in accordance with program goals and expectations. Because factors such as changes in economic conditions and in financial aid personnel affect an institution's ability to maintain desired levels of quality, "problem" institutions will appear sporadically and must be dealt with promptly and efficiently. Audits provide reasonable promptness, especially now that they are an annual requirement. Program reviews occur relatively infrequently because current Department of Education budgetary and personnel ceilings preclude regular reviews of all institutions. Yet, the review process has the greater potential to be proactive and to provide the useful instruction and technical assistance that promote quality and help to build a sense of partnership between the institutions and the department.

The audit and program review processes used by the Department of Education to enforce quality standards are marked by considerable duplication, ineffectiveness, and wasted effort. The independent audit of schools checks for internal controls and compliance with program regulations in a way that essentially duplicates parts of the program review process. Such checks are more effectively performed by knowledgeable reviewers and should be fully incorporated within the program review process. However, an effective review process would identify high-risk areas that could be part of the audit function.

Inspection is a deterrent only when a better job can be done. To maximize an institution's potential, the audit and review processes must be better integrated and redesigned with a sharper focus on addressing meaningful measures of quality and quality improvement rather than the current concept of measuring compliance with an unrealistic "zero defect" standard. To expend resources where risk is greatest, for example, data from past audits and reviews should be used to improve the methods for selecting institutions for inspection and the methods for sampling records at those institutions.

Further, the match between the capabilities of the inspector and the inspection function warrants careful attention. More information is needed about the reliability of independent auditor and reviewer findings. For example, are the relative frequencies of findings comparable between audits and reviews? While the audit function can provide timely information, program reviews are the only system of institutional quality checks that is entirely in the control of the Department of Education. Thus, the reviews should have the highest degree of reliability and objectivity, since all other systems rely on a considerable degree of good faith for self-reporting of problems or successes.

The panel believes the Department of Education should revamp its audit and program review systems in order to realize the potential of those activities to support its gate-keeping function and provide technical assistance to institutions and useful data to policymakers. The panel finds four areas in need of attention.

1. In response to the lack of usable data sets:

• To make efficient use of scarce resources, it is critically important that the Department of Education create more useful data sets and make better use of statistical sampling techniques in its inspection processes that provide the data. Selection of institutions for inspection is a key task. Reviews should continue to be focused primarily on problem institutions. Still, it is wise to include a purely random component in the selection process so that all institutions are on notice that they may be selected and to provide information that could be used to make inferences about all institutions. The majority of resources should be allocated to the highest risk areas, based on models that are derived from the best data available and are frequently refined to reflect the results obtained at previously selected institutions.

• Once an institution is selected for examination, various sampling techniques offer natural and effective means of ensuring that the time devoted to the examination is appropriate. For example, an initial sample can be chosen according to a prescription that uses the results of that sample to determine whether further sampling is necessary and, if so, how large the next stage of sampling should be. Such methods reduce significantly the number of records required on the average to provide accurate inferences about the total population of records in the category. Another plan, multiphase sampling, could be useful. Here, a large sample is selected for a "quick" review, possibly looking for known but simple indicators of problems. If the results of the large sample warrant it, a subsample is drawn for detailed examination. With either procedure, initial sample size should be based on knowledge of the variability of the problem and the risk it poses, not on a flat standard as is now done.

• The overly large number of review areas should be reduced. Areas not known to be error prone should be reviewed on a sampling schedule to provide an assurance of continuing compliance.

• Program reviews must result in the creation of a data base that can be used to do more than simply identify error patterns (national, regional, and type of school) within the group of schools reviewed. Incorporating a designed sample of institutions and recording the frequency of errors at the institutional level rather than just the occurrence of error would permit general conclusions about error levels. Currently, conclusions beyond a particular school are not statistically valid.

• Some details of successful compliance, especially in processes that are problematic at most schools, as opposed to "finding problems" only, should be reported as part of the review process.

• Reviewers should be experienced enough to look beyond prescribed review instructions to report unsound practices that undermine the intent of student financial aid programs even if they do not violate regulations or prescribed procedures.

• Better information on the cost of the audit and review functions and the liabilities actually collected should be maintained so resources can be allocated effectively.

2. In response to the lack of a good definition of "error":

• To provide much-needed clarity in the assessment of error, the inspection processes should maintain clear distinctions among errors of different types, for example, process errors as opposed to material errors and errors for which the institution is responsible as opposed to errors for which student applicants are responsible.

3. In response to the lack of standards:

• The review process itself should be subject to an organized effort focused on quality improvement. Sources of sampling and measurement error should be subjects of study to ensure that review outputs, incorporated into a well-maintained data base, adequately support regional and categorical comparisons, statistical estimates (e.g., of error rates), and policy decisions.

• Quality improvement activities should be part of the audit and review processes, from selection of the institutions to close out of the inspection, and should include verifiable standards for conducting the activity and for a higher level review of the results.

4. In response to the lack of follow-up:

• Reviews should seek to determine the cause of problems and report possible corrective action.

• Review findings, once they incorporate the prior suggestions for improvement, should be used as a basis for new policy and/or legislation.

• Finding violations should stimulate attempts to find causes and, if indicated, to identify systemic failure. There should be systematic follow-up on resolution of findings at each institution, and the results should be used to target areas for future reviews.

Because current program reviews and annual audits duplicate many activities and the skills required may not match the expertise of those doing the "inspection," the panel makes the following recommendation.

> *Recommendation 4-3: The Department of Education should redesign the current system of program reviews and independent audits. Program reviews should focus on compliance as part of an overall quality improvement program. Checks on institutional compliance and internal controls should be performed only in program reviews and audits should focus only on financial attestation.*
>
> *The Department of Education should also develop, test, and implement methods to systematize and standardize the program review process. The department should not interpret the 1992 reauthorization of the Higher Education Act as a requirement to review every school according to a fixed schedule. Risk-based statistical methods should be used to identify problem schools for more frequent reviews, and other schools should be selected randomly at a nominal rate that would fulfill the necessary "gate-keeping" functions. The department must improve the evaluative feedback and technical assistance provided to institutions during reviews. At the same time, the reviews should be used to accumulate data that provide the department with a continuous overview of error rates, compliance levels, and other information of significance for management in making policy.*

5

Alternative Perspectives on Quality in Student Financial Aid Programs

In the preceding chapter, the panel carefully defined the types of error that are encountered in the student financial aid system and then discussed the quality control and measurement procedures that are currently in use. In this chapter we consider quality from the perspective of three participants with major responsibilities for the control of error in the system—the Department of Education, the student applicant, and the postsecondary institution. We begin with a discussion of the attempts by the Department of Education to gauge the "state of error" in the system through sample surveys, particularly the most recent major study of the Integrated Quality Control Measurement Project. After a discussion of the shortcomings of that study and problems with the large-scale survey approach to error measurement in general, we turn to an examination of possible systemic causes of error by considering the complexity of the process from the viewpoint of the individual applicant. In the final section of the chapter, we consider some of the problems in maintaining quality that are faced by the postsecondary institution—the bearer of legal and moral responsibility for the just administration of financial aid. Not surprisingly, the perspectives of the three players differ in many respects. Each viewpoint, however, constitutes an important dimension of the "total picture" of quality in the student financial aid system.

SURVEYS OF ERROR

Thus far, the sole attempts to measure errors throughout the student financial aid system have been through a sequence of special surveys of aid recipients commissioned by the Department of Education. The panel first discusses these studies and then addresses the issue of nonrecipients. The early studies (see Table 5-1) focused on errors in Pell grants. More recent studies included estimates of error in Campus-Based and Guaranteed Student Loan awards as the survey designs were developed to select cases in those programs. Our focus in this discussion is on two of the department's

TABLE 5-1 Previous Quality Control Studies Commissioned by the Department of Education

Year(s)	Focus of Study
1975	Office of Education study. Compared IRS records with data from applicant. Repeated in 1977 and 1980.
1977	Report of Student Financial Assistant Group. Sources of data were public testimony, previous studies, and audits.
1979-80	Basic Educational Opportunity Grant study. Examined application data and institutional records.
1980-83	Pell Grant Quality Control Study. Studied error in the Pell Grant Program. The study, which consisted of two large national surveys, compared delivery systems, assessed options for redesigning delivery systems, and developed the *Institutional Quality Control Handbook*. The study concluded that error in the Pell program was significant, and aside from the need for program and policy restructuring, quality could be improved through implementation of verification and validation efforts.
1983-86	Stage One of the Title IV Quality Control Study. A national survey of recipients of Campus-Based aid and certified applicants of Guaranteed Student Loans (GSLs). This study examined error in the Campus-Based and GSL programs.
	Stage Two of the Title IV Quality Control Study. A national survey of recipients of Pell grants, Campus-Based aid, and certified applicants of GSLs. This study examined error in the Title IV programs.
1987	Stage Two of the Title IV Quality Control Study. Comparison with other federal programs and assessment of potential incentives and disincentives.
1985-92	The Institutional Quality Control Pilot Project. Assisted educational institutions in designing their own quality improvement programs and demonstrated the applicability of quality control procedures for financial aid at the institutional level.
1986	Guaranteed Student Loan Quality Control Project. Identified and measured error in the GSL program due to financial institutions, guaranty agencies, and the Department of Education.
1988-90	The Integrated Quality Control Measurement Project. Examined the extent of error in the delivery of Title IV aid, patterns and trends in error that point to systemic problems in the delivery system, possible causes of error and steps that can be taken to enhance quality in the future, and the extent to which prior actions have improved quality.

SOURCE: Based in part on Chauvin et al. (1989).

commissioned reports, *Title IV Quality Control Project: Stage Two, Final Report*, Vol. 2, *Corrective Actions* (Advanced Technology and Westat, 1987b) and *Integrated Quality Control Measurement Project, Findings and Corrective Actions* (Price Waterhouse, 1990b). We also rely on *Pell Grant Validation Imposes Some Costs and Does Not Greatly Reduce Award Errors: New Strategies Are Needed* (General Accounting Office, 1985). Each of these studies presents information on error by program, classified by student and institutional error.

The studies reviewed indicate that error in the Title IV student financial aid programs is sizable and persistent. In the 1988-89 academic year, for example, of the approximately $15.4 billion in aid distributed, Price Waterhouse (1990b) estimated that almost 11 percent of the program dollars were awarded in error. Possible inaccuracies in this and other estimates of program error are discussed later in this chapter, but there is little doubt that the errors, whatever their exact total, are considerable. At each step of the delivery process (applying, determining eligibility, calculating awards, disbursing awards, and monitoring educational progress), errors can be made. Despite the apparent magnitude of this problem, little has been done to prevent error—for example, changing procedures that seem to generate error. Instead, efforts have been focused on detecting errors in examined files and correcting those specific errors identified.

All the parties involved in student financial aid and its administration are potential originators of error, and indeed, a total quality management approach would hold each of them responsible for the efficient working of the system. Key players include the Department of Education, students applying for and receiving aid and their parents, third-party application processors, and the educational institutions. Historically, however, the emphasis in reporting has been on student and institutional error. Table 5-2 summarizes the results of various studies showing estimated student error, institutional error, and total error (i.e., resulting from either or both sources).

Student Error

Student errors may result from the use of incorrect data, difficulties in estimating and projecting data, or the complexities of the application and its instructions. Table 5-3 compares sources of student error over time in the Pell Grant Program, and Table 5-4 compares sources of student error in academic year 1988-89 by type of Title IV program. In all studies the important sources of error were relatively consistent over time, with the exception of dependency status, which was the most important source of error in 1982-83 and 1985-86 but dropped off the list of important errors in 1988-89, at least in part because the definitions of dependency changed considerably. Also note that the estimates of error cited from these studies

TABLE 5-2 Student and Institutional Error Found in Title IV Aid

Contractor/Program	Academic Year	Sample Size	Student: Cases with Error (%)	Student: $ Error (million)	Institution: Cases with Error (%)	Institution: $ Error (million)	Total (absolute): Cases with Error (%)	Total (absolute): Average $ Error per Recipient[a]	Total (absolute): Total $[b] (million)
Macrosystems[c]									
Pell Grant	1978-79	2,309	43	177	16	70	55	219	248
Advanced Technology[c]									
Pell Grant	1980-81	4,304	41	352	37	211	69	346	563
GAO									
Pell Grant	1982-83[d]	4,000	39.4	328	33.5	321	62.7	408	649
	1982-83e	4,000	27.3	327	17.2	202	40.4	518	530
Advanced Technology[f]									
Pell Grant	1985-86	3,200[g]	32.3	439	30.0	386	54.4	273	763
Campus-Based	1985-86	3,200	64.5	853	31.5	353	77.2	834	1,068
Guaranteed Student Loan[h]	1985-86	3,200	10.6	393	13.5	587	20.1	263	920
Price Waterhouse[i]									
Pell Grant	1988-89	3,310[j]	24.8	365	4.6	126	28.2	489	481
Campus-Based	1988-89	3,310	37.6	331	20.9	360	51	978	656
Stafford Loan	1988-89	3,310	11.5	337	9.6	447	18.3	1,223	742

[a]Based on cases with error.

[b]In some cases, this figure is the sum of student and institutional error.

[c]"All error figures are based on $2 tolerance and calculated without counting errors of missing affidavit of educational purpose or financial-aid transcript, which tends to understate error. The 1978-79 estimates are based on less rigorous verification of application data than those in the 1980-81 study (tending to understate student error in the former) and on discrepancies between verified application data and expected disbursements (the 1980-81 study examined actual disbursements)" (General Accounting Office, 1985:Table 2, p. 9).

[d]"Data are from the Department of Education and include all overawards and underawards added together, without allowing them to offset each other within a single case or in the aggregate. Error is defined as a discrepancy of plus or minus $2 from the best award" (General Accounting Office, 1985:Table 18, p. 55).

[e] "Data are from the Department of Education. Table includes all overawards and underawards added together, without allowing them to offset each other within a single case or in the aggregate. Error is defined as a discrepancy of plus or minus $100 from the best award. Totals may not add because of rounding" (General Accounting Office, 1985:Table 36, p. 108).

[f] "Error is defined as a discrepancy of plus or minus $50 from the best award" (Advanced Technology and Westat, 1987a:Exhibit 3-1, p. 3-2; Exhibit 3-4, p. 3-11; Exhibit 3-5, p. 3-14).

[g] The 3,200 sample size was the sum of each of the three program's samples.

[h] "Due to revision in the estimate of total GSL loan volume, these figures [the program wide estimates of $393 million student error, $587 million institutional error, and $920 million total (absolute) error] should be reduced by approximately 10 percent" (Advanced Technology and Westat, 1987a:Exhibit 3-5, p. 3-14).

[i] A $50 tolerance level was used (Price Waterhouse, 1990b:Exhibit II-2, p. II-4; Exhibit II-3, Campus-Based Need Error, p. II-7; Exhibit II-7, Stafford Loan Overaward Error, p. II-16).

[j] The 3,310 sample size was the sum of each of the three program's samples.

TABLE 5-3 Components of Student and Institutional Error in the Pell Grant Program

Academic Year	Error Item	$ Error (millions)
	Student error	
1982-83[a]	Dependency status	64
	Other nontaxable income	46
	Household size	34
	Number in postsecondary schools	24
	Home equity	18
	Assets of dependent students	17
	Adjusted gross income of parents and independent students	16
	Income of dependent students	12
	Taxes paid	2
1985-86[b]	Other nontaxable income	75.1
	Home equity	64.0
	Dependency status	45.4
	Dependent students' net assets	35.5
	Students' expected income	32.6
	Household size	29.9
	Adjusted gross income	20.6
	Number in college	18.4
1988-89[c]	Parents' number in college	72
	Parents' household size	70
	Parents' home value	47
	Students' 1987 adjusted gross income	44
	Parents' real estate/investment value	32
	Students' household size	31
	Students' 1987 other nontaxable income and benefits	24
	Parents' 1987 adjusted gross income	24
	Institutional error	
1982-83[d]	Missing financial aid transcript	95
	Incorrect determination of enrollment status	–39
	Incorrect calculation or disbursement of award	24
	Incorrect determination of cost of attendance	–21
1985-86[e]	Missing financial aid transcript	41.2
	Missing Selective Service compliance statement	30.5
	Missing statement of educational purpose	28.1
	Award to students with bachelor's degree	13.6
	Incorrect determination of enrollment status	9.6
	Incorrect determination of cost of attendance	8.3
	Loan default	4.7
	Incorrect calculation or disbursement of award	3.7

continued

TABLE 5-3 *Continued*

Academic Year	Error Item	$ Error (millions)
1988-89[f]	Missing statement of educational purpose	29
	Missing Selective Service compliance statement	29
	Award to students with bachelor's degree	29
	Missing financial aid transcript	14
	Incorrect determination of cost of attendance	9
	Independent under unusual circumstances	5
	Default/repayment	1
	Half-time enrollment	not observed
	Factoring other aid	NA

[a]General Accounting Office (1985:Table 20, p. 57).
[b]Advanced Technology and Westat (1987a:Exhibit 3-2, p. 3-5).
[c]These numbers are rough estimates based on those values found on the graph (Price Waterhouse, 1990b:Exhibit III-1, p. 14).
[d]Negative values are net underawards. General Accounting Office (1985:Table 22, p. 60).
[e]Advanced Technology and Westat (1987a:Exhibit 3-3, p. 3-8).
[f]These numbers are rough estimates based on those values found on the graph (Price Waterhouse, 1990b:Exhibit III-2, p. 16).

are based on sample data and thus are themselves subject to the sources of error associated with surveys. These problems will be addressed later in this chapter.

Assuming that errors are not made deliberately, several types of "student error" could not be corrected even with additional care on the part of the applicant. For example, some problems arise because, to apply for aid from some states and institutions, the application must be completed before the applicant completes his or her federal tax form. Thus, dependency status, taxes, and adjusted gross income are estimates and prone to error. Similarly, household size and the number in postsecondary schools are projections for the following academic year and are subject to change as circumstances change. In order to simplify the application procedure and include fewer items that are subject to error, the panel recommends the following:

> *Recommendation 5-1: For applicants who have filed a tax return in either of the prior two tax years, the information used to complete the application and determine the award should be based on the most recently filed of these income tax returns. When the earlier tax year is used, updated information should be required as soon as a new tax return is filed. The updated information should not be used to change the award before the next term. Further, "household size" and "number in postsecondary school" should be based on the situation as of the application date.*

TABLE 5-4 Components of Student and Institutional Error in the Federal Student Financial Aid Programs, 1988-89

	Dollar Error (million)		
Item	Pell Grants	Campus-Based Program	Stafford Loans
Student error[a]			
Parents' number in college	72	82	47
Parents' household size	70	60	52
Parents' home value	47	31	38
Student's adjusted gross income	44	29	88
Parents' real estate/investment value	32	13	27
Student's household size	31	31	52
Student's 1987 other nontaxable income and benefits	24	23	37
Parents' 1987 adjusted gross income	24	33	46
Institutional error[b]			
Missing statement of educational purpose	29	29	53
Missing Selective Service compliance statement	29	6	33
Award to students with bachelor's degree	29	1	0
Missing financial aid transcript	14	1	18
Incorrect determination of cost of attendance	9	21	86
Independent under unusual circumstances	5	1	7
Default/Repayment	1	5	9
Half-time enrollment	not observed	NA	107
Factoring other aid	NA	61	105

NOTE: "Home value" was removed from consideration under reauthorization.

[a]These numbers are rough estimates based on those values found on the graph (Price Waterhouse, 1990b:Exhibit III-1, p. 14).

[b]These numbers are rough estimates based on those values found on the graph (Price Waterhouse, 1990b:Exhibit III-2, p. 16).

For example, applicants for the 1994-95 school year would use 1992 tax year data if they have not filed 1993 taxes at the time of application.

Institutional Error

The most recent study (Price Waterhouse, 1990b) reported institutional error for three categories: procedural, calculation, and distribution errors. Procedural errors occur when institutions do not adhere to established guidelines for granting awards. Table 5-3 compares sources of institutional error over time in the Pell Grant Program and Table 5-4 compares sources of institutional error by type of Title IV program for the 1988-89 academic year. Note that for incorrect determination of enrollment status and of cost of attendance, the estimated net error in the Pell Grant Program for 1982-83 was negative, which indicates that the estimated underpayments (which we show to be underestimated later in this chapter) were greater than the estimated overpayments for these error sources. Enrollment status does not appear to have been a major source of error in the Pell Grant Program in later years, but it persisted as a troublesome issue in the Stafford Loan Program. According to the Advanced Technology and Westat (1987b) report, confusion regarding enrollment status generally occurs in cases involving students attending summer sessions or clock-hour students. Incorrect determination of cost of attendance causes a large dollar error to occur in all three Title IV programs.

Incorrect calculation and distribution of awards are also persistent problems for institutions. Calculation error, which Price Waterhouse (1990b) reported as dominating institutional marginal errors, occurs when incorrect information is used to calculate awards; for example, errors made in determining the correct cost of attendance. Factoring in other aid produces considerable calculation error as well. In the 1988-89 academic year, when a calculation error was made for 21 percent of applications, factoring error was found for 9 out of 10 applications in error.

Distribution error occurs when an incorrect award amount is disbursed. With respect to the expected award or certification, the Price Waterhouse (1990b) study found meaningful errors in the Campus-Based and Stafford loan programs, but acknowledged potential overstatement of the largest source. These errors do not affect the need calculations as do all the other errors discussed in the study. The panel will focus here on the award error components, since audits of financial administration were already discussed.

As can be seen from Tables 5-3 and 5-4, technical errors, such as a missing statement of purpose, certification of Selective Service registration, or financial aid transcript, have a large dollar impact, for when these documents are found to be missing, their absence renders the entire award erroneous. Such cases may or may not otherwise be eligible for financial aid, and for those who are eligible, the calculated award may or may not be the correct amount. The General Accounting Office (GAO) requested an analysis by the Department of Education of cases in which technical errors due to missing documentation were ignored and the files reanalyzed for substantive errors. The analysis indicated that the estimated dollar value of institutional errors dropped by about a third when technical errors were removed, and the percentage of cases with "institutional error" dropped by half (General Accounting Office, 1985). Underawards, when technical errors were ignored, were more frequent and had a larger dollar value than overawards. Department of Education staff mentioned that these administrative requirements are easy to observe during audits and review and can be indicators of more serious administrative problems. The panel believes that there is a need to refocus the effort used to detect technical errors. For example, potential improvements in the indicators of quality have been suggested by Goodwin (1991).

> *Recommendation 5-2: The Department of Education should determine which, if any, of the administrative requirements that can lead to "technical error" are useful surrogates for variables that deal directly with program goals but are difficult to measure. Administrative requirements that are useful in this sense should be retained, but others should be eliminated.*

The Most Recent Study of Error—The IQCMP

The Integrated Quality Control Measurement Project (IQCMP) is a large-scale survey of institutions and students who received financial aid during the 1988-89 academic year. The survey, designed and executed by Price Waterhouse in association with the Gallup Organization and Pelavin Associates, involved the first-stage selection of 350 academic institutions and second-stage selection of 3,310 students therein, for a total of 2,653 usable award analyses. The study attempts to evaluate the quality of the Title IV delivery systems for the (1) Pell Grant Program, (2) Campus-Based Programs (Supplemental Educational Opportunity Grant, College Work-Study, and Perkins Loan), and (3) Stafford Loan Program.

The IQCMP is by far the most ambitious undertaking of its type since the inception of the Title IV programs, and the panel wishes to emphasize at the start of this discussion that the contractors should be commended for their efforts to obtain measures of error that can lead to meaningful improvements in the system. Indeed, the panel considered the IQCMP to be so important to an understanding of the state of program error that it commissioned a special background paper (see Appendix A). Many of the comments that follow are based on that paper, although it should be read in its own right for a fuller understanding of some of the problems with the Price Waterhouse study.

Estimated Error

The IQCMP provides estimates of errors of overpayment and underpayment in the distribution of Pell grant and Campus-Based financial aid, and estimates of overaward errors in Stafford loans. The errors are reported in absolute terms—that is, both under- and overawards are assigned positive values as their measure of error in quality—and they are reported in terms of percentage of total dollars disbursed, percentage of awards in error, and mean dollars of error per recipient in error.

Components of Measured Errors A detailed description of the components of measured errors is contained in the report and need not be repeated here. However, it should be noted that the definition of error used in the study encompasses discrepancies between "actual" award and "best" award permitted under Title IV regulations. In some cases, this definition resulted in inclusion of some measured error that resulted from unavoidable projection errors. For example, an overaward resulting from a student or family incorrectly projecting household size is counted as an error in the IQCMP, whereas a good faith error of this type is not an error under the Title IV regulations. Other cases were labeled as error because of discrepancies between federal regulations and state or institutional rules. For example, the failure of an academic institution to follow its own internal rules—say, giving a certain student a Perkins loan that exceeds a stated maximum amount allowable—is not a violation of federal rules, but nevertheless is a measurable error in the IQCMP. Although the appropriateness of some of the cases of error may be debatable, in general the broader definitions result in measures that are more closely associated with "quality of delivery" than would be obtained under stricter statutory definitions. Further, since the sample consists only of recipients, it cannot be used to estimate errors of nonpayment to eligible nonrecipients. For these three reasons (the use of absolute error, the broad definition of error, and the exclusion of nonrecipients from the estimates) the error estimates from the IQCMP do not represent dollars spent in error.

Errors in the Estimation of Error In any sample survey aimed at assessing error in a process, there are two major sources of error in the summary measurement of the error of interest. To avoid confusion in the multiple use of the term *error* in the same sentence, we must distinguish between a "true" error in quality and an error in its observation. First, if a deviation in quality, when it occurs, can be detected and its magnitude observed with perfect accuracy (i.e., without error), then the only error of concern in assessment is the *sampling error* encountered when survey statistics are used to estimate population quantities such as averages and totals. Unfortunately, in most observational phenomena, there is another source of inaccuracy, called *nonsampling error*. Within the realm of nonsampling error, one can further distinguish among causes due to problems of *undercoverage*, *nonresponse*, and *mismeasurement*. For example, in the IQCMP the frame from which the sample was drawn excluded certain newer institutions. This exclusion can lead to an undercoverage error if the part of the target population that had no chance of falling into the sample is sizeable and has a different level or patterns of award error. The success of the "ratio estimation" method of correction for undercoverage mentioned in the IQCMP report relies on the validity of an assumption of similarity between the parts of the population that are covered and not covered by the frame.

The effects of nonresponse errors are much the same as those of undercoverage. It is reported that about 20 percent of the original sample of students was dropped from the study because either the students or their parents could not be interviewed. An overall interview response rate of 80 percent is usually considered quite respectable by modern survey standards, but if the nonrespondents differ dramatically from the respondents, potentially serious biases could exist in the reported results.

Finally, nonsampling errors can occur because repeated observations of the same phenomenon generally do not lead to the same reported measurement, especially if the required measures are based on human judgment. For example, *marginal error* was measured in the IQCMP study by comparing an award calculated with all reported values and the same award calculated with all reported values except for the substitution of one "best value" for the source of potential marginal error. Measurement error occurs in this observational process if repeated attempts at the same measurement result in variability of the marginal error from observation to observation. In many cases, two persons looking at the same award situation will not agree on the best value for a certain item.

It is important to have some idea of the magnitude of the contribution of this source of measurement error to the quality (technically called the mean square error) of the reported results. The IQCMP report provides little or no information concerning the possibility of serious measurement error in the survey field operations. Although it is often difficult to reduce or eliminate measurement error in sample surveys, it is possible to design the measurement procedures so that the components of variance due to measurement error and to sampling error can be estimated separately. For example, matches with official records can be used to estimate bias, and independent repeated measurements of a subsample can be used to estimate measurement variability. There is no indication in the IQCMP report that measurement error and its effect on accuracy were either controlled or estimated after the fact.[1]

Recommendation 5-3: Future studies commissioned for student financial aid programs should consider carefully and discuss the problems that result from errors of measurement. The studies should include

[1]There is a discussion of bias in the document on the sampling plan discussed below, but the bias under consideration is that of noncoverage of the frame, not bias due to systematic effects of measurement error.

estimation of components of the overall error in estimation due to nonsampling sources and discussion of assumptions underlying those estimates.

The IQCMP Sample Design

The design of the IQCMP survey is described in a separate document (Price Waterhouse, 1989). All the institutions, except the 50 institutions that were part of the quality control pilot project,[2] were grouped by geographic proximity into clusters ranging in size from one to four schools (but most frequently three). The clusters were then selected with probabilities proportional to the number of students in each program in institutions in the cluster. Second-stage selection rates for students were such that clusters had equal sample sizes and the rates were constant for samples in each of the three programs.

A technical discussion in the report on the sample design demonstrates that the measure of size used at first-stage selection ensures that the expected total sample size (across all program combinations) is constant for each cluster, thus balancing workload. The discussion also states that the design feature of constant overall direct selection rates for each program tends to increase the precision of the estimates of error rates. However, the design was complicated by including in the sample size for a particular program cases that were sampled for one of the other programs but were also found to be in that program. Analyzing a given program using students in multiple programs to augment the direct sample size results in differential weighting, and the ultimately weighted cluster sizes for that program are not equal. Thus, the final effect of the seeming elegance of the design on the precision of estimation is not clear.[3]

---

[2]The 50 institutions participating in the quality control pilot project (to be discussed in detail in Chapter 8) were considered to be selected at a first stage with certainty, and students were selected separately from each of the three programs proportionate to the program totals within each institution. A student who was selected for one program but also participated in one or more of the remaining programs, however, was used to augment the direct sample for the other programs. This required weighting the sample observations to account for differences in sampling probabilities.

[3]In Appendix A, Reiser discusses an error in the calculation of the probabilities of selection due to failure to consider the joint probabilities of selection of the same individual from more than one program. The effect of this error on the weights used in ultimate analyses is not known.

It should also be noted that the use of a sample consisting of direct and augmented cases for each program introduces some degree of dependency between error estimates across programs. This point may not be of great importance if the data are used to comment on each program separately, but it should be kept in mind if two or more programs are compared.

The description of the sample design includes a table that reports the expected (planned) sampling error as a function of various sample sizes (Price Waterhouse, 1989:Exhibit IV-2). The table shows that the expected half-width of a 90 percent confidence interval for an estimated percentage seldom exceeded 2.0 percentage points and never was greater than 2.5 percentage points. These prior estimates appear to have held (more or less) in the sole instances where estimated sampling variability is indicated in the final report (Price Waterhouse, 1990b:Exhibits II-1 through II-7). Reiser (Appendix A) observed, however, that in many other instances where reported standard errors would be helpful they are absent. It is especially difficult to judge the statistical significance of reported interdomain comparisons without knowing the standard errors of the differences.

The panel would like to have seen greater reporting of estimated sampling errors and design effects, especially when the total dollars and average error amount for recipients in error are reported. (The Department of Education has not insisted on computation of standard errors for all survey estimates.) The description of the "bootstrap simulation" method of variance estimation at the end of the sampling plan document is vague and confusing. The paucity of reported sampling errors implies that the method was not actually used on a large scale. Commonly used techniques in designs similar to those used in this study employ either the jackknife, balanced repeated replication, or Taylor Series methods of variance estimation after grouping first-stage clusters into random groups or pseudo pairs. The panel wonders whether consideration was given to those approaches and if so, why they were rejected. Software that computes estimates and estimated standard errors consistent with survey designs like that used in the IQCMP, such as SUDAAN or PC CARP, is available for personal computers.[4]

Recommendation 5-4: In future sample surveys commissioned by the Department of Education, the final report should contain estimates of sampling error for all important estimates. The report should also contain estimates of design effects resulting from the complexity of the sampling plan.

Other Troublesome Issues

Finally, we mention some observed inconsistencies in the reporting of the results of the IQCMP that were discovered by the panel staff. First, the

[4]At a minimum, some attempt at a more sweeping discussion of the precision of the estimation of the reported error rates and amounts, similar to the way in which generalized variance functions are used in the survey reports of many government agencies, would have strengthened the report, even though generalized variance functions are often of doubtful precision themselves.

1990 Price Waterhouse study purportedly breaks down and analyzes the components that are the principal contributors to student marginal error. Upon investigation, however, Exhibit III-1 in the Executive Summary of their report does not agree with the information in the cited exhibits in the main body of the report (Exhibits III-3, III-4, and III-5). For example, according to the Executive Summary, reported information on the *parent number in college* ranks as the most significant contributor to student error in the Pell program. However, Exhibit III-3 of the report ranks this component's percentage of dollars in error considerably lower, 0.6 percent—below that for parent-reported untaxed income (3.6 percent), parent reports on household size (3.4 percent), parent reports of home value (2.3 percent), parent reports of real estate/investment value (1.7 percent), parent reports of Social Security benefits (1.2 percent), student reports of household size (1.1 percent), and student reports of adjusted gross income (0.9 percent). Similarly, the Executive Summary cites *student's adjusted gross income* as the most significant source of student marginal error in Stafford loan overcertification error. Exhibit III-5 of the main body of the report, however, shows that it is exceeded in percentage of dollar error by five other components. Departmental staff investigated these problems and found that there were typographical errors in the information in the body of the report (the data in the appendix of the report being correct).

Inconsistencies may be found in the written text as well. For example, the Executive Summary specifies parent number in college and parent household size as the two largest contributors to student marginal error, while page III-12 of the main report indicates that the two top contributors are untaxed income and parent household size.

Upon consideration, these discrepancies lead us to question the reliability of these data and the analytic results. While the presentation of the data in these reports using Pareto charts is a very useful technique for determining the most serious problems, the department must be careful that acceptable judgments and conclusions are made based on the findings of the IQCMP.

Taking all these issues together, the panel doubts seriously that the various so-called quality control or error studies have very accurate measures of dollars spent or not spent in error. At the same time, through the history of these studies, the repeated finding of high error levels and the consistency of findings regarding contributing causes of error have been useful. In fact, the studies raised many issues regarding sources of error in program administration and are useful in identifying initiatives for quality improvement.

Failure to Estimate Error Leading to Nonaward

According to Department of Education data for fiscal year 1982-83, 42 percent of Title IV aid recipients received overawards and 21 percent received underawards. Typically, overaward has been estimated as much larger than underaward whenever such a classification has been made. There is, however, a serious defect in all the major studies of error in student financial aid programs that must be emphasized. The various surveys, including the most recent IQCMP, analyze only cases of awards; there is no coverage of students to whom financial aid was totally denied. Thus, it is not surprising that these studies find more overpayment error than underpayment error.[5] Department of Education staff indicated to the panel that the study design flaw was considered several times in the past, but no funding was provided to address this issue. On a more basic level, a major concern of the panel is whether the emphasis in the Department of Education on trying to measure and control possible overpayment errors leads to an underemphasis on measuring progress toward the program goals of access and choice in postsecondary education. Potential recipients mistakenly denied financial aid, despite actual eligibility, surely have restricted access and choice. The department should obtain some estimate of the number of such inappropriate denials and the dollar amounts involved. In the next section the panel will urge the department to go a bit further and try to ascertain the extent to which students who would have been eligible for aid had they applied nevertheless failed to apply, perhaps because of the perceived difficulty of the application process or perhaps because of ignorance of the available programs.

> *Recommendation 5-5: The Department of Education should improve estimates of "error" by including estimates of the coverage of student financial aid programs, that is, ascertaining the frequency with which eligible applicants are mistakenly denied financial aid and the underaward amounts associated therewith.*

Rethinking the Use of Surveys of Error

The cost of the IQCMP was approximately $2 million for planning, execution, and analysis alone, not including the efforts of Department of Education personnel in administering the contract. An important question is whether large-scale surveys that attempt to measure the state of error in the system and to identify the sources of that error are cost-effective. Do they result in estimates of sufficient precision and relevance that they can guide quality improvement efforts? Or would the resources be better spent on

---

[5]The GAO attempted to fill part of this gap by planning to survey by telephone some 2,000 eligible students who did not receive a Pell grant. They were able to contact only 42 of the young people, testimony to the difficulty involved in trying to get some measure of underpayment error (General Accounting Office, 1985). Such studies would be greatly enhanced if they were done immediately upon rejection of the application so that the problem of recontacting the respondent would be greatly reduced.

alternative approaches to total quality management? If such studies are deemed to be useful, how frequently should they be carried out, and on what scale?

The panel believes that the relevant information for informed policymaking can be gleaned from the surveys that historically have been used for estimation of aggregate error, but the methodological problems with the surveys and apparent limitations on the ability of student financial aid program managers in the Department of Education to detect and criticize the shortcomings leads the panel to make the following recommendation:

Recommendation 5-6: The Department of Education should not routinely embark on surveys of the type that have been used in the past to estimate total error levels in student financial aid programs. The resources are likely to be better spent on continuous monitoring—using data from audit and review activities, for example—and other approaches to quality improvement. Special studies should be done, but only when the study objectives are clearly linked to a policy evaluation or process improvement plan and steps can be taken to eliminate the methodological defects of past surveys.

Certainly, the National Center for Education Statistics has staff with the expertise to assist student financial aid program managers in developing studies and reviewing the reports of the studies.

THE APPLICANT'S VIEW

As the ultimate customer of financial aid services and as the provider of the data that puts the overwhelming inspection processes described in the previous chapter into motion, the applicant or potential applicant must weigh heavily in decisions concerning process improvement. The panel focused on two areas of importance related to the applicant's need for quality: early awareness and the application itself.

Nonapplicants for Financial Aid

Although not a part of the panel's original charge, the subject of students who may be eligible but never apply is an issue of particular concern to the panel. There may be potential students who could benefit from aid but who do not apply for any number of reasons, such as not understanding the process, misunderstanding requirements, believing that they are ineligible, thinking that college costs are too high, and so on. Such individuals, actually eligible, surely have restricted access and choice as a result of the error in award determination, which is contrary to the objective of federally funded aid. The panel's concern rests in the fact that little effort has been made to measure the frequency of these occurrences. Progress toward correcting the problem has been limited to outreach in selected areas, but it has not been consistent.

In 1990 the GAO reviewed several sources of information in an effort to determine what applicants and their families know about federal financial aid at various stages of the college choice process. The study found that gaps in specific knowledge exist at all stages, as well as misconceptions, lack of information, and misinformation about aid—all of which are critical components of higher education decision making (General Accounting Office, 1990a).

Among the GAO's findings was the fact that those individuals who were aware of the financial aid possibilities were more likely to enter postsecondary institutions. Low-income students aware of Pell grants in their sophomore year of high school and middle-income students similarly aware of loans were most likely to enroll in a postsecondary school upon high school graduation. Minority students and students whose parents had a high school diploma or less also enrolled in higher education more often when they had early knowledge of federal grants and loans.

More recently, in a statement before the U.S. House of Representatives, Subcommittee on Postsecondary Education, the GAO's assistant comptroller general for program evaluation and methodology (Chelimsky, 1991:1) noted that, "Currently, knowledge of available student aid is limited and inaccurate, and many students who probably could benefit from higher education end their schooling early." Clearly, this is a problem that must be addressed. In order to move closer to the goal of higher education being accessible to all, changes must be made in reaching and advising potential students and their families.

Although the studies cited above seem to imply that it is obvious that causation runs from knowledge of the programs to enrollment, a word of caution is necessary. It may well be that preexisting intention to enroll encourages early knowledge seeking. A longitudinal study, at least, would be needed to determine the influence of early information on enrollment decisions.

Recommendation 5-7: The panel commends the Department of Education for its recent efforts to improve early awareness of federal financial aid programs, such as providing financial aid software to high schools. The panel recommends increasing those efforts. Studies of the effectiveness of the efforts and users' reactions to the timeliness, accuracy, usefulness, and clarity of outreach and counseling services are needed.

Very few ongoing data sets are available from which to obtain information about students who have not applied for financial aid. The Department of Education maintains administrative records on only those students applying for financial aid, and the IQCMP studies discussed earlier collected data only on aid recipients.

The only sources of data on students not applying for federal financial aid are National Center for Education Statistics surveys—the National Postsecondary Student Aid Study (NPSAS), High School and Beyond, and the National Longitudinal Survey. The NPSAS asks students who did not apply for aid why they did not. Departmental staff indicated to the panel that the unweighted frequency of responses to the question regarding the most important reason for not applying indicates that the overwhelming majority stated either that their families paid for their education or that their income was too high to receive aid.

In addition to collecting self-reported data on why students did not apply for aid, the Department of Education is currently using the NPSAS to analyze the characteristics of postsecondary students who appear eligible for Pell grants but did not receive them. Preliminary results from this comparison reveal that eligible nonrecipients were much more likely than recipients to be part-time and/or part-year students. The eligible nonrecipients were also much more likely to be financially independent, attend less than four-year schools, and to have greater income and assets than Pell recipients.

Recommendation 5-8: The Department of Education should gather data on the reasons for nonutilization of student financial aid by potential recipients. Consideration should be given to ways of estimating the number of potentially qualified applicants who are discouraged for one reason or another from applying for financial aid in the first place. Further, the department should consider ways of estimating the number of potential students who do not even attempt to enter a postsecondary school because of their ignorance of available financial aid. Also, data on the knowledge of aid should be collected from students and their families before the student finishes secondary school. Such data could be obtained in a variety of ways, including ongoing national surveys. The resulting information will be important in devising a program for reaching those who are eligible but do not apply.

Applying for Federal Student Financial Aid

For the 1992-93 award year, students who wished to apply for the Federal Pell Grant, Federal Stafford Loan, Federal Supplemental Educational Opportunity Grant, Federal Work-Study, or Federal Perkins Loan programs could make application in one of three ways:

- Students could complete the Application for Student Financial Aid (AFSA) produced and distributed by the Department of Education.

• Alternatively, students who wished to apply for the above programs could complete an application form produced by one of the multiple data entry (MDE) contractors. Federal regulations require that MDE-produced forms incorporate verbatim all instructions and data items from the AFSA. However, a major difference between AFSA and MDE-produced forms is that the latter can include additional items needed for the administration of student aid programs, including nonfederal programs, at campuses served by the MDEs. Thus, MDE-produced forms tend to be longer, and more complex, than the AFSA.

• In the 1990-91 award year, the Department of Education introduced the Electronic Data Exchange application process. This process, which is available at an expanding number of schools, enables participating schools to enter and review federal student financial aid application data using a personal computer or mainframe computer.

Panel members were concerned that the design of the three application methods could cause confusion among applicants and financial aid officers, lead to inadvertent errors in financial aid decisions, and deter some students from applying. Such up-front errors could then lead the Department of Education to perceive a need for more inspection. Testimony before the panel, as well as the panel's own deliberations, suggest that the application forms for student financial aid might have been difficult to complete, especially for the typical lower income applicant, and that the design of the form might complicate the work of student financial aid officers who advise students about financial aid, check the accuracy of applicants' responses on application forms, and attempt to correct erroneous data. As a result, the panel undertook a study of the federally produced AFSA and the Electronic Data Exchange process (see the report in Appendix C).

The 1992-93 AFSA

The AFSA for the 1992-93 academic year became available to applicants in late 1991. The form is available in English and Spanish versions, although the panel examined only the English version during its deliberations.

The English version of the 1992-93 AFSA consists of a four-page application form and a preaddressed mailing envelope stapled in the middle of a 12-page booklet, which consists mainly of instructions, definitions, and worksheets needed to fill out the attached application form. The packet contains only a limited amount of information on the five federal programs for which the AFSA is the relevant application, and students wishing more information on those programs are directed (on page 11 of the booklet) to write to the Department of Education for a free copy of another booklet, The *Student*

Guide: Financial Aid from the Department of Education - Grants, Loans, and Work-Study 1992-1993 (U.S. Department of Education, 1992-93). The *Student Guide* is a 60-page booklet describing the five programs for which the AFSA is the relevant application, as well as Supplemental Loans for Students and Parent Loans for Undergraduate Students.

The AFSA package and the *Student Guide* provide different types of information, and information from both is needed if students are to make informed decisions about financial aid applications. For example, the *Student Guide* describes federal financial aid programs and discusses key eligibility requirements and borrowers' rights and responsibilities. It also lists telephone numbers for Federal Student Aid Information Centers, numbers that are not given or referred to in the AFSA packet, where the need is probably much greater. On the other hand, the *Student Guide* does not provide definitions of several key terms or discuss special circumstances that can trigger flexibility in student aid eligibility requirements. Instead, those are discussed in the AFSA packet. The important point here is that an applicant who relied only on the documents provided by the federal government in order to apply for student financial aid would apparently need 72 pages of information and instructions in order to complete an informed application for student financial aid from the federal government.

More important, the four-page AFSA form appears dauntingly complex. A cursory inspection of the form by panel members revealed that the form is crowded in appearance, uses a potpourri of response formats presented in multiple colors, and sometimes contains confusing or incomplete directions and inconsistent wording of questions. Moreover, only one copy of the form is included in the AFSA package. Thus, no working copy is available for use as a draft or to keep as a record should verification or correction be required. Despite this, the instructions specifically state that applicants are to use a pen in filling out the form, and a standard black-and-white photocopy of the AFSA would not adequately reflect the multicolored format. As a result, many applicants routinely request two copies of the entire 12-page AFSA package, thus wasting 12 pages to secure another 4-page form.

In summary, the panel's initial work suggested that the AFSA had been produced without sufficient regard for well-known form design considerations or sufficient attention to the accuracy of the wording of items or clarity of directions to the applicant. To confirm this impression, the panel requested and received help from 13 federal agencies and research organizations known to have expertise in the design, collection, and processing of information similar to that collected by the 1992-93 AFSA. In mid-March of 1992, the panel mailed those organizations a letter that stated, in part:

> The panel is especially interested in expert advice concerning the complexity of the form and instructions, especially for the typical applicants (low-income, high school graduates and their parents).... Comments or sugges-

tions based on your organization's experience with the collection and study of similar data would be helpful to determine whether errors made by applicants or data processors might be reduced through revisions in wording, sequence, instructions, format, or other aspects of the application and related tasks.

In general, the reviewers were critical of the AFSA and accompanying instructions. For example, reviewers commented as follows:

- "The aid application forms and processes are much more complex and onerous on applicants than they need be, more onerous than a 1040 tax form. Ironically, [many] of the students seeking aid come from low income families which either file no tax return or file a 1040EZ. The student aid application form is probably the most complicated financial form they have ever seen."
- "We agree that this form and accompanying instructions are exacting and complex due to the myriad of financial requirements which must be documented by law. As a result, student-level applicants and low-income parents are likely to encounter much difficulty in both understanding and completing the AFSA."
- "I found the form to be difficult to follow. Part of the difficulty is due to the amount and complexity of the information required, but the overly complicated appearance and structure of the form also contribute to confusion."
- "Looking at the form, I don't think any of the questions are very difficult. But it has the appearance of being overpowering. The first page is cluttered and the rest is red and grey. From the face of it, my guess is that it is confusing."
- "I think the similarity to income tax forms might underline the importance of completing the form correctly, but many people are intimidated by tax forms. I am concerned that this general similarity and the overall lack of "white space" make the task appear more formidable than it is."
- "Needed improvements would require a total redesign of all features mentioned in the letter—wording, sequence, instructions, format, and so on."
- "The form itself appears manageable for typical applicants.... The instructions that accompany the application form are quite difficult and complex. We would expect significant confusion and incorrect responses if the instructions are not modified."

Other, more detailed comments were offered by the reviewers, as were specific suggestions for changing the AFSA and accompanying instructions (see Appendix C). Although the reviewers did not cite statistical research demonstrating the extent of error in responses to items similar to those included on the AFSA, several suggested that review and research should be undertaken on this point. The following statements exemplify reviewers' comments:

- "... a careful review should be conducted to determine minimum data requirements; then extensive questionnaire design work should be undertaken to develop a form that collects these data in a way that is simplest for applicants to provide. The questionnaire design work should address not only wording of questions but also form layout and general instructions provided. Cognitive psychology techniques could be very useful."
- "Pretest with respondents typical of those who would use the form. If you can observe them completing the forms, and probe where they appear to be having difficulty or are making errors, it may help explain why errors are made and how to correct or avoid them."

The informal testing methods suggested by the reviewers are not necessarily expensive to conduct, and they have been employed by many federal agencies. Use of such techniques was discussed in the Office of Management and Budget's *Statistical Policy Paper 10* (DeMaio, 1983); the examples in that report include the Social Security Administration's group interviews with teenagers and adults prior to a revision of the application for a Social Security form. Papers commissioned by the panel describe Internal Revenue Service (IRS) experience with the informal testing of forms (see Appendix E) and two redesign projects conducted at the Behavioral Science Research Center of the Bureau of Labor Statistics (BLS)—the IRS Schedule C study and a BLS survey (see Appendix D). Such research centers are sometimes referred to as cognitive labs.

The AFSA and related documents have never been field-tested among students. A predecessor of the AFSA, the basic grant form, was field-tested under contract in 1981, but far fewer data elements were required by legislation to be collected at that time, and the prototype was an uncrowded, two-page form (Rehab Group and Macro Systems, 1981). Nevertheless, much helpful information was gathered during this field-testing and used to improve the form. In addition, the contractor that conducted the field test made a series of suggestions for future activities designed to improve the application for student financial aid. Those suggestions included using routine activities to gather information on problems applicants are having with the form, engaging in research on the effects of variations in forms on respondents, and reviewing comparable benefit application forms as a means of improving the forms used to apply for federal student financial aid. The panel concurs with those recommendations and believes that, over a decade later, they should be implemented by the Department of Education. Similar concerns were expressed by the General Accounting Office (1985).

The 1992-93 Student Aid Report

The panel also examined the Student Aid Report (SAR), which is sent to applicants after the paper version of the AFSA is processed. If an AFSA is not rejected for one of a variety of technical reasons, an applicant can expect to receive a SAR from the processor within about four weeks. The SAR contains the data given by the applicant on the AFSA, information from the Department of Education about the applicant's eligibility for federal student aid, and instructions about what to do next. At this step, applicants also might receive either an Information Review form or an Information Request form on which to provide additional information or make corrections and to verify any assumption edits that were inserted during processing. Applicants who appear to qualify for Pell grants based on their initial application receive a payment voucher at this time. If corrections or additions to an application are needed, applicants can expect to wait two to three weeks after they submit changes for receipt of a revised SAR.

As part of its study, the panel reviewed the comments of over 600 applicants who wrote to the Department of Education in 1991 in response to an invitation in the SAR to voice their comments or ideas for improving the SAR. Three-fourths of the comments referred to confusion in reviewing or correcting data due to a lack of correspondence between the item sequence on the SAR and the item sequence on the AFSA. Apparently, as students work their way through notations on the SAR, they must move back-and-forth within the AFSA to make corrections, all the while paying careful attention to the AFSA's color coding scheme. Thus, in line with the recommendations above, the panel also suggests that the Department of Education review the SAR with the goal of relieving the burden on the applicant. Suggestions about potential changes to the SAR are discussed in Appendix C.

Electronic Version of the 1992-93 AFSA

In addition to examining the paper versions of the AFSA and the SAR, the panel also reviewed the Department of Education's Electronic Data Exchange application process—also known as Stage Zero (for details of this review, see Appendix C). According to the user's manual, the electronic application form for 1992-93 is "intended for student use in the financial aid office environment, with monitoring and counseling done as needed by financial aid staff. Some institutions may want to have aid administrator staff walk through the questions as the student enters his/her information. Others may have staff members use this entry mode while interviewing applicants" (U.S. Department of Education, 1991a:15-1). In practice, most applicants work from an already completed paper version of the AFSA.

Alternatively, an "expert" entry mode is provided so financial aid personnel can quickly enter data from applications initally submitted on paper.

An advantage of the Stage Zero process is that it includes an Electronic Needs Analysis System, which enables financial aid personnel to use data already keyed by students to calculate a number of expected results for a given applicant. Using this system, financial aid personnel can calculate an expected family contribution using the Congressional Methodology. Other financial calculations, such as an estimated Pell Grant Index for determining Pell eligibility, as well as an estimated Pell award amount, can be calculated (the Congressional Methodology and the now unused Pell Grant Index were discussed in Chapter 3). In addition, Stage Zero allows verification selection criteria to be applied on-site. While the calculations are not official, they do provide immediate information to applicants. Further, an important incentive for using this system is that it can considerably shorten the time from application completion to receipt of federal aid.

Stage Zero also can be used for electronic filing of renewal applications, a process that was introduced for the 1992-93 school year and is available to returning students at selected institutions. Renewals for other students require filling out the entire paper AFSA, no matter how much of the data previously filed are still correct. In the electronic renewal process, only changes in data need be entered, after which a copy of the completed form is generated by the computer.

Learning to use Stage Zero is easy. Experience with a keyboard is helpful, but even hunt-and-peck typists and others inexperienced with computers should be able to adapt to the system easily. Answers to most questions are precoded and those that are not do not generally require lengthy answers. The first screen displayed by the program contains simple instructions on using the system, and additional information is provided through help messages. On the screens that follow, the wording, sequencing, and numbering of items match the contents of the paper version of the AFSA. A limited number of questions appear on each screen, which overcomes the "crowded" look of the paper AFSA, and answer cells are consistently located on the right-hand side of the screen (except for long items, such as names and addresses), which eliminates the varied formats of the paper AFSA.

Although the panel's review of Stage Zero revealed several minor problems, the electronic application process appears to have many advantages over the paper process. Data entries can be proofread on screen, and errors can be corrected simply by backing up and rekeying the entries. In addition, edit and query messages automatically appear on screen to alert the user to incorrect, incomplete, inconsistent, or suspect data. In some cases, previously inserted data are entered automatically when called for in later items. In addition, the complex skips called for in the paper version are performed automatically, and help messages are available throughout the program. The program also contains worksheets that do the mathematical calculations called for in some parts of the application and then automatically insert the totals into the proper box on the application form.

When using Stage Zero, an applicant can stop at any point in the program, although if the application is not completed, the entries made cannot be saved. The Department of Education should determine whether this is a shortcoming in need of action. At the conclusion of the program, applicants are asked if they want to review the application. Choosing "yes" causes the display to return to the beginning of the form. Corrections can be made easily, and when the applicant okays the data, the program automatically informs the user that the program is being validated. Corrections can also be made if inconsistencies are flagged during the validation process.

If the application passes the validation stage, the program automatically saves the file and prints a summary of the data entered on a two-page printout, which also contains a certification statement for the student to sign. The Quality Control Guidelines in the user's manual instruct the applicant to then compare the answers on the printout with the responses on the applicant's paper form. However, this is a difficult task because item numbers are not shown on the printout and section names do not match those on the paper version of the AFSA. Moreover, applicants are instructed to make written corrections on the printout, but that is not always possible due to a lack of space.

Completed and validated applications can be sent to the Department of Education's Central Processing System automatically, or data files on floppy diskettes can be mailed. Applications can be processed and an Electronic Student Aid Report returned to the institution within 72 hours using the Electronic Data Exchange System.

The Stage Zero process has many advantages. Many of the advantages are nullified, however, by having an applicant first fill out the paper AFSA and get the necessary signatures before filling out the electronic application. The panel believes that this does not take advantage of the many Stage Zero features that make it easier for the applicant to understand the information required on the application or to provide that information accurately. If applicants could start with Stage Zero, working from notes, and fill out the paper form concurrently or subsequently, errors and burden might be reduced.

Moreover, the use of Stage Zero is currently limited to postsecondary educational institutions participating in student aid programs. However, a slightly modified version of the software might be appropriate for off-campus use. In fact, many home and most office personal computers meet the requirements for installation of the 1992-93 Stage Zero version, and with appropriate modifications, it might be possible for high schools, churches, community organizations, civic groups, and mentors with access to a computer to assist aid applicants in filling out the forms.

Recommendations on Financial Aid Forms

Based on its analyses of the various forms used in the federal student financial aid application process, the panel makes two recommendations:

> *Recommendation 5-9: The complexity of the forms, instructions, and information booklets leads to excessive burden for applicants and is a cause of error. Thus, the Department of Education should consult experts in form and question development, such as those found at cognitive research laboratories, to aid in its efforts to improve the application materials.*

> *Recommendation 5-10: The Department of Education should continue to improve and expand the availability of its electronic data exchanges, making sure to address the issue of appropriate balance between the potential for improved data and additional burdens that might be placed on the schools.*

Although the panel was unable to estimate the amount of error caused by current versions of the AFSA and SAR or the reduction in error due to use of Stage Zero, the evidence reviewed above suggests that attention to these recommendations has considerable potential to reduce applicant burden and improve the quality of data. The reduction in burden, alone, is a quality dimension that should be of interest to a governmental agency. Improved data quality can reduce inspection and correction activities during SAR and verification reviews.

POSTSECONDARY INSTITUTIONS

Institutions are increasingly burdened by the administrative complexities imposed by the federal government. From an original promise to administer the Pell eligibility requirements centrally, the government has moved to an increasingly complex student aid report, which must be verified by school personnel. The addition of information unrelated to student need, such as Selective Service status, resulted in a form which has grown from two pages to four. In addition, hard copies of applications and related "underwriting" materials must be physically retained for long periods of time, which creates the need for expensive warehousing in the financial aid offices.

Postsecondary institutions have other concerns as well. Various layers of aid and the complexity within each layer contribute to a cumbersome aid structure. Additionally, with continuous regulatory changes and requirements, schools must often adapt to changes in rules and accurately administer financial aid simultaneously. All factors considered, the system inevitably becomes error prone. In the remainder of this chapter, the panel relates concerns of the institutions that were repeatedly expressed by representatives of institutions and during visits to student financial aid offices and looks at the available measurements of those concerns.

Administrative Cost and Regulatory Requirements

Federal and Local Costs

The program of oversight of the federal student aid programs appears to impose unreasonably high costs for inspection of processes. Contributing to the high costs of inspection are layers of redundant review. An individual applicant, for example, may be subject to repeated data and process examination of initial information—as a student loan recipient, as a Pell grant recipient, as a part of internal audits, and as a part of federal audit requirements or program reviews.

Cycles of reexamination are also problematic. Applications undergo separate inspections at each institution if the student is applying for or considering transfer to several institutions of higher education. Even a student who applies for and attends only one institution is not immune from repeated cycles of review of data each time credit load varies, income changes, a new award is received, or for a myriad of other conditions. Revision of each student award five times per academic year is not uncommon. Besides adding to the institution's work, these changes add uncertainty to the financial planning of the student.

State and School Program Coordination

Although the subject of this study is the federal student aid process, it is important to note that to the student and institutional participants, the federal government, while dominant, is nonetheless only one provider of student aid (see Tables 5-5 and 5-6). Assessment of the perceived quality of the aid process must consider all sources of aid because many students with high financial need would simply not be able to participate in higher education with federal funds alone, even with maximum funds available. This is especially true for a student living away from home at a private university, but it is also true for some public universities. The packaging of the various aid sources, however, adds to the administrative burden of the institution.

State grant programs vary in the proportion of financial aid they provide, but almost every state provides some level of support in addition to

TABLE 5-5 Profile of Aid Packages, All Students

Number of Students with Aid Combination (000s)	Average Dollars per Recipient, by Program			
	Pell Grant	Campus-Based	Stafford and SLS Loans	Other
10,578	0	0	0	0
2,912	0	0	0	2,854
607	0	0	3,646	0
592	0	0	3,763	3,891
50	0	1,265	0	0
141	0	1,495	0	3,461
92	0	1,600	4,180	0
295	0	1,598	4,114	4,374
613	1,243	0	0	0
636	1,339	0	0	1,763
490	1,545	0	2,805	0
485	1,434	0	2,572	2,095
189	1,551	1,135	0	0
353	1,525	1,325	0	2,085
187	1,603	1,085	2,481	0
370	1,545	1,465	2,563	2,819

NOTE: SLS=Supplemental Loans for Students Program; "Other" includes state, Veterans' Administration, and institutional aid.

SOURCE: Data from 1990 National Postsecondary Student Aid Study; provided by Daniel Goldenberg.

the federal programs. In part that is due to the incentive structure of the State Student Incentive Grant Program, a federal grant that requires state matching; however, most states match a much higher proportion of federal aid than is required. States direct funds to needy students, to perceived manpower needs, and to students with high academic performance, in the main. Thus, the states add their own regulations. It is possible that the level of state regulation has been minimized due to the high burden on institutions and on the states themselves from federal student aid regulation. Nonetheless, institutions must often resolve conflicts inherent in federal and state regulations. Further, the student recipient often perceives the layers of state and federal regulation as confusing or, worse, as a roadblock. For students at high-cost institutions, additional information requirements may be requested in order to ration scarce school resources. For example, a student whose parents are divorced encounters federal and state requirements to provide information from his or her custodial parent and stepparent (if any), but, in addition, may be required to provide parallel data from his or her noncustodial parent and stepparent to meet the institution's needs.

TABLE 5-6 Profile of Aid Packages, Full-Time Undergraduates

Number of Students with Aid Combination (000s)	Average Dollars per Recipient, by Program			
	Pell Grant	Campus-Based	Stafford and SLS Loans	Other
3,698	0	0	0	0
1,206	0	0	0	2,648
380	0	0	3,067	0
353	0	0	2,722	2,792
35	0	1,400	0	0
107	0	1,482	0	3,259
54	0	1,352	2,902	0
199	0	1,396	2,805	3,758
360	1,379	0	0	0
471	1,427	0	0	1,823
416	1,597	0	2,868	0
405	1,459	0	2,599	1,965
153	1,621	1,214	0	0
301	1,570	1,402	0	2,115
163	1,630	1,121	2,514	0
336	1,568	1,480	2,552	2,746

NOTE: SLS=Supplemental Loans for Students Program; "Other" includes state, Veterans' Administration, and institutional aid.

SOURCE: Data from 1990 National Postsecondary Student Aid Study; provided by Daniel Goldenberg.

Extensive and Ever-Changing Regulations and Policy

A significant factor in the ability of financial aid administrators in institutions of higher education to perform their jobs thoughtfully, accurately, and compassionately on behalf of students is the extensive and ever-changing regulations and policy governing the student aid programs. Change is rapid and accountability is immediate. Regulations or statutes frequently go into effect within 30 days of being issued or are retroactive, and changes often take effect months before the information required to implement them is received. As a result, financial aid offices and officers must often function with unclear directions. For this reason, the quality and timeliness of information on regulatory changes should be improved, including the interpretation of the regulations and guidance on how to establish administrative systems to implement the changes.

The Higher Education Act, which authorizes funding for federal student financial assistance, is reauthorized every six years. If changes in the student aid programs were limited to a six-year cycle, the process could be manageable and would allow administrators to use their expertise to perform the best job for all students. However, the reality and ideal are very far apart. In the past 10 years, over 20 new responsibilities for student aid administrators have been enacted. Ryan (1988) lists the following examples:

- verification of data used to award Pell grants, guaranteed student loans (GSLs), and all federal Campus-Based aid;
- increased Pell program reporting and documentation;
- implementation of a determination of satisfactory academic progress;
- multiple disbursements of Guaranteed Student Loans;
- implementation of the Supplemental Loans for Students and Parent Loans for Undergraduate Students programs;
- verification of citizenship;
- documentation of independent student status;
- adherence to changes in the Federal Tax Reform Act, which affected scholarships and grants;
- new refund and repayment policies; and
- collection of Selective Service compliance and antidrug statements.

Ryan indicates that these duties not only required changes in procedure at institutions, they also required reeducation of students and retraining of staff. In some cases, changes to computer systems and informational handouts were needed.

Although a deadline of December 1 for any policy or regulation to go into effect for the next academic year (starts on July 1) was established during the 1986 reauthorization, the deadline is frequently ignored. Often, regulations are either deemed too significant to delay or budgetary savings take precedence over the need to provide sufficient lead time for implementation. As a result of concerns regarding extensive and ever-changing regulations and policy, the 1992 reauthorization act requires a master calendar for financial aid rules and that the Department of Education engage in negotiated rule making.

Another issue raised by ever-changing regulations and policy is the inappropriate use of common-cause regulations to effect special-cause events.[6] Over the years, added layers of regulations have been placed on students and institutions as a whole as a method of achieving compliance from small segments of the student and institutional population. Whether it is worth burdening all to ensure the compliance of a few is questionable.

Common-cause regulations do not adequately deter schools with undesirable outcomes nor reward those that exhibit good management of federal programs. Guidelines are not designed with the intent of improving the

[6] Recall the discussion of common-cause and special-cause problems in Chapter 2.

administration of financial aid programs by setting performance standards; rather, penalties are assessed for noncompliance as an attempt to motivate good performance.

Financial aid offices struggle to keep up with the burdensome administrative requirements. Administrative costs reportedly have risen faster than the overhead recovery rates allowed by federal regulation; consequently, institutions are forced to allocate resources to the financial aid office that could be spent on instructional purposes. This is particularly serious due to the significant financial crisis facing many, if not most, colleges. Only institutions that award a high proportion of their own funds, as contrasted with federal funds, appear able to invest in improvement. Some institutions believe that some loans, for example Perkins loans, are too cumbersome for their limited financial aid staff to administer and therefore they do not offer them.

Burden and Error

Given the complexity of the student financial aid system and the large number of players involved throughout the process, many concerns arise regarding administrative burden and error. How much burden is acceptable? Who should bear the burden? How real is the problem associated with error?

A recent assessment of regulatory burden (Price Waterhouse, 1991) found consensus among all types of institutions regarding such issues as mandatory in-person counseling and the complex determination of dependency status. Mandatory in-person counseling of all loan recipients upon entering and leaving the institution was found to be burdensome, unproven in reducing defaults, and inappropriate for institutions with low default rates. Similarly, collecting documentation each year to prove that a student is independent, when the student has already proven independence in previous years seems to be an unnecessary burden, particularly given that the rules are difficult to administer.

Other issues of concern agreed upon included the manual reporting and recordkeeping requirements associated with the financial aid transcript and Student Aid Report, and the burdensome need to collect numerous signed statements from the student regarding illegal use of drugs, educational purpose, and other items. To alleviate much of the burden associated with manually keeping records, Price Waterhouse (1991) proposed instituting the use of an electronic system and recommended that changes to specific statutes and regulations be evaluated for their potential to reduce unnecessary burden.

When addressing the concerns related to obtaining signed documentation from students, the issue of *technical error* arises. Technical errors, or categorical errors as some studies refer to them, are a component of procedural error which occurs when an institution fails to adhere to established guidelines. As noted earlier in this chapter, when any one of the following documents, required by the Department of Education, is not present in a student's file, the student is considered to be categorically ineligible: financial aid transcript, statement of educational purpose, statement of registration for Selective Service, and documentation of independent status under unusual circumstances. These causes of error have the greatest impact on total error because when they occur, the entire amount of an award is considered to be in error. Categorical errors account for about two-thirds of the institutional errors found in Department of Education commissioned studies. Three reports—General Accounting Office (1985), Advanced Technology and Westat (1987b), and Price Waterhouse (1990b)—all found that although the frequency of categorical errors is low, the dollar impact was significant.

In the 1982-83 academic year, 3 percent of Pell grant recipients received awards in error due to a missing financial aid transcript, and the net estimated error equaled $95 million (General Accounting Office, 1985). In the 1985-86 academic year, net marginal error due to a missing financial aid transcript was $41.2 million and affected 2 percent of Pell grant recipients; for GSL recipients, 1 percent had categorical errors totaling $142.8 million (Advanced Technology and Westat, 1987b). In the 1985-86 academic year, some form of categorical error occurred in 4 percent of Pell grant cases, which resulted in $114.2 million in institutional payment error. Estimates related to the error due to a missing financial aid transcript for the 1988-89 academic year by aid program are presented in Table 5-7. Although the dollars in error appear large, as a percentage of total dollars they are no more than the percentage of students with error. Since dollar error is nested

TABLE 5-7 Pell Award Error Due To Missing Financial Aid Transcript, 1988-89 Academic Year

Program	Percent of Recipients with Error	Percent of Dollars in Error	Average Error per Recipient with Error
Pell	0.4%	0.3%	$ 875
Campus-Based	0.3%	<0.05%	$ 664
Stafford Loan (overcertification only)	0.2%	0.2%	$ 3397

SOURCE: Price Waterhouse (1990b).

within this small number of students, error reduction strategies still require finding those students in error. Further, once the appropriate documents are obtained and added to the student's file, the technical error is corrected and the award is no longer considered to be in error.

While the Department of Education requires institutions to collect signed statements regarding illegal use of drugs and educational purpose, the certification is not of direct use to the institution because it neither prevents drug use nor ensures that the student has a valid educational purpose. Since regulations such as these are driven by statute, Congress must take action if changes are to occur. Under the current system, institutions bear a considerable burden in obtaining and storing this type of certification. There is, however, no reason why the depository cannot be changed so that a centralized process developed by the Department of Education can take on an equitable amount of responsibility for federal requirements not related to the education of the student. (This action is discussed in Chapter 9.)

In an effort to improve the existing system along the lines suggested above, Congress has made some progress in initiating changes. The 1992 reauthorization of the Higher Education Act calls for increased utilization of verification mechanisms in which student statements and supporting documentation can be verified through record matching, by using either an automated or other system. These provisions include requiring that data base matches with the Selective Service be made and that the Social Security Number of all aid recipients be verified. With this advancement toward electronic data transfer of student financial aid information, the burden imposed by the collection of student certifications could be greatly reduced and the value returned for these activities could be increased.

In general, technical errors are an administrative problem that can be solved by obtaining the appropriate documentation. Record matching is often an easy way to obtain the documentation. When this error is corrected, most student award amounts will not change (except in cases in which an award is incorrectly given to students who already have a bachelor's degree). Although technical error is not as severe in its impact on the intent of the programs as other types of error found in Title IV aid administration, it is a regulatory violation that troubles policymakers who are locked into an enforcement/penalty approach.

Recommendation 5-11: The Department of Education should increase its efforts to remove unnecessary burden from students and institutions by further development of automated data matches whenever possible.

The panel will expand on this recommendation in Chapter 9.

6

Financial Aid Data Systems

The panel has discussed the extensive body of information available to student financial aid program managers from special studies and the edit and verification processes. The Department of Education also asked the panel to comment on the organization of information about award error and the usefulness of such data bases for making program decisions. In a similar investigation, the General Accounting Office (1985) found the department's approach to issues regarding the quality of award determination to be unsystematic. That study found that decisions that might affect improvement were hindered by a lack of goals and analyses that were hurried because of operational demands. The study cited problems in coordinating the activities of offices within the department that needed to work together and labeled the resultant reactive decision making "remedial" and "not preventive."

The panel, after discussions with Department of Education personnel and review of earlier studies, also found no particularly well-organized use of the data that focused on improving quality of award decisions. It is evident that operational demands continue to limit proactive thinking. While attempts are being made to bring the parts of the department together to work on cross-organizational issues, comments by departmental staff to the panel indicate that there is no strong management awareness of the data resulting from the quality control activities described in Chapter 4, nor is there direction in cross-functional efforts.

Yet, there exist formally organized data sets related to some student financial aid programs. In this chapter, the panel reviews the data system for entering applicant data—the Central Processing System—and that used with the loan programs. Department of Education personnel reported to the panel that there is no applicant data base for Campus-Based programs—they know how many get aid, how much money goes out, and forgiven loan amounts, among other things, but not who receives it or items useful for quality improvement analyses.

THE MANAGEMENT INFORMATION SYSTEM

The Management Information System (MIS), the main tool used by the Department of Education to monitor and control the Title IV application processing system, draws data from virtually all aspects of the Central Processing System (CPS). The MIS is part of a coordinated set of management controls, called Project Control Information Services; the other parts are quality control, configuration management, and process control. (The CPS and the MIS are operated for the Department of Education by a contractor.)

The MIS enables the Department of Education to monitor data, (e.g., number of applicants, eligibility rates, and turnaround times) generated during production processes. Massive amounts of data are condensed into coherent tabulations and presented in four groups, which are aimed at various management levels (National Computer Systems, 1990-91a and 1990-91b). The four groups of data are as follows:

- highly summarized information to give top management a snapshot of key CPS operational and program areas;
- operating management data (e.g., summary information for monitoring funding level and detailed contract, quality control, and project information) to allow monitoring of day-to-day operations and the performance of data entry contractors;
- detailed statistics for monitoring the effect of applicant characteristics and behavior on program costs, compliance with regulations, the effect of system changes on applicant population characteristics, and quality control by contractors; and
- detailed information for monitoring the receipt, handling, and mailing of applicant documents.

The contractor submits printouts of these routine MIS reports to the department at appropriate intervals, such as weekly or biweekly, during the award cycle. Some data from previous cycles are included to permit comparisons. A few process-monitoring tools, such as control charts, are included in the reports on an ongoing basis, but their use seems limited, identifying occasional shocks to the system from causes such as peaks in work flow of applications. Several staff members have used the MIS to draw samples for additional inspection in areas exhibiting some unusual characteristics in the periodic MIS reports. Special reports are produced on request, usually through a task order to a contractor. At the end of the award year, the contractor prepares a final report.

The MIS reports are also available to Department of Education staff on-line. The information can be

- viewed on terminal and workstation screens,
- printed via menu selection, and
- downloaded in ASCII format and translated to other formats (e.g., a worksheet or data base file), manipulated, analyzed, or graphed.

Some of the department's information needs can only be met through use of the entire applicant data base. However, many of the tabulations do not require an exact count; an approximation with a sufficiently small confidence interval provides adequate information. Such tables are produced from a Sample Data Base of approximately 50,000 cases drawn several times during each processing cycle.

The department also has information needs that require statistical analysis and programming involving numerous data transformations and complex statistical procedures. The Sample Data Base can be used in such analyses with a high degree of precision and at a reasonable cost. Access to the Sample Data Base is provided through the on-line terminals and personal computer workstations at the department, which enables staff to run tabulations and perform statistical analyses. The Statistical Analysis System is used as the major data base management and reporting tool for the Sample Data Base.

The panel commends the Department of Education and the CPS contractor for what appears to be a thorough development of an MIS data base that presents operational data targeted appropriately to the functions of various management levels. Improvements have also been made in recent years in the presentation of the data. The panel is concerned, however, that the data base is underutilized. While appropriate data seem to be captured with the system (almost all the data are captured), and the system recognizes the need to target data to the differing needs at various levels of management, the reports produced tend to be dollar and timing oriented and not focused on improvement of the system by identifying potential causes of error in application and award processes. There are seemingly unbounded opportunities to mine the data set to find ideas for process experimentation and the potential to improve by finding and removing true causes of error.

Use of any data base requires some degree of expertise with computers and knowledge of statistical methodology. Use of a sample data base and a high-level statistical package as a tool for access and analysis raises the level of expertise needed. More fundamental, use requires hardware, the lack of which the panel heard mentioned by Department of Education staff. Further, the utility of the Sample Data Base for special projects is not fully appreciated. The panel, when discussing this data base with departmental personnel often found a lack of appreciation for the usefulness of such a data base. There was a tendency for departmental personnel to be concerned that 50,000 records in the sample data base were too few of the over seven million applications, without appreciating the degree of precision that such a large sample can have for most purposes.

It appears that much of the analysis of MIS data is done through contracts. While contracting for such analyses in itself may not be bad, a data-driven organization should encourage the development of expertise within its own staff. Several contractors commented to the panel that the department does not always encourage their innovative suggestions and that some lack of communication within the department hindered their efforts to provide effective analysis. One contractor did comment that there has been a recent move toward encouraging its input, and that its contract now requires that it allocate time to consider improvements. When technical expertise, either statistical or computer, is obtained from outside sources, the department should consider the technical advisors as partners in the process and encourage unsolicited suggestions for creative analyses.

The MIS has the potential to provide appropriate information to the appropriate levels of management. While the current implementation has noticeably improved over the past few years, users of the system seem hampered by a lack of equipment, methodological knowledge, and time. Similar problems were observed in other areas of the department's financial aid programs. (The panel makes a recommendation addressing these problems in Chapter 9.)

STUDENT LOAN DATA

The panel reviewed several studies of student loan programs that commented on the data systems needed to monitor the loan programs, and it spoke with Department of Education personnel about those systems. In one study, the General Accounting Office (1990b:3) describes the loan data system this way:

> As part of its monitoring of the program, the Department each year collects Stafford loan information from guaranty agencies and consolidates this information into the Stafford loan data base, commonly referred to as the tape dump. This data base is maintained by a contractor for approximately $900,000 a year and is primarily for the internal use of the Department. The contractor edits the data base's information to check whether guaranty agencies are reporting complete data. For fiscal year 1988, the Department required guaranty agencies to report 95-percent-complete data for 10 data fields the Department considered critical, such as students' social security numbers and loan amounts guaranteed. However, these edit checks can only determine completeness, not accuracy.

The department primarily uses information in the loan data base for routine trend analysis (e.g., the number of students obtaining loans). These analyses can be found in the *Annual Guaranteed Student Loan Data Book*, which is prepared by a contractor. Departmental staff reported to the panel that at least some individuals within the department were dissatisfied with the quality of the data, lack of some data items of interest, and the lack of analysis with the existing data.

PROBLEMS WITH THE DATA SYSTEM

The General Accounting Office (1990b) and various officials at the Department of Education (e.g., Thompson, 1991b; Winkler, 1991) have written detailed critiques of several of the problems in the operation of guaranteed student loan (GSL) programs. Briefly, the findings indicate the following:

- Financial management capabilities and maintenance of accounting records are poor.
- Computer systems are inadequate. Data elements in the systems are either old, unreliable, or not collected at all. The systems are not easily adaptable and require major reprogramming to provide information when policy, regulatory, or financial analyses raise complicated questions.
- Data and analyses are inadequate to (a) monitor guaranty agencies and lenders, (b) predict more accurately default and interest costs, (c) improve collections, (d) forecast volume, (e) outline borrower characteristics, (f) analyze proposed legislative and regulatory changes, and (g) evaluate program effectiveness.
- Guaranty agencies are not allowed access to the loan data base, a procedure that would help prevent making a loan to someone who is in default or in excess of loan limits, and thus ineligible.

To remedy these problems, the General Accounting Office (1990b) recommended that the Secretary of Education:

- direct guaranty agencies to ensure that their student loan data are as accurate and complete as practical, with special emphasis given to data on defaulted borrowers, and provide updated information to the department.
- report the ability of ineligible borrowers to obtain loans as a material internal control weakness under the Federal Managers' Financial Integrity Act.
- analyze the data the department now has and provide to guaranty agencies on a periodic basis the data needed to prevent defaulters from obtaining new loans.
- develop a more comprehensive annual report that gives guaranty agencies the data they need to more efficiently detect loan limit abuses, and require guaranty agencies to use the report.

A PROPOSED SOLUTION

The 1986 amendments to the Higher Education Act authorized the Department of Education to develop a national student loan data system (NSLDS), a computer system that would make national student loan data accessible to guaranty agencies. The purposes of the system include improving data on default rates, reducing defaults, and reducing overpayments. The system could be used to assist lenders and guaranty agencies in guarding against borrower abuse. The General Accounting Office (1990b:3) notes, however, that "because the 1986 amendments contained a provision that the Department could not require guaranty agencies to use the system before guaranteeing new loans, the system was not developed. The 1989 Budget Reconciliation Act, however, allows the Department to require guaranty agencies to use such a system before approving new loans. The Department plans to develop the new system by 1993; the guaranty agencies will have to use this system before guaranteeing new loans." A contract to develop the system was awarded in early 1993. Winkler (1991) notes that data content, applications, and linkages with other GSL-related systems must be defined for an NSLDS, and the prospective cost of the system must be scrutinized carefully.

Thompson (1991b) suggests that the Department of Education should expedite the development of the NSLDS in order to protect the integrity of the program more effectively. He notes that the system is crucial in providing departmental officials with part of the information they need to prevent student-borrowers from abuses, such as exceeding statutory loan limits and receiving additional loans when they are already in default.

The need for an NSLDS, as included in the 1986 amendments to the Higher Education Act and as reemphasized in the 1992 reauthorization of the act, will be even greater in the future. While the direct lending demonstration project authorized in the act would affect the loan distribution system, there will still be difficulties with students' address changes that have to be kept up-to-date as they leave school, enter the work force, reenter schools, and/or change schools. Generally, young people at this point in life are difficult to track. In addition, the vast increases in amounts authorized under the Parent Loans for Undergraduate Students program will require very careful attention if default rates are to be kept in check. Parents who borrow $25,000 or more and are not able to pay it back may go into default as much as a year before the current tracking system could identify that default and deny another $25,000 loan.

Recommendation 6-1: The panel believes that a totally integrated applicant data base is essential for problem identification, the development of solutions, and monitoring progress—important activities if true quality improvements are to take place. The data base would compile information from all the Title IV aid programs and across years to provide, for each applicant, a complete history of participation in the financial aid system, thus facilitating a broad range of cross-sectional and longitudinal statistical analyses. The Department of Education should allocate sufficient resources and personnel to accomplish this task without further delay.

PART III

Toward an Improved Delivery System

In Chapters 7 through 9, the panel considers various approaches to system improvement. In Chapter 7, we compare quality control activities in the student financial aid programs with those found in other "similar" systems, such as welfare programs and private financial institutions. Our discussion in Chapter 8 centers on the Department of Education's Institutional Quality Control Pilot Project, an experiment aimed at improving the quality of institutional activities. In Chapter 9, we consider the expected effects on system quality resulting from changes legislated by the 1992 Reauthorization of the Higher Education Act and propose further initiatives for the Department of Education and Congress to consider that will lead to system improvement.

7

Quality Control in Other Monetary Distribution Systems

There has been increasing awareness of the importance of quality management in industry, including service industries, and in federal need-based social programs. Recognizing these developments, the Department of Education has been interested in the lessons that might be learned from other organizations involved in activities similar to those of the student financial aid system. In response to past recommendations that ideas for improvement be sought, the department commissioned a study that compared several family assistance programs and student aid programs (Advanced Technology and Westat, 1987a,b). The department asked the panel to address similar issues.

A complete benchmarking with other programs would be difficult because service industries, social programs, and student financial aid programs differ in regard to goals, concerns, and approaches. Further, the panel's resources limited the amount of information that could be collected. Yet, in its review of several family assistance and veterans benefit programs, mortgage, insurance, and other financial entities, the panel found two practices that the Department of Education should incorporate as operating strategies. First, the organizations reviewed do not hold themselves to an unattainable zero-defect standard. Second, monitoring functions are generally allocated based on the risk the activity presents to achieving important organizational goals. This chapter describes the activities of the organizations reviewed, and it suggests a framework for making comparisons across programs and within which lessons can be drawn for the student financial aid programs.

FEDERAL NEED-BASED BENEFIT PROGRAMS

The Congressional Research Service has identified more than 75 federal benefit programs (including student financial aid) providing aid in the form of cash and noncash that are directed primarily to persons with limited income (Burke, 1991). In fiscal year 1990, those income-tested benefit programs cost $210.6 billion, 72 percent in federal funds and the remainder in state or local funds. Total spending on those programs amounted to almost one-eighth of the fiscal 1990 federal budget.

Of the spending for those programs in 1990, about 9 percent was invested in "human capital" programs, including education, jobs, and training. Forty-one percent was used for medical services. Cash, food benefits, and housing aid together accounted for almost 47 percent.

More than 90 percent of the programs have an explicit test of income, of which there are five kinds:

- income ceiling related to one of the federal government's official poverty measures (Census Bureau poverty thresholds or federal poverty income guidelines);
- income limit related to state or area median income;
- income limit related to the lower living standard income levels used by the Bureau of Labor Statistics;
- income below absolute dollar standard; and
- income level deemed to indicate "need" (typically, student financial aid programs use this type of income test).

All of these tests require that data on family or individual income be obtained, and that the income data be verified for all or a sample of applicants. The programs have different definitions of income and time periods for which income is reported.

The panel could not look at quality control procedures in all of the programs identified by the Congressional Research Service. Thus, we chose to examine the quality control activities of several programs that were the subject of prior studies by the National Research Council (NRC) of the National Academy of Sciences. The very proliferation of programs, however, suggests potential duplication of verification and quality control processes for those aid recipients who receive more than one type of aid (especially if one type is not based on receiving another type). Although the panel did not have the resources to explore this area in depth, we believe coordination of verification activities and sharing of information about the development of these activities in the various programs would benefit all agencies in their attempts to improve quality. The following discussion describes the eligibility, verification, and quality control systems used in the family assistance programs.

Quality Control in Family Assistance Programs

Quality control in family assistance programs offers a useful basis for comparison with the system used in the student financial aid programs. Both sets of programs serve low-income populations and involve very large commitments of federal dollars. The family assistance programs, however, pose quite a contrast in their verification strategy. First, they rely heavily on rigorous front-end verification, in general, before individuals receive any cash assistance. Then, they apply systematic and extensive post hoc reviews to a sample of recipients in order to assess the correctness of eligibility and benefits received. Finally, they assess stringent penalties against the administering agencies (states) in cases of error above prescribed tolerances.

Three federal benefit programs were studied by the NRC from 1986 to 1988—Aid to Families with Dependent Children (AFDC), Food Stamps, and Medicaid (Affholter and Kramer, 1987; Kramer, 1988). Together, they represented nearly $50 billion in fiscal 1987 federal dollars. In the AFDC and Medicaid programs, states and localities pay a substantial addition in benefit amounts (between 50 and 83 percent depending on a formula based on state per capita income), and they pay 50 percent of administrative costs in all three programs. At the time of the NRC study, there were nearly 11 million recipients of AFDC, 22 million participants in Medicaid, and 20 million recipients of Food Stamps.

Caseload monitoring and payment determination in these programs can be extremely complex. First, eligibility and benefit payments are determined monthly (although comprehensive determinations are not repeated each month) and must reflect what is a frequently changing profile of income and household composition in recipient households. Second, the three programs are administered by separate federal agencies and frequently have little connection at the federal level although they are targeted at similar populations and the same individuals commonly participate in all three programs concurrently. At the state and local levels, the programs may be administered separately or by the same public assistance agency, and their services may be delivered through a unified state system or by county and local agencies with differing rules and procedures. Thus, from a quality control perspective, there are two main difficulties. First, eligibility and payment levels are constantly changing. Second, federal policies and benefit payments may be delivered through a network of hundreds of different federal, state, and local service delivery designs, which involve differing capabilities and, in many cases, differing and at times incongruent policies and procedures.

The quality control system in each of the programs employs a two-tiered review process. The system is used to monitor the correctness of eligibility determinations, correct identified errors, calculate error rates, and assign penalties against the states. State staff sample and review cases monthly, and the federal agencies review a subsample of those cases and determine error rates and penalties. States also maintain a staff, in most cases separate from the program staff and separate from the quality control reviewers, to design and supervise corrective action. Error rates are calculated using a combined value of the state and federal reviews, although the federal estimate from the subsample prevails in cases of disagreement.

When error rates exceed specified thresholds, penalties are collected dollar-for-dollar against the federal share of benefit payments for AFDC and Medicaid and against the federal administrative share in the Food Stamp program. States are required to correct AFDC underpayments and recoup overpayments promptly, whatever the cause or identifying source, including the quality control system. There are limits on the amount of overpayment that may be recouped from current recipients at any one time; large overpayments are recouped over a number of months. In the Food Stamp program, a percentage of the value of recouped overpayments may be kept by the state under certain circumstances. Only the Food Stamp program offers rewards for good performance, and until 1988 and 1990 (when separate legislation for Food Stamps and AFDC, respectively, changed the situation), underpayments did not figure in the calculation of error rates for purposes of assessing financial penalties. In both the AFDC and Food Stamp programs, neither improper terminations nor denials (so-called negative case actions) are counted as errors in determining sanctions.

Eligibility

Eligibility rules for each of the three programs are different. Each has differing income and asset tests, inclusions and exclusions, and periods of coverage. Thus, processing and verification requirements also differ and pose special challenges to the administering agencies. For purposes of illustration, the following brief description focuses on the AFDC and Medicaid programs.

Eligibility for AFDC and Medicaid, beyond broad limits established in federal law, is determined by the state. But states define their own standards of need and income and resource limits (within federal limits), and they set their own benefit levels within those standards. States are not required to pay 100 percent of their determined standard of need, and about half the states do not.

Eligibility for AFDC is determined prospectively, based on the best estimate of the income and circumstances for the month assistance will be paid, except that for the initial one or two months states may use a retrospective budgeting method to compute the benefit payment. Generally, eligibility must be redetermined at least every six months, and a face-to-face interview is required at least once a year. States may require certain families to file eligibility reports monthly. Families with earned income must report monthly, generally by mail, any changes in income or resources, unless specifically exempted from this requirement. The agency must adjust the payment accordingly or terminate assistance, as appropriate. Since recipients typically move in and out of employment and sometimes on and off the benefit rolls, income and resource changes are a large source of error.

Determining income in order to calculate AFDC benefit amounts is a two-step process: determining that gross income does not exceed 185 percent of the state's standard of need and determining that net income does not exceed 100 percent of the same standard. *Total family income* includes gross income before taxes from a variety of specified sources (e.g., wages, child support, certain subsidies, and some income of others who are not necessarily in the assistance unit, such as stepparents, an alien's sponsor, or the parent of a minor parent, that is deemed available to the applicant household), some at state option. There is a variety of exclusions, such as grants, loans, scholarships, and income or subsidies from certain other assistance programs (e.g., Social Security Insurance, or SSI, payments, nutrition subsidies, low-income energy assistance, and at state option, certain job-training program income). Certain other income is disregarded, such as income that offsets a limited amount of work, training, and dependent care expenses. A limited amount of earned income from a job is excluded as an encouragement to work.

Except for specified exclusions (e.g., primary residence and the value of an automobile up to $1,500), an AFDC assistance unit cannot have resources in excess of $1,000 or a lesser amount determined by the state. In general, the resources counted are those that can be converted into cash; essentials such as clothing and furniture, as determined by the state, may be disregarded.

In addition to income and resource determinations, AFDC eligibility requires establishing the dependency of a child, which poses special challenges. To qualify as a dependent child, a child must be "deprived of parental support or care" by the death, continued absence or incapacity of one or both parents, or by the unemployment of the principal wage-earning parent.

Frequently, the most difficult task in establishing eligibility is determining who should be included in the household unit and be considered to be contributing to household income. Agencies may deny aid because of insufficient verification of continued absence of a father, for example.

States must provide Medicaid to all so-called categorically needy. These include all AFDC and SSI recipients (or, at state option, all aged, blind and disabled, using stricter criteria, and all others who meet AFDC income and resource requirements). However, states may, at their option, extend coverage to others—such as those eligible for but not receiving cash assistance, those eligible except for their institutional status, and others whose income is up to 100 percent of the poverty level. States may also extend coverage to those deemed medically needy—those whose income is otherwise above the standards but whose income after deducting or "spending down" their medical expenses puts them below the state's income standards for assistance.

For the categorically needy in Medicaid, AFDC and SSI rules apply. But for all others, determining income for Medicaid eligibility is further complicated. For example, parental and spousal income are considered available to Medicaid applicants. Complex rules related to family contributions and transfers of assets are used to determine eligibility for institutionalized persons. For the medically needy using the spend-down provisions, income is determined prospectively for up to six months.

Verification

Verification is done at the point of initial application (and at required periodic reporting and redeterminations) by the eligibility worker, and through complete reviews of cases in the quality control sample and federal rereviews of the subsample.

In order to demonstrate eligibility, an individual applying for AFDC benefits must demonstrate U.S. citizenship or legal alien status and furnish a Social Security Number for each member of the assistance unit. Applicants are further required to demonstrate dependency of a child, and their ability and willingness to work or receive educational and training services, and are required to assist the state in securing spousal support payments.

In all cases, with certain exceptions for incapacity, applicants apply for assistance in person, generally at a local office that administers applications for all three programs, and provide required documentation to corroborate their family status at that time. Applicants may also have to allow a home visit. If an applicant does not comply during the application process with agency procedures for demonstrating eligibility, the application is denied. Failure to comply with requirements to document continued eligibility results in case closing. Nationally, failure to comply with a procedural requirement is the most common cause of case closing, even though the applicant or participant may be substantively eligible.

Income is further verified through matching systems. State agencies administering AFDC, Medicaid, and Food Stamps must operate an Income and Eligibility Verification System (IEVS). The system is used to verify the accuracy of client income for the purposes of eligibility and benefit determinations by matching application files with data from the Internal Revenue Service (IRS), Social Security Administration (SSA), State Wage and Information Collection Agency (SWICA), and Unemployment Insurance Benefit (UIB) data bases.

Since the programs serve individuals presumed to be in immediate need, a variety of requirements exist to speed application processing despite mandated verification requirements. Applicants are required to be notified of eligibility for AFDC within 45 days of application. Benefits for the first month are prorated from the date of application. The eligibility determination process may not be interrupted or delayed by IEVS checks, and data from all sources must be requested at the first available opportunity (the SWICA and UIB process requests twice a month and the IRS once a month). The SSA's Bendix system generates automatic notices to the state when updated information becomes available.

Up to 20 percent of the cases may be carried beyond the prescribed application period if warranted by delays in third-party verification. If verification data are received after an applicant is determined to be eligible, a review must be completed within 20 days. Federal law ensures the right to a fair hearing of any adverse decision of the administering agency, and appeals processes can be fairly extensive.

The Food Stamp program is administered by the state agency responsible for administering federally aided public assistance programs. The federal sponsors, the U.S. Department of Health and Human Services (HHS) and the U.S. Department of Agriculture (USDA), are required to develop a system of single interviews to determine eligibility for AFDC and Food Stamps. Further, they must develop procedures that may permit, at state option, a single application form for Food Stamps, AFDC, or other public assistance programs, as well as permit, again at state option, a single verification based on the public assistance application. The secretaries of HHS and USDA are also required to consult in issuing regulations to ensure, to the extent feasible, that definition, valuation, and calculation of income and assets under both programs are comparable.

For Food Stamps, the law specifies that states must verify income and resources to the extent practicable, prior to issuance of coupons. To verify eligibility for Food Stamps, states must request information available from the state employment service, the SSA, and the IRS. States must set up a system to protect against receipt of benefits in more than one jurisdiction, as well as a plan for automated data processing and retrieval. States are encouraged to have systems that include data elements for the determination of eligibility, calculation of benefits, issuance of benefits, computer matches for income and asset verifications, reconciliation procedures, and other purposes. States may not require additional verification where the state already has current verification. Further, they may not deny an application because of noncooperation from an individual outside the household. As with AFDC, timeliness and hearing requirements are intended to ensure prompt processing of applications and receipt of benefits, but they differ slightly from those for AFDC.

For Medicaid, applications must be processed and notification given within 60 days for cases involving disability and 45 days for all others. Payment procedures ensure that 90 percent of claims are paid within 30 days of receipt and 99 percent within 90 days. States must provide for procedures for prepayment and for postpayment claims review. States are also required to check for third-party liabilities and recover monies due for services that have been paid by Medicaid.

The Quality Control Systems

Although HHS still does AFDC audits annually or less frequently, as determined to be necessary, the principal means of monitoring and recouping misspent funds in the AFDC and Food Stamp programs is through the quality control systems. The Medicaid program has a variety of separate additional monitoring systems and audit procedures. Some are designed to detect fraud and abuse by service providers. The program also has a mechanized claims processing and information retrieval system and a utilization control program. Other systems monitor the use and appropriateness of Medicaid services and are intended to control cost and monitor the level and appropriateness of care. Finally, other mechanisms monitor quality of services as part of the certification of facilities that participate in Medicaid.

The quality control systems for all three programs are based on the system developed originally for the AFDC system and thus are relatively similar. For purposes of description here, they will be treated as the same system unless major differences warrant mention.

History The current system—except for changes in error rate thresholds legislated after completion of the mandated NRC and administration studies—was developed in the early 1970s in the face of one of the largest increases in caseloads and costs for the AFDC program. The quality control system was specifically designed to address ineligibility, fraud, and abuse. Indeed, although early studies of the system were inconclusive about the level of error, the fact that true error rates were hard to establish only added to concern about ineligibility, fraud, and abuse, and the need for systematic error rate monitoring.

The original quality control system design, developed in the 1960s, used caseworker actions, rather than active cases as is currently done, as the sample units. Such a design is better suited to management improvement but less useful for assessing overall error rates because the status of active cases between formal redeterminations is not considered. Concern for true case error rates was heightened when the AFDC program went to a simplified eligibility system, a so-called declaration system, whereby eligibility determination was reduced largely to a clerical process, and many means of verification, such as home visits, were eliminated.

In revisions begun in 1970, national error standards were set at 3 percent for ineligibility and 5 percent for over- and underpayments. Corrective actions rather than financial penalties were imposed for states failing to meet these thresholds. Financial penalties were imposed through regulation in 1973, but they were never collected because, set only in regulation and not in law, they were ruled arbitrary and capricious by a federal court in 1976. They were reimposed by statute in 1979 and became effective in 1981. The new error thresholds were gradually made more stringent over several years, resulting in 3 percent for AFDC and Medicaid by 1983 and 5 percent for Food Stamps by 1985. Recent legislation, described below, has changed these thresholds.

Sampling and Review The quality control systems for all three programs are concerned with whether eligibility is properly determined and benefit payments are being properly paid. Monthly samples are selected on a continuing basis in each state. Using a separate quality control staff, states sample from their list of active cases and draw a separate, smaller sample from their negative case actions (households that were denied or terminated). Utilizing data from state quality control reviews of this sample and federal re-reviews of a subsample, the federal agency estimates a payment error rate, which is used to determine the disallowance. The system also measures underpayments and erroneous negative case actions. Underpayments were only recently added to the formula that determines AFDC financial disallowances. Negative case actions still do not contribute to disallowances.

Depending on caseload sizes, standard sample sizes, which are required if states use systematic sampling (the chief method used), range between 300 and 2,400 cases. States may use other sample designs and reduce the sample size, but never below the minimum sample sizes for AFDC active cases (between 300 and 1,200). Some states use larger sample sizes when they desire information for subpopulations or subregions. Many states use an integrated quality control system (IQCS) for the three programs. The federal re-review sample is a subsample of the state sample and also a function of the size of the caseload; for AFDC, it ranges from 140 in states with caseloads below 7,000 to 360 for caseloads of 40,000 and over. Negative case actions are sampled separately from a much smaller subset.

Federal guidelines state that "permissible state practice" is to be used as the primary basis for determining eligibility and benefit amounts in AFDC.

A standardized worksheet provides a systematic means for the state's quality control reviewer to analyze elements of eligibility and record case findings. The quality control reviewer conducts a desk review of each case, analyzing case record documentation and determining the specific elements that must be verified during a field interview.

Except in special cases, *all* sampled cases in which a payment was issued in the review month must receive a full field review. The interview of the recipient is used to (a) establish identity, relationship, and living arrangements; (b) ensure that all significant elements of eligibility have been explored and ascertain any changes; and (c) obtain statements, documents, and other evidence and cooperation and consent for identifying collateral sources of information. The reviewer must try to contact collateral sources to verify elements of eligibility and payment when documentation in the case record does not meet verification requirements. When a face-to-face interview is not possible, verification is attempted through other means, such as records on property ownership, work program participation, school attendance, and earned income.

Verification must attempt to use primary evidence, such as a birth certificate to verify age or a bank account to verify income. Secondary evidence may be used, such as a school record to verify age, when primary evidence is unobtainable. The required verification varies depending on the recipient's specific allegation. If, for instance, he or she claims no earned income, the reviewer must document the allegation. Evidence could include employment records from the state, the IRS, or the SSA. Consultation with a supervisor and other special determinations are required when documentation is questionable or circumstances make certain verification unobtainable, but the special determination cannot be used unless there is already at least one piece of evidence on the element in question.

For cases in the negative sample, that is, those that were denied eligibility and benefits, the quality control review consists only of analysis of the case record and only for reasons for denial and adherence to notice and hearing requirements, not for correctness of the decision. Limited field investigation can be used if the record cannot be clearly established.

In the Food Stamp program, documents from a governmental or public agency constitute primary evidence, and collateral information constitutes secondary evidence. When primary evidence is unavailable, at least two sources of secondary evidence must be used. The U.S. Department of Agriculture's Food and Nutrition Service (FNS) specifies minimum standards of evidence for each element of eligibility, but states may use stricter standards, and thus, standards vary across states. The depth of the investigation depends on the nature of the applicant's case. For instance, affirmative statements of earnings may be documented with pay stubs, but for denials the quality control reviewer must establish a work history, contact previous employers, and query the state employment service or the SSA records of reported wages. Reviewers are also instructed to look for other indications of employment, such as frequent or regular absences from home during working hours, which would indicate employment. Federal reviewers use the same standards of evidence. As with AFDC, however, the federal review is not independent of the state review since federal reviewers work only from the completed quality control files submitted by the states, and they may or may not seek any additional evidence.

In each program, state and federal reviewers calculate the value of errors identified in the review process for purposes of assessing penalties. They also distinguish between "client-caused" and "agency-caused" errors, make judgments about willing misrepresentation, and characterize the major sources of error, such as income, resources, deductions, and numerical miscalculations.

States must submit their findings from active and negative AFDC cases within 75 to 120 days from the end of the sample month to ensure timely release of national error rates. The state quality control findings for 90 percent of the sample are due within 75 days of the end of the sample month (for active cases) and for 95 percent of the sample within 95 days. The Administration for Children and Families (formerly the Family Support Administration) attempts to issue error rates within one year after the quality control reviews for the final month of a fiscal year are completed, although interim findings on individual cases are provided to the state as they are completed. The rules are generally similar for Food Stamp reviews.

Federal Re-Review The federal agency, through its regional offices, reviews and approves state plans specifying acceptable procedures for eligibility and benefit determinations and state sampling plans and procedures for quality control. The federal agency, as noted, also re-reviews a sample of state quality control cases and conducts management assessments of state quality control systems. The federal re-review consists of selection of a subsample of cases for review each month, analysis of the state quality control review file and case record, interviews and collateral contacts as necessary, redetermination of eligibility and recalculation of the correct benefit amount, and sending a "difference" letter to the state if state and federal findings vary. For AFDC cases, federal reviewers may make extensive use of collateral contacts by mail and telephone; home visits are the exception. Except for Guam, Puerto Rico, and the Virgin Islands, negative AFDC case actions are not re-reviewed at the federal level, and negative Food Stamp cases are rarely reviewed.

Error Rates and Sanctions Both case error rates and payment error rates are reported by the states. The official error rate, which is used to estimate financial penalties, is produced using a regression methodology that combines federal and state findings on payment error rates. The regression procedure in theory allows the smaller subsample to borrow strength from the larger sample. Where there is a difference in findings, the federal finding prevails.

Different resolution and appeals procedures apply to each program. With recent legislated changes that somewhat relax error tolerances, appeal procedures have been simplified and limited somewhat. Beginning with fiscal 1981, and through the time of the NRC study, states were mandated to reduce their payment error rates (overpayments and payments to ineligibles) over three years, reaching 4 percent by fiscal 1983 and 3 percent by fiscal 1984. A number of "good causes"—such as natural disasters, significant caseload growth, and other conditions that are beyond a state's control—may be used to waive some or all sanctions.

In AFDC, overpayments must be recovered promptly—no later than the quarter following the quarter in which the error was found. States are urged to give priority to overpayment cases involving current rather than former recipients. Overpayments are collected from current recipients by reducing the amount of future aid to specified levels. States are expected to take appropriate action under state law against the income and resources of former recipients, unless the state can show that recovery will cost more than the overpayment itself. States must attempt to correct all cases involving recipient fraud. For Food Stamps, state agencies are also required to restore promptly benefits that were improperly denied, terminated, or underissued. The quality control system is also expected to refer cases in error to the appropriate state counterpart for action and follow-up, including referring cases involving fraud or legal liability to special administrative units for action.

Historically, states were required to file annual corrective action plans (and six-month interim reports) in which they identified major concentrations of errors (by type, including distinguishing between agency and client errors) and their basic causes. Subsequent to the NRC studies and a round of legislated changes that principally changed error rate tolerances, the requirements for corrective action plans have become less stringent.

Performance Over Time and System Reform

For fiscal 1980 through 1984, the measured national payment error rate declined for all three programs—from 7.8 to 6.0 for AFDC, from 5.1 to 2.7 for Medicaid, and from 9.5 to 8.6 for Food Stamps (although the decline was not consistent over the five years) (Kramer, 1988). The national trends, however, mask a variety of different rates among the states due to a variety of different influences on state performance. (The state rates sometimes mask extreme variation in performance across localities and local offices with differing administrative designs and differing capabilities). No state showed consistent improvement in all three programs, and only six states showed steady improvement in two programs. By 1985, when Congress mandated studies by the NRC and the administration, the states' total financial liabilities were estimated to be at least $3 billion, every state but one had been found in error in one or more of the programs, almost all states had filed administrative appeals, and many had already joined in lawsuits against the federal government.

Criticism of the program, by the states (in the lawsuits) and by the NRC panel, focused on the measurement and estimation systems, including the two-tiered review structure described above, the rationale for the specified thresholds, the imbalance between rewards and punishments, and the lack of incentives to meet all program objectives (as would be created, for instance, by incentives to reduce underpayments or improper denials as well as overpayments and payments to ineligibles). It also included substantial debate over the proper definition of error. As with the student financial aid programs, many so-called technical errors—procedural errors, such as failure to provide a Social Security Number, that may or may not represent true eligibility errors—are included in the measurement of error and the assessment of penalties.

The NRC panel recommended eliminating the two-tiered review structure, changing error tolerances to reflect performance, and remedying the imbalance between incentives and disincentives to meet all program objectives. It also recommended giving states the tools—both resources and better technical designs (such as sample designs)—to improve the overall ability of the systems to identify the sources of error and assist in corrective actions (Affholter and Kramer, 1987; Kramer, 1988).

Error thresholds and the components of payment error used to generate penalties were reviewed by Congress following the mandated NRC and administration studies, and several important changes were legislated. Beginning in 1991, states with AFDC error rates above 4 percent became subject to sanctions based on a sliding scale reflecting the degree to which their error rates exceed the national average. Error rates are then partially adjusted on the basis of the state's rate of underpayments, child support collections, and recoupment of overpayments. There are no financial rewards or incentives in AFDC or Medicaid. However, all sanctions prior to 1991 were waived, and limited grace periods are to be provided after the new regulations are imposed. The new laws for the Food Stamp (discussed below) and AFDC programs mandate studies to determine the feasibility of measuring improper terminations and denials for purposes of sanction.

For Food Stamps, as a result of the Hunger Prevention Act of 1988, states are liable for penalties beginning with fiscal 1986 if their total dollar error rate (using the point estimate of overpayments and underpayments combined) is more than one percentage point above the weighted (by caseload size in each state) national average for the year (or the weighted national average of any previous year, if lower). Beginning with fiscal 1988, states can receive increased federal funding for administration (up to a maximum of 60 percent depending on their rates of terminations and denials) if their error rates are below 5.9 percent. As with AFDC, there are limited grace periods granted to allow states to adjust to new regulations before penalties are imposed. But, states are liable for interest on unpaid claims 30 days after an administrative appeal is completed, and rulings on good cause are not subject to legal appeal.

Alternative Incentive Systems

Much has been made of the use and effectiveness of stringent penalties to achieve desired performance. The Department of Education previously commissioned a study of the quality control systems in other federal benefit programs, including family assistance programs, in order to develop some alternative incentive and disincentive structures that could be considered for the student financial aid programs (Advanced Technology, 1987). Some of the conclusions of that report were based on the experiences of a pilot project in which selected educational institutions assessed their management controls, estimated error rates in a subsample of awards, and developed corrective actions in response to the level and sources of error found. For the pilot project, relief from verification requirements was used as an incentive for participation in the project. (The pilot project is discussed in detail in Chapter 8.)

The Advanced Technology study suggests a set of four optimal characteristics for a system of incentives and disincentives: (1) reward and punish only the party responsible for the action; (2) rewards and penalties should be progressive and continuous (i.e., minor penalties for minor infractions); (3) rewards and penalties should be symmetrical (equal number of incentives as disincentives); and (4) incentives and disincentives should be feasible to implement and effective in achieving desired results.

Item four addresses a central conclusion of the NRC panel study (Kramer, 1988). The NRC study found that the error tolerances were not based on capability; they did not reflect system-imposed common causes of variation. Hence, the financial penalties were insufficient incentives for the programs to meet desired levels of performance. However, the Advanced Technology study suggests a strong bias against the use of sanctions, which is inconsistent with the NRC findings. The central point of the NRC finding is that tolerances, upon which sanctions are based, must be set in relation to capability *or* necessary resources must be provided to improve capability. When either of these conditions is met, sanctions should prove to be effective.

The Advanced Technology study also generated a set of five criteria of feasibility, against which the researchers assessed 32 alternative incentive and disincentive strategies. To be feasible, alternatives had to have low budgetary impact, be consistent with program intent, require minimal operational difficulties or legislative change, have a high cost-benefit ratio, and pose minimal political problems. The 32 alternative strategies extended through each step in the delivery process: institutional eligibility determination, allocation of funds, disbursement, application, eligibility and benefit determination, benefit disbursement, verification, beneficiary account reconciliation, quality control, audit, evaluation of institution, corrective action planning, and agency review of corrective action implementation.

It is difficult to comment on the study's assessment of each of the 32 alternatives because the empirical basis for the study's conclusions is not made clear. The panel's comments on the conclusions are thus also founded on little other than commonsensical reactions except where the earlier NRC study or other analyses can make specific contributions. In the following description the panel aggregates the study's findings into three classes of approaches and comments on them as appropriate.

- *Tying institutional participation to performance*. The study assessed strategies that would either wholly exclude institutions based on performance or adjust allocations based on performance. Few of the strategies stand the study's tests for political or operational feasibility because, in general, they threaten participation of individuals to whom the programs are aimed. Yet, such action would be appropriate for institutions that are clearly engaging in fraudulent behavior. One strategy—reallocation of funds based on performance—met the tests, according to the researchers, of program intent and political acceptability, but it is difficult to see why denying some institutions reallocated funds would threaten desired individual participation less than other approaches reviewed.

- *Tying financial and oversight controls to institutional performance*. The study assessed tightening or lessening regulatory and other oversight controls on institutions according to performance. The options included were graduating disbursement authority according to performance, altering required quality control sample size, allowing alternative documentation for verification, altering the percentage of beneficiaries that must be verified, reducing regulatory and audit requirements, allowing reduced quality control sample sizes along with diminished appeals rights, altering administrative allowances or allowing bonuses related to performance, allowing fund transfers across programs based on performance, and allowing flexibility in corrective action planning requirements, including waiver of sanctions tied to performance.

Most of these strategies were viewed favorably by the study. Many, however, create perverse consequences that might not enhance the ability of the institutions to improve performance. First, as the earlier NRC panel found, tampering with administrative funds as a carrot or stick to influence performance can be tricky if such strategies result in reducing funds to poorly performing institutions just when those funds are needed for desired corrective action. Also, using restrictions on or rewards for certain corrective action planning is useful in principle but often difficult to achieve. As the earlier NRC panel found and as the Advanced Technology study is also sensitive to, mandating details of program administration from above frequently creates inappropriate rote responses from the administering organizations. And, review of corrective plans by those unfamiliar with the details of the administering organizations creates other problems.

• *Tightening reporting requirements of applicants and strengthening the financial consequences of misreporting.* Current law establishes a $10,000 fine and/or imprisonment for misreporting by applicants for student financial aid. In general, the study views this disincentive as unenforceable and does not consider increasing reporting requirements universally or otherwise increasing beneficiary responsibility as a means of reducing beneficiary error. Imposing substantial and immediate penalties on the applicant for clearly willful misreporting would, however, be consistent with the family assistance programs and would, it would seem, be consistent with public fiduciary responsibilities. Rather, the strategies considered in the study include various means for restricting future eligibility or benefit amounts, or increasing reporting requirements after beneficiary errors occur, and conversely, reducing future reporting requirements if the beneficiary establishes a history of correct reporting. Further, they would correct errors on future benefit amounts but not correct overpayments made to individuals who have graduated from or left the institution.

Of 12 suggested approaches for increasing the obligations of the applicant, the study finds 4 that pose operational or budgetary problems. These include recovering institution-caused overpayments from the institutions rather than the beneficiary and assessing a premium to be paid to the beneficiary by the institution for underawards due to institutional error. The study also assesses the utility of collecting overawards against tax refunds or the garnisheeing of wages. The study deemed both budgetarily and operationally difficult. Both would also affect only the subset of students with tax refunds or wages against which to collect. (Since the Advanced Technology study, legislation has been enacted that mandates the IRS to use tax refunds to offset defaulted student loans. Also, Department of Education staff report that the department is conducting a pilot activity on garnisheeing of wages.)

PRIVATE SECTOR MONETARY DISTRIBUTION SYSTEMS

Private systems that involve the distribution of money differ from federal programs in many ways, most notably in profit motives and often by having an asset upon which the transaction is based. There are, nonetheless, important comparisons that can be considered in assessing governmental performance. For example, the assistant comptroller general of the General Accounting Office (Thompson, 1991a) stressed that the quality of governmental services would benefit from program management that keeps in mind four principles found, in general, among quality leaders in the private sector:

- management continuity and consistency,
- long-range planning and visions for the future,
- orientation toward serving customers, and
- systematic strategies for measuring performance.

In its inquiries the panel was repeatedly told that these principles were not characteristic of the Office of Student Financial Aid's activities related to award errors, nor its general activities. Without implying that any of these principles are more important than the others, it is the last principle on which we focus attention here.

Many monetary distribution systems in the private sector have processes and quality problems similar to those found in the student financial aid system. For example, credit card lenders, mortgage bankers, auto loan providers, and insurance companies also face the problem of incorrect data being supplied by applicants and have difficulty maintaining and improving quality in a distributed network of service centers. As for student financial aid, these organizations require an application and have eligibility rules that the applicant must meet to qualify for the service (e.g., loan, policy, credit line). These systems also experience a nesting of errors within service centers and individual applicants. The panel called on a number of quality practitioners to ask about good practices in their service industries.

Although no one organization provides a model for immediate use in Department of Education applications, the panel believes that two major concepts used in quality service organizations are instructive. First, organizations create a quality group that reports directly to senior management and is involved in decision making, especially in recommending and approving actions needed to remove defects or procedural weaknesses.

The second concept is targeting risk. The amount of money at risk of being lost and the propensity of an individual or service center toward "error" are the considerations. While instances of fraud were reportedly under 1 percent in, for example, the mortgage industry, the applicant is subject to intensive review prior to obtaining funds. Still, dollar losses can be considerable. Thus, while the service organization must approve applicants to generate income, the applicant must meet certain guidelines for a profit to be made. The guidelines will vary by industry, amount of money provided, and the timing of the payment. For mortgages, credit history and employment are verified, and the value of the real property is subject to an independent appraisal. Risk considerations are used to structure the transaction to increase the expected return on the loaned funds. For example, the portion of the appraised value that is approved for a mortgage varies, thus providing a default deterrent and a cushion against losses if a default occurs. Higher risk clients are often charged higher interest rates, which are set to provide the desired return on investment within a class of loans.

Credit card companies rate credit histories to develop classes of individuals to which they offer their services. Interest rates and credit limits can vary to provide expected profits within the groups. Insurance companies have sources of information for verifying key application information, for example, motor vehicle department records of accidents and violations and consumer-reporting agencies to investigate other items. For large policies, a health examination, or an inspection of the property, may be required. Still, the insurance company is at risk only when paying a claim, and it can concentrate its inspection efforts effectively at that time.

Many of the service industries the panel reviewed place the responsibility for proper documentation on the local service provider. Often, this provider is an independent contractor, whose profits are based on volume. Thus, the industry also focuses on errors nested in the service center. Mortgage-purchasing organizations have well-defined procedures for measuring the quality of underwriting as a whole and by individual servicers. The goals are to not only identify problem servicers, but also provide feedback and work toward problem resolution. Where training and such feedback do not achieve the mortgage purchaser's standards for quality, the servicer can be asked to repurchase problem loans and, in extreme cases, removed as a service provider. In addition to having such compliance monitoring responsibilities, the central organizations show concern for their own quality by using surveys to measure the satisfaction of the servicers as their own customers.

LESSONS FOR STUDENT FINANCIAL AID PROGRAMS

In comparing any quality control strategy with that used in student financial aid programs, at least three issues should be explored. First, how well are the programs doing compared with other programs with similar missions? In fact, the comparative magnitude of error in programs differs markedly, but programs view errors differently in terms of who they serve and what they count. Thus, simple comparisons across programs may prove problematic—implicit as well as explicit tolerances of error must be understood. Second, what practices of quality control and quality monitoring are worth borrowing from other systems? Many systems have well-developed verification schemes, and some attributes may be applicable to the student financial aid system. But, verification and monitoring schemes are often very program specific; thus, simple transferability may also be problematic. Third, what incentives and disincentives are most effective in improving performance? Do stringent penalties work? Are there other incentives that also work to improve performance? The structure of incentives and the imposition of explicit penalties and rewards create important consequences for managing the institutions and for the ultimate consumers of their services. Those practices must be understood in order to keep them consistent with overall program objectives.

To illustrate the first issue, comparing error levels, the definition of error itself creates wide variation in how the magnitude of the problem is perceived. For example, in the family assistance programs and the student financial aid programs, technical (procedural) error is intermingled with actual payment error. The earlier NRC panel that studied the family assistance programs argued, in effect, that the definition of error for the purpose of assessing financial accountability ought to be based on those measures that are direct surrogates for payment error. It reasoned that certain procedural requirements may provide a form of internal control that may be important in ensuring payment accuracy. Thus, certain procedural requirements, such as the provision of a Social Security Number for certain members of the household, may give agencies a useful tool for checking for unreported income. But, extending that requirement to all members of the household, including infants and children, enlarges the magnitude of payment error, due to a procedural requirement that only partially reflects true payment error.

To further illustrate the first issue, the universe from which errors are measured may be markedly different in different programs or institutions. Some institutions limit their risk by limiting risky participants. Others may simply ignore areas of potential error if bottom-line profitability is not affected by the errors. Many commercial insurance carriers simply refuse to underwrite certain classes of applicants rather than make individual determinations of risk to guide insurance offerings. Banks have histories of so-called redlining of geographic areas or real estate markets in order to avoid altogether areas of potentially high risk. Mortgage-purchasing associations stop buying loans from servicers who do not meet basic standards.

The family assistance programs, and to a large extent the student financial aid programs, do not have such options. The family assistance programs must require that administering agencies be scrupulous in attempting to discover all sources of income and assets in order to ensure that the deserving poor are served and all recipients are deserving. They also subject administering agencies to perhaps the most stringent error tolerance levels of any public loan or grant program. However, many errors stem from the number of households with earned income and the volatility of the caseload as recipients move in and out of work and on and off the rolls. Both outright eligibility and benefit amounts can change month to month as income and resources change. In the AFDC and Food Stamp programs, more errors are associated with households with working recipients than with other households. The single largest type of error in the Food Stamp program is that associated with income and with appropriate deductions from income. In the Medicaid program, a large proportion of resource errors are associated with elderly participants (provider error is measured elsewhere). The earlier NRC panel attempted to make adjustments for differences in capability among the states caused by the proportion of their caseload with error-prone characteristics. The panel recommended setting performance thresholds for groups that are differently prone to error (e.g., households with reported earnings, nonearning households with elderly recipients, and all other households) and adjusting thresholds applied to the states to reflect those differences (Kramer, 1988).

With regard to the second issue, quality control practices, there are surely some quality control and monitoring techniques that can be borrowed by student financial aid programs. Techniques such as simplifying application forms and improving the training of frontline workers are generic approaches to process improvements that are useful tools to address problems in student financial aid programs. Newsletters, workshops, and other tools to disseminate best practices have been used in the family assistance programs.

Different state and local welfare systems, however, have required different remedial approaches. Few techniques in the family assistance programs are used across all states or all local offices. Approaches that are appropriate to the context must be identified through careful research to determine common sources of error and effective techniques to control them. Other techniques for improving performance, such as an aggressive federal role in the transfer of technology across states, have also been used in the family assistance programs, but they were viewed with uneven enthusiasm by state quality control administrators.

Perhaps most important in comparison with the student financial aid programs is the emphasis in the family assistance programs on front-end verification. More responsibility seems to be placed directly on the applicant for family assistance than on the applicant for student aid. Although the administering agencies do use independent verification techniques (e.g., matching data with IRS and UIB data), a variety of documentation intended as surrogates for truth of eligibility status is required of all welfare applicants at initial presentation. In the student financial aid programs, such documentation may be a weaker proxy and is only required of applicants selected for verification. (In Chapters 8 and 9, the panel addresses the lack of such extensive and up-front verification data in student financial aid programs.)

The agencies administering family assistance are responsible for ensuring compliance with application requirements. The quality control reviewer then undertakes—on only a sample of cases—a full field investigation. The cost of administering rigorous front-end verification and other improved application procedures is important but difficult to assess. Some costs are clearly trivial, others are not. In the case of family assistance, the federal government has been willing to pay half of the costs of administering the quality control systems through its usual 50 percent share of all administrative costs, and even more for a variety of other improvements, such as automated data processing and fraud investigation and prosecution, in order to encourage the states to upgrade their monitoring capabilities.

One inexpensive and useful technique that the panel believes is worth exploring is matching application data with the data collected by other agencies. While use of credit bureau and other such commercial data bases may not be appropriate in student financial aid programs, except for some loans, further use of matches with federal data sources seems worth attention. Student financial aid programs do some matching, but they do not match with IRS records. Such matches are done by the family assistance programs and by several Department of Veterans Affairs need-based programs. The cost is minimal, about one cent per record for the data, and the data supplied are regarded as highly accurate by the users. Differences between reported data and the official record are often ranked by priority and assigned to field staff for investigation. (Note that such matching, while found to be accomplished with minimal procedural problems, would likely require a legislated mandate for the IRS to provide the data to the agency.)

With respect to the third issue, use of incentives and disincentives, consequences other than payment error are born of the relationship between basic program objectives and verification requirements meant to serve quality control, and they must be considered in any assessment of rewards and penalties built into a quality control system. For example, although many program requirements have been legislated over the years to ensure participation by those who are eligible for family assistance, including explicit outreach requirements in the Food Stamp program, the intended combined effect of eligibility determination procedures and quality control monitoring is to limit participation. Until recent changes, described above, the quality control systems did not count underpayments in the penalty system at all. Improper terminations and denials of benefits are still not counted. As the earlier NRC panel found, when overall program objectives and quality control requirements are in strong conflict, improving performance is particularly problematic. The penalty structure, the earlier NRC panel concluded, distorted incentives to serve other program objectives—for example, to serve all who are eligible.

Further, the emphasis in the quality control systems in the family assistance programs is on sanctions for poor performance. Until recently, the programs had minimal, or no, explicit rewards for good performance. Although few, including the earlier NRC panel, have argued against sanctions, and error rates have declined substantially over the history of the quality control systems, the stringent (financial) penalties have had varying effects, depending on their severity and on the resources and capabilities of the states to improve their performance. At the time of the NRC studies, it was widely held that the states had done all they could to improve performance with the resources they had available. The states clearly thought they had nothing else to do but to protest. At the point that the earlier NRC panel was asked to review the quality control systems, those systems had become the source of a fierce federal-state battle, and few penalties had ever been collected because most states had appealed either administratively or in the courts.

Although the earlier NRC panel did not recommend against sanctions, it stressed that for sanctions to be effective, error tolerances must be tied to program capabilities or sufficient resources must be provided to help states improve their capabilities to desired tolerance levels. The NRC panel recommended a simplified review structure and a much more extensive quality improvement program to improve capability. In its view, to improve program performance further, the federal government and the states would have to spend at least as much on quality improvement strategies as they had spent in preceding years on quality control.

We do not make specific recommendations based on the comparisons in this chapter. In Chapters 8 and 9, we use the principles discussed here to guide our system improvement recommendations.

8

A New Strategy for the Department of Education

The Department of Education's current strategies for ensuring quality are characterized by

- centralization of authority,
- reliance on retrospective inspections to bring about quality, and
- onerous sets of frequently changed regulations that focus on compliance with process requirements.

Under the current strategies, the student financial aid delivery system is burdened with a multiplicity of process checkpoints, which add to the cost of running the system, for schools and for the government, and also contribute to a tendency for the relationships between customers and suppliers in the system to be perceived as confrontational. Moreover, there has been an emphasis on meeting stringent national standards that fail to take into account the often substantial differences among schools, in regard to their student profiles and missions. As Department of Education staff reported to the panel at its first meeting, the deficiencies of these strategies have led some within the department to seek new strategies.

One of the difficulties in developing new strategies to improve quality is conceptual. In the absence of a statutory definition of *quality*, regulatory efforts fall into the trap of allowing no margin for error. As reported to the panel, the department has been operating with a "zero error" standard, which is unattainable in practice and therefore not effective in promoting quality improvements. Departmental staff reported to the panel on efforts to develop new strategies, which have been characterized by delegation of authority and responsibility, the "ownership" of performance measures by those who are performing the functions of the system, and a deregulation of the aid delivery process that empowers an institution to determine how best to accomplish program objectives. The new strategies, as found in the department's Institutional Quality Control (IQC) Pilot Project, focus accountability on results rather than process and emphasize the continuous collection of data useful for quality improvement at participating institutions. In place of the usual imposition of external quotas, these strategies are intended to form proactive partnerships rather than confrontational relationships and to focus on service improvements for the end customers. At the same time, they are intended to meet the need to assess overall system performance by measuring quality on an ongoing basis.

THE INSTITUTIONAL QUALITY CONTROL PROJECT

The panel was asked to study the Department of Education's IQC Pilot Project, a management experiment that seeks to implement a system of accountability at the institutional level to ensure quality performance in the administration of student financial aid. The panel's study consisted of a review of materials concerning the project (workbooks, instructional manuals, three recently contracted studies, and an earlier study that was brought to the attention of the panel late in the panel's deliberations), discussions with departmental and contractor staff, and visits to financial aid offices. The Department of Education expressed interest in two main questions:

- Is the IQC concept viable as an oversight strategy?
- Is the IQC concept viable as an improvement strategy?

Participation in the IQC project is voluntary and assumes that the commitment to ensure data quality already exists at the school. The aim of the program is to shift the responsibility for quality control from the federal level to the educational institution by providing assistance and the flexibility to develop quality control programs that are tailored to the institution. With this experiment, the Department of Education hopes to reduce the burden on educational institutions, encourage the development of innovative management approaches, improve service to students, and reduce error in the delivery of Title IV financial assistance (Price Waterhouse, 1990a:1).

The IQC project was created by the Department of Education in 1985 and now involves some 80 institutions. Ideally, the institutions benefit from the opportunity to learn more about their processes by performing a detailed investigation on a random sample of their current student financial aid applicants. While the department acknowledges that all institutions are not suited for inclusion in such a project, its long-term desire is to involve a group of institutions that would account for 60 percent or more of all federal student aid funds.

Those involved in developing the project in 1985 (volunteer postsecondary institutions, a steering committee, and other parties) agreed that shifting the responsibility for quality control from the federal level to the educational institution would enable institutions to focus their resources on the factors that caused error at their respective institutions. The pilot approach differed from the prevailing integrated verification approach to quality control, in which institutional actions were determined centrally through the application processing edits developed by the department (Price Waterhouse, 1990a).

The IQC pilot schools must perform four major activities:

1. Conduct a management assessment—review the procedures and practices of the financial aid office, assess internal controls, and identify enhanced management procedures. This step helps to build team commitment and to make the project more visible throughout the institution.

2. Measure error caused by students, institutions, and the delivery system—select and review a random sample of student aid recipients to quantify the level of error and the major sources of error. A minimum of 203 students must be sampled, with the minimum rising with the number of aid recipients at the institution. The goal is to identify the types of errors that have the greatest impact on the accuracy of aid awards.

3. Identify corrective actions—develop plans to reduce error, focusing primarily on the major error sources identified through error measurement. With this step, the institution establishes a process for identifying systematically the causes of significant errors.

4. Monitor system status—repeat the management assessment and error measurement activities annually to determine the effectiveness of prior management enhancements and corrective actions. This review helps to determine whether further procedural changes are needed. Institutions then revise the corrective actions as appropriate.

Eligibility to participate in the IQC project is currently limited to the larger participants in Title IV programs who have shown low levels of financial liability and a commitment to ensure data quality. To be eligible in recent years, an institution had to have at least 2,000 recipients in the Pell and Campus-Based programs and combined program awards of at least \$2 million. The institution must also participate in all five aid programs, and an assessment of less than \$150,000 in audit liabilities is required during the two years prior to application for the program. Finally, an eligible institution must agree in writing to follow the IQC pilot program requirements.

Objectives of IQC

The Department of Education recognizes that its role has been perceived by the educational institutions as strictly regulatory in nature. Indeed, the department has viewed it to be the job of the institutions to find the errors that are sure to exist in their student aid files. The program reviews done by the department and the required independent audits have traditionally offered little help to the institutions in terms of what they should be doing to improve their financial aid delivery systems. The IQC project was offered as a demonstration project to help the institutions determine where problems lie in their systems and to encourage development of innovative management approaches. Of course, the accuracy of the Title IV student aid award process would improve if the discovery of filing and other errors led institutions to make changes in their own systems. Unfortunately, the panel found that many of the changes that are needed are outside the institutions' control or of little real consequence.

The panel believes that the primary purpose of the IQC activities should be to conduct a management assessment (task 1 above), but it appears that the institutions focus on satisfying the requirements of the data gathering and monitoring activities (tasks 2, 3, and 4). That is, the IQC project seems to force the institutions to focus initially on the results of the review of a sample of student aid recipients. The intent of the project is to help the institutions determine the types of errors that are inherent in their records so that they can work toward eliminating or reducing them in subsequent years. The methods for the sampling schemes and procedures described in the IQC workbook reflect statistically valid approaches, but the statistical knowledge available in most student financial aid offices is very limited, and the institutions are provided with few tools to help them determine either the causes for the errors or appropriate solutions. Thus, the panel found that, despite the periodic training programs offered by the department, the IQC institutions will not be able to utilize fully the instructions and software provided to them for statistical analysis of their sample data without further help.

Incentives and Disincentives

The Department of Education offers incentives to encourage institutions to participate in the IQC project. The incentive most often mentioned is that institutions are not required to verify applications as selected by the central processor, the task required on up to 30 percent of the total federal financial aid applicants at nonparticipating institutions. Recall that for nonparticipating institutions, the central processor identifies a number of applications that are recommended for review, then the institutions select additional applications to ensure that at least 30 percent of the applications have been reviewed. For an institution with a large number of selected students, this process is labor intensive and not likely to provide valid information about how to change its activities, for two reasons. First, the review process must be cursory in nature for individual data items on the application because of the number of applications reviewed. Second, the nonrandom selection of the applications makes it difficult to project the results to other applications not selected.

Although the incentive to reduce verification is in place, in practice many institutions in the pilot program apparently continue to verify applications selected by the central processor. Also, if the department would want institutions with small numbers of aid students to participate in pilot activities in the future, this incentive may not work. Such institutions will perceive that they have little to gain from participating in the project. For example, since the IQC sample size can be no fewer than 203 applicants, institutions that normally have fewer than 203 centrally selected cases for review will not benefit from this aspect of participation in the IQC.

The Department of Education looks at retention statistics as an indicator of success in the pilot's development. Figure 8-1 shows cohort retention of institutions accepted into and starting the pilot activities in each of the

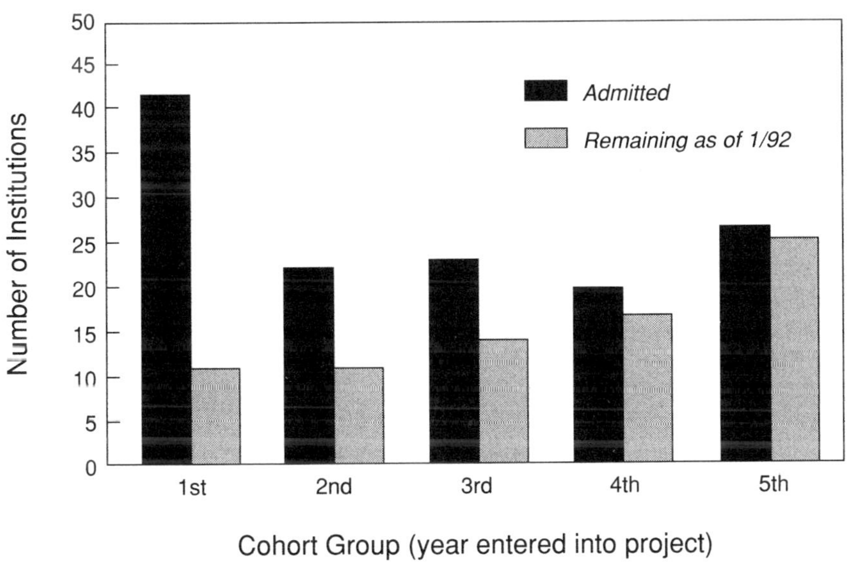

FIGURE 8-1 Cohort retention, Institutional Quality Control Pilot Project. SOURCE: U.S. Department of Education.

first five years. This information leads the department to believe that after discounting the problems that one would expect in first-year activities (only 11 of the 42 institutions in the first cohort participated in the program in the fifth year), there has been steady improvement in acceptance of the pilot project by participants. For institutions in the first cohort there were no minimum size standards, thus providing an opportunity to evaluate the methodology of various sizes and types of institutions. Many of the institutions found that the burden of participation exceeded their commitment to participate. In addition, the first cohort did not have the benefit of automated error calculation tools, which were not developed until mid-1986 (Price Waterhouse, 1990a). The panel requested additional data on year-to-year retention within each cohort (Table 8-1), which did not indicate that the likelihood of dropping out after one or two years in the pilot has been greatly reduced.

Although long-term retention rates may not exceed 70 percent, the rates should not be a dominant consideration in judging the success of the program. More important are the benefits to the institution and the department's success in achieving its desired compliance objectives. Some institutional changes have been made as a result of information learned from the IQC sample, but panel members, in visits to institutions and discussions with aid officers, found that many if not most of the institutions were not sure how to proceed or even how to generate useful reports using the IQC software and that the amount of work required to complete the IQC process is generally greater than the institution had anticipated. Finally, the incentives for compliance may not be appropriate. Penalties imposed on those in the IQC sample with problem accounts may cause concerns at the institutions because the independent audits that the institutions are subjected to are not reduced even if they exhibit desirable results over time.

TABLE 8-1 IQC Project Retention, by Cohort

			Number/Percentage Remaining			
Cohort	Date Admitted	Number in Cohort	After 1 Year	After 2 Years	After 3 Years	As of Jan. 1992
First	Jan. 1985	42				11/26%
Second	Dec. 1986	22	19/86%	17/77%	15/68%	12/55%
Third	July 1988	23	17/74%	16/70%	14/61%	14/61%
Fourth	July 1989	20	18/90%	17/85%		17/85%
Fifth	Sept. 1991	27				26/96%
Total		134				80/60%

SOURCE: U.S. Department of Education.

Prior Studies of the IQC Project

Looking beyond retention in the program as an indicator of the value of the IQC project, the Department of Education has commissioned several studies of the effectiveness of the project (Pelavin, 1989, 1991a, b, and 1992; Price Waterhouse, 1990a). In this section the panel briefly critiques some of the methodology of the studies and comments on the most important findings on which panel members were in agreement.

Pelavin (1991a) looked at the 19 institutions that had data for the 1987-88 through 1989-90 program years. Point estimates were provided for "errors" in terms of percentages and dollars but standard errors were not presented. Comparisons were made between 1987-88 and 1989-90, and the 1988-89 data were not included because the department believed that improvements would take two years to become evident. The follow-up report (Pelavin, 1991b) does provide some standard error information and 1988-89 data. This report found, as a whole, less reduction in error between 1988-89 and 1989-90. The panel is concerned that the multiple comparisons made across institutions and programs may have overstated statistical significance since no adjustments were made to the variances to reflect the multiple comparisons. The reports conclude that the "IQC Project is showing improvements in the delivery of Title IV student aid, albeit slowly" (Pelavin, 1991a:7). A major concern of the panel is that no attempt was made to determine the extent to which the error rate in all institutions, including those not participating in the IQC pilot, was declining (as indicated in larger studies). One would expect such results when program changes are made over the years.

The Price Waterhouse (1990a) report is commendable for looking at error rates at similar-sized, nonpilot schools and relating those data to estimates of national error rates. The study looked at changes in the percent of dollars in error at institutions participating in the IQC pilot during the 1987-88 and 1988-89 award years, but it made no estimate of standard errors for these differences. Most of the percentage differences were less than 2 percent, which concerned the panel because some subgroup comparisons surely had too large a sampling error to infer that changes had occurred since there was a small sample (412) of applicant files studied. Still, the panel concurs with several of the recommendations made in the report: (1) reassess the effectiveness of the IQC pilot in reducing student error and (2) reassess the objectives of the IQC pilot and determine the extent to which it is meeting those objectives.

There is little evidence in any of the studies that student error can be greatly reduced by pilot or additional verification activities, yet the potential exists to reduce institutional errors through pilot activities. Of equal importance, pilot schools provide the possibility of early and repeated measurement of the system and any changes made to the system, and they provide the opportunity to test and evaluate innovative approaches to delivery systems. In short, the pilot has more to offer than what appears to be the Department of Education's primary goal—error reduction.

Pelavin (1992) compared data for 32 schools for which information was available for 1988-89 through 1990-91. However, only point estimates for comparing 1988-89 and 1990-91 were provided. The panel believes that the methodology used to compute standard errors, *t* values, and degrees of freedom was incorrect. The report concluded that the data "strongly support the precept that the IQC Project is significantly increasing accuracy in awarding and disbursing Federal Title IV student financial aid. The IQC Project—a deregulated approach to quality improvement in the Title IV programs—provides [the department] with necessary accountability measures, extends institutions needed flexibility, and produces quantitative results that document and confirm its success" (p. 3). The panel disagrees with the contention that the data "support" such broad conclusions.

Despite the problems with the studies, the Department of Education should take note of the messages they convey: The schools need more help; student error is not likely to decline as a result of these activities; and the objectives of the pilot project should be rethought. Given the difficulty of using subgroup estimates from studies with such small sample sizes, the panel doubts that further such studies could provide more detailed information of sufficient quality to justify the substantial investment in terms of the cost to the department and the time of the institutions involved in providing the data. Any further analysis of the data from existing studies should use appropriate statistical tools and interpretations.

> *Recommendations 8-1: The Department of Education should develop the capabilities needed to ensure that proper statistical methodology is used in future evaluative studies of the Institutional Quality Control project. In addition, future IQC activities should go beyond the emphasis on reduction of verification error rates to improvement of a wide range of financial aid management tasks and investigation of other quality concerns, such as the complexity of the forms and the need to improve outreach activities.*

Support of the IQC Project

The Department of Education has instituted many positive activities in support of IQC institutions, including training programs for new and continuing institutions, providing software, developing recognition and awards processes, publishing a newsletter, holding state and regional meetings, and providing technical assistance (using departmental and contracted personnel). The IQC personnel within the department are continually updating their support mechanisms so they can offer more help to the institutions. The panel, based on discussions with financial aid office staff from various institutions, has some suggestions for improving those activities.

Training Sessions

The training programs are generally regarded by the institutions as good; the sessions are appropriate for the areas that are currently covered. Breakouts into special topic/interest sessions seem very worthwhile, and the agenda for those sessions seems well thought out and subject to improvement as new ideas are available. The emphasis now is on how to avoid making certain types of errors during the next cycle of financial aid applications. More emphasis should be placed on discovering ways to improve the institutions' processes and systems.

Quality Control Software

The software used by all institutions in the project is developed by a Department of Education contractor. The panel's questions to the contractor resulted in friendly and helpful service. The software was designed specifically for the original requirements of the project. Updates to the software have reflected changes in the law and other requirements. A manual provided by the contractor attempts to explain in detail how various parts of the software's output should be interpreted, including the calculation of various errors, although some of the descriptions of error types and reasons are confusing to some users. The manual describes the two types of data that can be used by the institution for verification: original data from the students' records or "best" data from an updated source, such as the quality control sample. The panel was informed of several issues regarding the software that the department should address, including inappropriate double counting of variances (in the accounting sense), the need to improve the procedure for updating the software and the timing for delivering updates to institutions, the fact that computer memory requirements often exceed the hardware capabilities in aid offices, the need for a help feature in the on-line access software, and the need to provide software to automate worksheets and quarterly reports.

Recognition and Awards

Although recognition and awards are often used in IQC pilot activities to encourage participation and commitment to new approaches, the recognition and awards should be monitored carefully. A financial aid office that merely adds more inspection or review activities in an attempt to "improve" the error rates without improving the process should not be encouraged. Recognition and awards should be given for substantial changes to a financial aid process that result in noticeable improvements for the customer.

Newsletter

The newsletter has great potential for increasing communication and understanding among the various organizations participating in the IQC project. More use should be made of this vehicle to educate IQC institutions about the value of making real changes which improve processes. Newsletter materials should encourage other suitable institutions to join the IQC project. Articles prepared by participating institutions that describe the positive and negative aspects of participation in the IQC project would be useful. Articles on how the Office of Postsecondary Education is using the IQC results for its internal processes would increase the credibility of the project. Also, articles on the distinction between the uses of the IQC sample and the uses of the verification process would be helpful.

Meetings

Sponsoring national, regional, and state meetings is one of the important service functions of the Department of Education. At such meetings there is an opportunity to highlight the role of the IQC project and to showcase success stories. Although these meetings are not intended only for those in the IQC project, they could be used more to generate interest in the IQC program. Local and regional networks are an important way for people to learn and help each other, and they should be encouraged by the department, with departmental time and resources if necessary.

Technical Assistance

Participation in the IQC project will inevitably lead to questions and concerns. The department recognized this from the beginning and has attempted to provide assistance. Departmental staff involved in technical assistance efforts exhibit enthusiastic dedication to providing good assistance. However, the department must acknowledge that many institutions view it not as a partner in the process of improvement, but as a judge. This inhibits communication in an area where there should be mutual trust. In addition, departmental staff and contractors should be better informed about how the IQC process actually works. In the struggle to keep up with project demands, technical assistance personnel are not afforded enough time to gain hands-on experience with the process at an institution.

Recommendation 8-2: The Department of Education should periodically make complete revisions of the IQC software and instructional material, rather than engage in continuous patching, and it should seek assistance from software evaluation and improvement specialists and involve the users in redesign decisions.

Recommendation 8-3: Institutions in the IQC pilot program should have more at-hand statistical support, and institutions volunteering to participate in IQC activities should be required to show access to statistical expertise in sampling and data analysis as a condition of being in the program. To some extent this can be accomplished by improving the training of internal staff. Adding training material on basic statistical skills to the training program could help, but more effective strategies might include subsidizing locally obtained coursework for financial aid office staff or developing cooperative agreements with local quantitative departments to provide ongoing assistance. The Department of Education should assist the IQC institutions in these efforts by helping develop the cooperative ties and providing monetary support.

Types of Errors Noted in the IQC Project

The types and severity of the errors, including institutional and student errors, in the IQC process have been delineated in studies of the process and are reasonably well understood by all involved. However, the IQC project does not seem to provide any measures of improved service to students, families, institutions, the Department of Education, or the community at large. Errors created by the complexity of the process are, for the most part, ignored or attributed to the institutions or students. Errors caused, as discussed earlier, by the application form itself or by accompanying explanations about items on the form may contribute to a large share of the overall errors noted. Some aspects of the forms, although not necessarily causing an error, do cause frustration and confusion. In many cases operational definitions of terms, such as "support," seem confusing and subject to interpretation by the department or the data entry contractors.

Errors associated with such items as a missing financial aid transcript, missing Selective Service statement, and missing statement of satisfactory academic progress may not result in misspent aid dollars, yet they are counted as serious errors. Getting the quality control software to calculate the summary tables without including such errors is at best awkward and perhaps impossible. Also, cut-off points for errors in declared assets and income seem somewhat arbitrary.

Error types should be defined so that they are clearly understood by all involved. For example, errors that do not affect the amount of the aid award should not be given equal weight with errors that do. Also, other measures that deal with improvements to the process should be added, and they could perhaps be determined by the institutions themselves. For example, the time it takes to process certain portions of the application might be a useful measure.

SUMMARY OF THE PANEL'S REVIEW OF THE IQC PROJECT

The panel examined the IQC project at great length and gave much consideration to its future. Should it be dropped, continued as a pilot program, or be incorporated as a basic approach to quality improvement? Does the IQC project release institutions from too few of the regulations to have any effect? Has it had a noticeable effect on any measures of improvement, or is it impossible for structural changes that are limited to activities within the financial aid offices to result in noticeable improvement?

The fact that there has been a high attrition rate in the project raises several questions. Are the institutions participating because they expect to make changes for the better, are seeking relief from the 30 percent verification process, or for other reasons? Does the incentive to join the IQC project come mostly from benefits offered by the Department of Education (external) or from the institutions' desire to seek improvement (internal)? What would happen to attrition if the department paid some of the administrative costs of the program? What incentives might be used in addition to regulatory relief? Facts known about various types of incentives will influence what the department does in the future to maintain and build the IQC process. Clearly, the incentive structure should be reviewed.

Even though first-year schools are paired with a more experienced school, possibly the IQC process is overwhelming. Perhaps local assistance should be considered since many institutions will have quantitative staff who could learn more about the financial aid programs as they assist. Other institutions may have to ask for outside help. Statistical expertise should also be developed at the department to permit generation of the appropriate statistical information about IQC institutions and the sharing of aggregate results.

The measures of success should also be reviewed. As examples of possible measures of success, what effect has the IQC process had on default rates or customer service? Institutions should target their own areas for improvement rather than use the Department of Education's numerical goals exclusively.

The IQC project offers a chance for the Department of Education to be more proactive (compared with its usual reactive and regulatory mode), but the department may not be making the best use of the chance. For example, because there are strict admission standards, the schools selected for pilot activities could be allowed more freedom from regulatory and management burdens. The panel is concerned that the department may be more interested in expanding pilot activities as a means of regulatory relief than it is in learning from pilot activities. Where regulations are a burden, the department should address the problem by improving the regulations so all institutions may benefit.

Further, selection of small groups of the pilot institutions to participate in special studies should be considered. In addition, the design of the studies should be rethought in order to maximize what is learned from each study. This is especially important until the department better develops its internal analytic capabilities in these areas. Possibly, it could pretest the application form in a special study. Perhaps the training sessions could be used as a mechanism for obtaining suggestions from the institutions about improving the IQC process. Institutions in the pilot might show evidence of systemic problems, but they will not be able to correct such problems effectively. Systemic improvements will require fundamental changes to systems, many of which will have to made by the Department of Education.

The IQC project is a valuable source of information for the Department of Education. While it may help schools to lower their error rates, that is but one role. The department must remain aware of the two-track system that the pilot creates. The entrance requirements and commitment needed to participate are likely limiting participation to the most quality-conscious schools, and surely the largest. This limits the use of data for inference about the progress of quality improvement. Will policies found useful in these special schools be as useful if tried in nonparticipating schools? Wouldn't the philosophy of risk-based management encourage selection of the worst of the nonparticipants as pilot possibilities so issues of quality related to the larger universe of schools might be addressed? These issues lead to a fundamental issue that should be addressed by the pilot activities. The pilot project should make data available from which to infer "common-cause" problems so that the department can consider system improvements and determine what works and what does not work when innovations are attempted.

Recommendation 8-1: The IQC program should be retained and given the support of top management. However, when the common-cause regulatory burdens imposed by audits and reviews are eliminated (for details see Chapters 4 and 5), the incentives to join the pilot project will change. Thus, the following improvements should be considered:

- *Incentives for institutions to join the IQC should be reexamined with the aim of encouraging schools with known administrative difficulties to seek help from Department of Education staff.*
- *The department's measure of success in the IQC program should*

be reexamined with the aim of going beyond measuring retention in the IQC program to identifying ways to improve processes.

- *More use should be made of IQC data. For example, the Department of Education should inform all institutions about the progress of the IQC program and suggest use of measurements and practices found to be successful in addressing specific concerns about quality.*

9

Further Initiatives for Improvement in the System

In its review of the issues related to quality in the delivery of student financial aid, the panel has endorsed a customer-oriented focus that is consistent with a mission of supporting the educational needs of the student applicant while making the most efficient use possible of taxpayer dollars. A customer service philosophy must embrace all of the internal customers of the system: students, postsecondary educational institutions, lenders, guaranty agencies, various relevant units within the Department of Education, and the Congress.

In this concluding chapter of the report, we discuss the directions for change that we believe are most likely to improve the quality of the student financial aid award determination system. We also provide a final set of recommendations designed to achieve that end.

REAUTHORIZATION OF THE HIGHER EDUCATION ACT

The most recent reauthorization of the Higher Education Act occurred in 1992, as the panel was engaged in its deliberations. One of the main goals of the reauthorization legislation was to simplify the student aid programs. The House Committee on Education and Labor defined the issue as follows.

> Many students and their families are denied access to student aid because they cannot navigate through the bewildering complexity of the current student aid forms and delivery system. This complexity has become a new barrier to educational opportunity (U.S. Congress, 1992).

As a result of the passage of the bill, some of the concerns already expressed in this report concerning the complexity of the application and its effect on student error have been reduced or even eliminated. Following are some of the simplifying features of the 1992 reauthorization:

- *A single needs analysis* replaces the two methodologies, Pell and Congressional, with one formula.[1] The analysis is used to determine a family's eligibility for all federal student aid.
- *Expansion of the simplified needs test* leads to a less complex analysis for families with adjusted gross income under $50,000 who file either a 1040A or 1040EZ income tax form. Prior to the 1992 reauthorization, the simplified needs test was restricted to students and families with income of less than $15,000. The simplified calculation, when it applies, excludes all family assets in determining eligibility.
- *The "effective family contribution" is automatically zero* for the lowest income dependent students and independent students with dependents other than a spouse. This treatment will be based on an income equal to or less than the income allowed for receiving the maximum earned-income credit under IRS rules.
- *A single form* is used to determine the need and eligibility of a student for Title IV financial assistance and the need for guaranteed student loans. The bill also requires that the secretary of education develop a separate, single loan application document for all students applying for the guaranteed student loan program.
- *Eligibility for federal aid is to be determined at no charge.* No student or parent will be charged a fee for the collection, processing, or delivery of federal financial aid.
- *A streamlined reapplication process* simplifies subsequent applications for federal student aid.
- *A direct loan demonstration project* will help determine whether there is any advantage to having the U.S. Treasury, through the Department of Education, fund and administer loans directly to students without use of private institutions, such as commercial lenders or guaranty agencies.

A new section ("H") was added to the Higher Education Act. This section is designed to improve accountability and integrity in the student aid programs without precluding needy students from receiving the education they deserve and without preventing quality institutions from providing the educational services that foster productive and contributing citizens. Section H, entitled "Program Integrity," focuses on strengthening the process by which institutions of higher education are allowed to participate in fed-

[1] Recall the description of the two methodologies in Chapter 3.

eral student aid programs through state licensure, accreditation, and federal eligibility, certification, and program review processes. The panel hopes that enactment of this section will lead to development of performance-based statutes that avoid affixing common-cause solutions to special-case events and that aim at achieving measurable and meaningful outcomes rather than additional layers of bureaucracy. Examples of meaningful outcomes would include lower default rates, higher graduation and employment rates, and improved customer satisfaction.

In response to the problem of regulations being changed without providing sufficient notice for the institutions to adapt to those changes, the reauthorization calls for a master calendar. With this requirement, any Title IV regulatory changes not published in final form by December 1, prior to the start of the next award year, will not become effective until the beginning of the second award year after that December 1 date. This provision, along with negotiated rule making (which requires public involvement in the development of proposed regulations), should reduce the burden on institutions and result in the reduction of error, if the mandate is not violated.

TOWARD A NEW APPLICANT PROCESSING SYSTEM

Important measures of increased quality in the student financial aid system include the reduction of the time required to complete the application process and the reduction of unnecessary work or burden (such as that measured in person-hours). In the applicant verification and loan certification process, considerable work and redundancy add time from the point that the student initially applies to the point of certification or noncertification of eligibility, but they add little or no value to the product. Consider, for example, a student applying to five universities. The student may iterate several times in submitting and resubmitting the student aid application to one of the multiple data entry (MDE) contractors. After this first step, the student then sends the resulting Student Aid Report (SAR) to each of the five institutions. For all centrally selected SARs, each institution is required to verify the data up to a maximum of 30 percent of applicants, although they often verify more. Thus, this student's application could be chosen for verification by all five of the schools. Imagine five student financial aid officers all sitting next to each other verifying the same file. Although in reality the five financial aid officers are at different schools, the result is the same as five inspectors doing the same work. This is redundant and wasteful of time that could be better spent in counseling students or in other value-enhancing work.

Prior verification results are not used to form a risk-based strategy for selection of reapplicants for verification. Thus, the verification process may be repeated at the school where the student is attending (or at other schools if the student wishes to transfer) for another three or four years. This is because the student has to reapply for financial aid each year, iterating again with the MDE contractor and institution. The process adds uncertainty and time delays to the student's decision making, as well as burden for the institution.

A "New" Approach

While some further improvements are possible, the current institutional verification process is fundamentally redundant and inefficient, as described above. In addition, errors in the system are seldom corrected until long after they occur. To improve the system, a greater emphasis on cooperation and coordination between customer and provider is crucial. In addition, there must be a move to deemphasize ineffective, time-consuming, and expensive efforts to eliminate 100 percent of error through inspection and reinspection. A process that treats program participants as miscreants rather than customers must be changed.

The panel suggests that the Department of Education weigh more heavily the comments made in many of the commissioned studies that have addressed verification. Those studies have indicated that (1) large errors remain even after verification, (2) the cause of much of "student error" lies in the complicated application process, and (3) data items that must be forecast (e.g., estimated income, household size, and number in college) are main contributors to student error. The studies have produced little evidence that institutions can develop procedures that will further reduce student error very much. Thus, the panel believes that further improvement possibilities, that is, true corrective actions, lie mainly in the hands of the Department of Education and Congress, since only they can make the necessary systemic and legislative changes.

Ideally, the process could be greatly simplified if the MDE contractors or the central processor (also a contractor) took over most if not all of the verification/certification steps. Only one resource would be used rather than up to six as in the previous example (i.e., the data entry contractor plus five institutions). Under the revised process, the data entry contractor would send the SAR to the student and the institutions after the student and the contractor had performed the correction and verification steps. Thus, the extra steps involved in having the student send the SAR to the schools after the contractor has sent it to the student would be eliminated. (We note that the contractor currently sends the SAR data to the schools indicated on the application, but a signed SAR sent by the student is required to meet Department of Education recordkeeping requirements.)

To summarize, while institutional verification removes some, but not all, of the error made by the student when initially applying, the process has several critical flaws. Most important, the system does not have a management strategy and associated data feedback aimed at developing corrective actions. Corrective actions taken to increase the reliability of the initial data would remove problems, such as reliance on expensive and duplicative inspection efforts and time delays in making the award. In assessing possible solutions to these problems, the panel found that the Department of Education can best work on reducing the causes of error by developing centralized and up-front verification of applicant-reported data. Indications of how the department might proceed in these areas are presented next.

Reducing "Student Error"

The Department of Education must move from a system that focuses on detecting errors after awards have been made to a system that prevents error to the extent possible. While some error could be removed by making the application materials more user friendly, as suggested in Chapter 5, and by the increasing use of electronic application systems, additional action is needed. A combination of changes to some data requirements and changes to the activities associated with the SAR and verification can result in large reductions in errors, for example, of the types reported in Tables 5-3 and 5-4. We begin with some ideas on reducing error by changing data requirements.

Prospective data have been identified as a source of student error in past studies. The Department of Education and Congress, recognizing such problems, have made changes in recent years to reduce such errors. For example, income is now reported for the tax year preceding the school year and applications must not be sent before January 1 following the tax year. In the past, applicants had to estimate income for the current year, an obviously error-prone activity. Yet, several states still have aid programs that require applicants to apply for federal aid early in January. For many of the applicants, taxes are not completed and even Wage and Tax Statements (W-2s) may not be available. Thus, such applications are some of the most error prone and have an impact on the strategy for selecting records to be verified. The Department of Education should work with states to set a due date that would eliminate such problems or allow data from a year earlier if tax forms are not yet completed. In the latter case, applications in subsequent years should be required to use the tax form for the year after the one used the previous year.

The Department of Education might also explore the placement of electronic application systems at service sites for other need-based programs. Thus, low-income applicants, potentially having no tax form, who are subject to the verification processes of the other programs could have their student aid eligibility efficiently determined by their eligibility for those other programs.

Another prospective data item is the number of other family members in college. The department should consider asking for the Social Security Number of all family dependents expected to attend postsecondary schools. If any of the listed dependents is not found in the application system, the applicant could be asked to report the school that person attends. The school could then be asked to report to the department the attendance status of these nonapplicant students along with the status of students who are applicants for aid at that school. The central processing system could link all applicants affected by a change in this data item, recompute their eligibility "indices," and notify the school in a timely manner.

The department might also consider a separate form for applicants from families with multiple dependents in college. Parents would then supply their financial information only once on a form separate from that of the student's finances. This would currently affect as many as 35 percent of the dependent students and 10 percent of independent students. It would reduce unnecessary burden on parents and reduce transcription errors.

Household size is also a major contributor to the error estimated in past studies. This data item entails prospective error, as in asking for the number of persons who will be supported from July 1 to the following June 30. Problems may also be caused by the complex definition of the item. The prospective error can be eliminated by using a past date, such as the January 1 start of the application process. Reducing definitional problems might require using tax code definitions of *dependents* or a listing sheet to identify the individuals claimed and their relationship to the household.

Home value is no longer a consideration because the 1992 reauthorization removed this data item from need calculations. To some extent, *other real estate* and *investment value* have diminished as causes of error in the federal application process because they are not reported unless income exceeds $50,000. The panel is concerned that some state and institutional aid programs will continue to require these data items, which will complicate the application process as it appears to the student who must explore all sources of aid. Even though the federal application form will collect some state-required data items (eight items, at the time this report was written), the Department of Education, Congress, and the other sources of aid should continually work together to improve the system. The long-term goal should be to create a true one-form system that simplifies the process for the applicant but also results in a fair distribution of aid dollars from all sources.

Rather than removing from the application form items that are error prone or perceived as unfairly restricting aid awards, the department should consider ways to allow more tolerance in reporting those items. For example, raising the threshold amount before an asset affects the calculation of need would reduce errors because it is effectively the same as removing the item for applicants with small asset values. Applicants with very large assets would still be identified, which would provide the potential for a more fair determination of eligibility for aid. Yet, using thresholds presents problems regardless of the cutoff level because a few dollars in error at the threshold results in a large error in determining eligibility. Consideration could be given to creating relational decisions that might fairly assess the ability to use assets. For example, the aid formula could cap *home value* at some multiple of the applicant's income that is related to mortgage availability. Such a computation should be less affected by error in the reported asset value and should more reasonably assess the amount of the asset available to the applicant. Data from the Survey of Consumer Finances (Kennickell and Shack-Marquez, 1992) could be useful in defining the applicant's ability to pay and in setting thresholds for use of assets in needs analysis.

Errors in reporting other nontaxable income have been reduced in importance due mainly to the removal of the married-couple deduction from the tax form. This item was the largest of the nontaxable income error items (Price Waterhouse, 1991). Errors in some of the other nontaxable income items could be identified if Internal Revenue Service (IRS) forms were available, as could some errors in the existence of assets, the last of the items in the listing of major student errors.

A break-out of tax form items could be collected from all applicants, or applicants could be required to submit the 1040 page of the federal tax form. Useful tax information could then be entered with the application data. While this would add to data entry costs, the information would certainly help to improve the current verification selection methods and would result in more efficient use of time at the institutions. Yet there may be a more efficient approach. The panel believes that the Department of Education should develop a front-end match of applicant data with IRS data tapes. Such matches are being performed at several federal agencies and are reportedly very successful. (The panel recognizes that the department will likely need the help of Congress for such matches to be possible. Legislation directing the IRS to allow these matches may be needed. Requiring a match of the data elements used to determine student aid eligibility with tax requirements would help. Otherwise, nonmatches would require personal attention in verification to ensure a fair determination of eligibility.)

The timing of applying for aid and filing tax forms also needs attention. Early aid applicants often will not have filed the federal forms for the tax year. Even when tax forms have been filed, there is some delay before tax information can be retrieved. A match with the previous year's tax data could be done for those applicants. Questionable applications could be identified for verification or a later match with the current tax data. Alternatively, the applicant might be allowed to use the prior year's tax data for aid determination. Although the effects of such a change on the award distribution among students should not be great, this option should be studied further before being acted on.

Thus, the panel believes that the "problem of student error" falls into the hands of the Department of Education and Congress. The department must take actions that affect the system in order to reduce student error appreciably, not impose unnecessary requirements on the institution in the verification and compliance-review procedures.

Recommendation 9-1: The Department of Education and the Congress should work together to effectuate changes in data requirements that should simplify award determination and increase accuracy. Development of a system that requires applicant data to be matched with IRS data should receive top priority.

Reducing "Institutional Error"

Each error item associated with students in Department of Education contract studies generally had the same level of award error in all the aid programs (Pell, Campus-Based, and Stafford Loans). In contrast, the most important institutional error items varied in level of award error across programs (see Table 5-4). As with student error, many of the causes of institutional error can be removed through systemic changes initiated by the Department of Education. Errors that are caused by a piece of paper being missing from a student's file, such as the statement of educational purpose, are prime targets for action. Institutions must utilize resources to keep such forms although they have no relationship to the institution's mission. If the signed statements for educational purpose, Selective Service compliance, reporting of any drug offenses, and so on, were required with the application, considerable burden would be removed from the institution and from audit and review activities. Thus, the auditors and reviewers would be freed of trivial activities and would have more time to focus on the more important quality issues of effectiveness of educational programs, institutional integrity, and the value of the service purchased by the student and taxpayer. (See Schenet, 1990, for further description of these issues.)

Data base matching is currently mandated by Congress in Title IV legislation to identify applicants who have failed to register for Selective Service. Federal concerns internal to the Department of Education, such as prior aid received as measured by the financial aid transcript, should be identified from the department's own records, much like the matches with loan default records. Here too, Congress has instructed the department, through Title IV legislation, to improve its internal data bases that contain information on defaulted loans. (A contract for the National Student Loan Data Base was awarded early in 1993.) The applications identified in these automated processes as "problem cases" should be referred to the institutions for follow-up. This process should be satisfactory to the schools since the Price Waterhouse (1991) study indicated that institutions agree that some type of verification is needed but that the current system requires substantial institutional resources and is not well targeted.

The remaining major sources of institutional error (computing the cost of attending the institution, monitoring enrollment, determining special-situation exceptions, determining whether the student has a bachelor's degree, and packaging of aid) are associated with information and actions most easily handled at the school. With the reduction of other unnecessary activities, the Department of Education and the schools could concentrate on developing effective methods to reduce errors in these activities. Both systemic and special-cause actions are needed. As an example of a systemic action, Price Waterhouse (1990b) recommended that schools be required to report each item in the cost-of-attendance computation separately so individual item limits that are exceeded could be determined early. Although the panel did not explore this possibility, the Institutional Quality Control Pilot Program could be used to explore such activities.

Reduction of special causes of error requires knowledge of where the errors are located. An unusual clustering of errors is likely to indicate the existence of a special cause. For example, Advanced Technology and Westat (1987b) discovered that clock-hour schools were four times more likely than credit-hour schools to have underawards due to incorrect determination of enrollment status. They speculated that the regulations were developed with credit-hour schools in mind and thus were confusing when applied at a clock-hour school.

Centralized Verification

With the removal of many of the underlying causes of student error and the availability of "external" sources of data, the verification strategy changes. Information is at hand on most of the remaining error-prone data elements. Besides the obvious items, such as income and number of dependents, interest or dividends reported and tax schedules that indicate business or rental assets should be good indicators of problems with reported asset information. The automated checks on such items as Selective Service registration and student loan default could determine the records that will need further verifying documentation. Rather than flagging the record for institutional action during verification, the SAR could request corrections that are currently made much later in the process. The changes could be processed centrally, which would result in an initial award determination that would be considerably more accurate than the one produced by current procedures. It is likely, as mentioned previously, that some applications will require assignment to institutions for further examination to resolve special situations that might otherwise delay the determination of award. An example of such an application is one involving separated parents who filed a joint tax form. In this case, the aid application is required only to report the income of the parent with which the applicant lived most of the prior 12 months.

While up-front data processing costs might increase under this proposal, the Department of Education should consider total cost and service improvement in making decisions on implementation. Repeated processing of SARs would likely decrease. Financial aid administrators, freed of burden, would be able to concentrate on the special cases that always exist. Awards might be determined sooner, a service improvement for applicants. Consistency of verification and documentation would be better controlled. Finally, award error would be controlled on all applications, not just those selected for verification, as is now the case.

> *Recommendation 9-2: The Department of Education should begin the development of a front-end and centralized verification system in which the schools' verification burden is drastically reduced. Under a new system, the department would identify exceptional cases, far fewer than the current 30 percent, for institutional review activities.*

STUDENT LOANS

The 1992 reauthorization emphasizes the use of loans even more than in the past. By expanding loan limits in all programs and by eliminating loan limits completely in the Parent Loans for Undergraduate Students Program, the average future aid package will likely contain a higher percentage of loans than in the past, which increases the possibility for errors of the kind encountered under the terms of the old programs. Therefore, the need to redesign the Department of Education's management of these programs so that they focus on students, parents, and recipient institutions is greater than ever before.

In general, the panel believes that the same remedies recommended in this report for other parts of the Title IV student financial assistance programs also hold for the loan programs. The difference is that the structure of the loan programs is more complicated because of the public-private partnerships that have been developed over the years since the first Higher Education Act (1965). The involvement of the private enterprise banking community, state guaranty agencies, and secondary markets, in addition to the school financial aid offices and the MDE contractors, makes the loan programs even more complex to manage than other parts of the system.

The Department of Education requested that the panel focus on delivery systems leading to awards rather than payment processes; thus, we have said little in this report about quality assurance in lending and guaranty agencies. In some respects, the department's procedures for dealing with these entities are even more highly skewed toward inspection than those problematic systems dictated by federal rules for institutions of higher education. Considering the level of federal expenditure to leverage capital into the student aid loan programs that rely on private enterprise and nonprofit organizations, the panel believes the following comments on the need for greater use of quality systems in this part of the program are in order.

One possibility for addressing issues of quality in the current loan programs is a model similar to that in the Institutional Quality Control Pilot Project: high standards for participation, clear rules for ongoing federal oversight, and deregulation incentives for participants. This process could lead to insightful review, "best case" examples that might be instituted by other agencies, and new avenues for working relationships in the development of federal rules.

While the existence of additional partners from the private and nonprofit sector is often cited as adding to the complexity of the federal student loan programs and instances of poor loan servicing do exist, the strongest of the private and nonprofit entities have developed greater managerial and data processing capabilities with respect to loans than are currently possessed by the Department of Education. Thus, the importance of instituting quality management programs within the department to enable it to engage the assistance and cooperation of that expertise is vital. This is especially true given the direct loan demonstration project mandated by Congress, in which the Department of Education is charged with administering loans in their entirety.

The direct loan program is one current effort aimed at resolving problems in the loan process. Direct loan programs are an experiment in an attempt to increase student benefits and simplify the aid application process. Overall simplification of processing and registration while improving the quality of the outcome is certainly in order. The success in these areas has yet to be measured.

TOP MANAGEMENT LEADERSHIP

Despite the genuine movement toward quality improvement that the 1992 reauthorization will bring about, the panel believes that there is much more in that direction to be accomplished. For example, a major detriment to sustaining the desired focus on quality is a lack of stability in leadership positions that influence student financial aid programs. Changing leadership may cause inconsistency in long-term vision. In recent years, the positions of assistant secretary for postsecondary education and deputy assistant secretary for student financial assistance, for example, were often filled by someone in an acting capacity or by a regular appointee of short tenure. During this time there was also a major reorganization of the Office of Postsecondary Education and a number of shifts in line management assignments. While, in themselves, these changes might not be bad, and some might be necessary, the panel sensed that the long-term vision for quality in financial aid programs often took a back seat to problems resulting from frequent turnover. That type of situation is not unique to student financial aid programs. It occurs in many government agencies. The assistant comptroller general for human resources programs of the General Accounting Office, in testimony before the Committee on Ways and Means, House of Representatives (Thompson, 1991a), urged Congress to help agencies overcome such problems in striving to improve service to the American people. The panel agrees with Thompson's recommendations that Congress

- encourage the development of management systems to help cushion the effects of leadership transitions.
- use oversight to promote constancy of purpose in agencies, with emphasis on long-term vision.
- encourage a customer-service focus.
- work with agencies to develop meaningful performance measures.

The panel found that while the Department of Education requires schools to invest heavily in *inspecting* the quality of their activities, the resources the department allocates for *improving* quality are very limited. Obtaining an accurate accounting of expenditures for these activities was not possible, but departmental personnel made it clear that such activities amount to much less than 1 percent of the operating budget of the Office of Postsecondary Education. Budgets for quality improvement activities in organizations known for quality leadership are often in the range of 2 to 5 percent of operating budgets. While 2 percent may be too much to allocate with new funds, a substantial increase is needed at least for a period of development. A successful effort should be expected to find enough cost-reducing efficiencies to fund continuing activities thereafter.

The panel has also pointed out inadequacies in the information technology available to the Department of Education in almost all the areas studied in this review. In addition, the department's own internal assessment (Winkler, 1991) indicates such problems and recommends that staff at all levels of the Office of Student Financial Aid be reinforced, particularly the numbers and kinds of staff necessary to handle the increased load to be placed on the office by new emphasis on analytic, quantitative, and managerial skills. This staff must meet the new demands to be placed on the organization for increased intensity in monitoring, data gathering and analysis, and financial management.

Recommendation 9-3: To signal top management's commitment to a Total Quality approach at the Department of Education, the department should initiate a Total Quality training program that starts with the leadership group and rapidly includes everyone in the department. In this way the fundamentals, vocabulary, and principles of Total Quality will be integrated into the department. Corporations have found this to be a critical first step in implementing quality improvement. Such a training effort should include leadership's role in the commitment to change, process-improvement and problem-solving methods, Total Quality tools, focus on customer satisfaction and its measurement, teamwork, and quality planning/deployment.

Recommendation 9-4: In its review of survey activities, verification procedures, and management information systems, the panel was disappointed to find a paucity of statistically trained personnel available to the student financial aid programs to analyze data and to interact with contractors. The Department of Education should develop a much greater in-house statistical capability to manage contracts that demand high levels of statistical expertise, and the data developed by contractors should be thoroughly documented and made available for in-house analysis. The department should also strengthen the analytic capabilities of its entire work force, including those who will not be expected to attain the level of statistical "expert" but yet should be skilled in handling and interpreting data. Specifically, the department should perform a needs analysis of statistical and computer literacy. Then it should develop training programs to improve abilities and purchase the hardware required to carry out the necessary analytic tasks.

The panel recognizes that technical improvement cannot begin without some initial funding targeted toward efforts such as pilot projects, data base improvement, and hiring staff with appropriate skills to help in these efforts. Thus, the panel requests that Congress take action to help make this possible.

Recommendation 9-5: Congress should ensure that there is adequate funding and staffing to develop the quantitative information needed to manage and review the student financial aid programs effectively.

The panel found an absence of performance measures linked to long-term planning. Setting long-term plans that transcend leadership changes is important. To make sound decisions on necessary changes to the programs, a new top management team must gain experience and familiarity with the system and its processes. A thorough understanding of a system as complex as the student financial aid programs takes time.

Recommendation 9-6: To ensure the development of and commitment to long-term planning, the politically appointed position in charge of the student financial aid programs (the assistant secretary for postsecondary education) should have a fixed (commonly five-year) term.

References and Bibliography

Advanced Technology, Inc.

1987 Title IV Quality Control Study. Stage Two, Management Option 1, Developing a performance monitoring system for the Institutional Quality Control Pilot Project: Assessment of potential incentives and disincentives. Submitted to the Division of Quality Assurance, Office of Postsecondary Education, U.S. Department of Education. Advanced Technology, Inc., Washington, D.C.

Advanced Technology, Inc. and Westat, Inc.

1987a Title IV Quality Control Study. Stage Two, Final Report, Executive Summary. Submitted to the Division of Quality Assurance, Debt Collection and Management Assistance Service, U.S. Department of Education. Advanced Technology, Inc. and Westat, Inc., Washington, D.C.

1987b Title IV Quality Control Study. Stage Two, Final Report, Vol. II, Corrective Actions. Submitted to the Division of Quality Assurance, Debt Collection and Management Assistance Service, U.S. Department of Education. Advanced Technology, Inc. and Westat, Inc., Washington, D.C.

Advisory Committee on Student Financial Assistance

1990 *Ensuring Access: Challenges in Student Aid in the 1990s* A report to the Congress of the United States. Washington, D.C.: Advisory Committee on Student Financial Assistance.

1991 *Priorities for the 1990s: Recommendations for Reauthorizing the Higher Education Act of 1965*. A Report to the Congress of the United States. Washington, D.C.: Advisory Committee on Student Financial Assistance.

Affholter, D. P. and F. D. Kramer, eds.

1987 *Rethinking Quality Control: A New System for the Food Stamp Program*. Committee on National Statistics, National Research Council. Washington, D.C.: National Academy Press.

American Council on Education

1991 *Higher Education and National Affairs* 40 (20).

American Institute of Certified Public Accountants

1992 *Compliance Auditing Applicable to Governmental Entities and Other Recipients of Governmental Financial Assistance.* Statement on Auditing Standards No. 68. New York: American Institute of Certified Public Accountants.

Anderson, U. and R. Young

1988a Internal audit planning in an interactive environment. *Auditing: A Journal of Practice & Theory* 8(Fall):23-42.

1988b Strategic auditing: A different game. *Internal Auditing* 4(Fall):14-24.

Brinkman, P.T. and L.L. Leslie

1988 *The Economic Value of Higher Education.* New York: American Council on Education and Macmillan Publishing.

Burke, V.

1991 *Cash and Noncash Benefits for Persons with Limited Income: Eligibility Rules, Recipient and Expenditure Data, FY 1988-90.* CRS Report for Congress No. 91-741 EPW. Education and Public Welfare Division, Congressional Research Service. Washington D.C.: U.S. Library of Congress.

Carr, D.B. and C. Sutton

1992 Selection Procedures for Verification of Pell Grant Applications. Unpublished paper. George Mason University, Fairfax, Va.

Chauvin, K., D. Iwamoto, and G. Galfond

1989 Quality Measurement for Postsecondary Education Financial Aid Programs. Paper presented at the Symposium on Quality Assurance in the Government, Washington Statistical Society, Washington, D.C.

Chelimsky, E.

1991 Student Aid Information and Private Tuition-Guarantee Programs. Statement before the Subcommittee on Postsecondary Education, Committee on Education and Labor, U.S. House of Representatives, Washington, D.C., May 15.

The College Board

1992 *Trends in Student Aid: 1982 to 1992, Update.* New York: College Entrance Examination Board.

College Scholarship Service Council

1992 *The Future of Student Aid Delivery.* New York: College Entrance Examination Board.

Congressional Budget Office

1991 *Student Aid and the Cost of Postsecondary Education.* Washington, D.C.: Congressional Budget Office.

DeMaio, T., ed.

1983 *Approaches to Developing Questionnaires.* Statistical Policy Paper 10. Prepared by Subcommittee on Questionnaire Design, Federal Committee on Statistical Methodology. Available through NTIS Document Sales, PB-84-105005. Washington, D.C.: U.S. Office of Management and Budget.

Deming, W.E.

1986 *Out of the Crisis.* Cambridge, Mass.: Center for Advanced Engineering Study.

Edelman, M.W.

1987 *Families in Peril: An Agenda for Social Change.* Cambridge, Mass.: Harvard University Press.

Fitzgerald, B.K.

1990 Equity and Efficiency: An Analysis of Simplifying the Pell Grant Eligibility Formula. Unpublished EdD dissertation. Graduate School of Education, Harvard University, Cambridge, Mass.

Frasier, F.
1990 The Stafford Student Loan Program. Statement before the Subcommittee on Permanent Investigations, Committee on Governmental Affairs, U.S. Senate, February 20.

General Accounting Office
1985 Pell Grant Validation Imposes Some Costs and Does Not Greatly Reduce Award Errors: New Strategies Are Needed. Report to the Honorable Paul Simon, former chairman of the Subcommittee on Postsecondary Education, Committee on Education and Labor, U.S. House of Representatives, Washington, D.C.
1990a Higher Education: Gaps in Parents' and Students' Knowledge of School Costs and Federal Aid. Report to the Chairman, Permanent Subcommittee on Investigations, Committee on Governmental Affairs, U.S. Senate, Washington, D.C.
1990b Stafford Student Loans: Millions of Dollars on Loans Awarded to Ineligible Borrowers. Report to the Chairman, Permanent Subcommittee on Investigations, Committee on Governmental Affairs, U.S. Senate, Washington, D.C.
1991 Student Financial Aid: Education Can Do More to Screen Schools Before Students Receive Aid. Report to the Chairman, Subcommittee on Postsecondary Education, Committee on Education and Labor, U.S. House of Representatives, Washington, D.C.

Gladieux, L. and T.R. Wolanin
1976 *Congress and the Colleges: The National Politics of Higher Education.* Lexington, Mass.: D.C. Heath.

Goodwin, D.
1991 Beyond Defaults: Indicators for Assessing Proprietary School Quality. U.S. Department of Education, Office of the Under Secretary, Washington, D.C.

Hiniker, J.P.
1987 The Selection of Returns for Audit by the IRS. In Proceedings of the Symposium on Survey Research Methods, American Statistical Association, Alexandria, Va.

Kennickell, A. and J. Shack-Marquez
1992 Changes in family finances from 1983 to 1989: Evidence from the Survey of Consumer Finances. *Federal Reserve Bulletin* 78(1):1-18.

Kirsch, A.
1984 A Critical Review of Research Report: *Quality in the Pell Grant Delivery System.* George Washington University, Washington, D.C.

Kramer, F. D., ed.
1988 *From Quality Control to Quality Improvement in AFDC and Medicaid.* Panel on Quality Control of Family Assistance Programs, Committee on National Statistics, National Research Council. Washington, D.C.: National Academy Press.

McPherson, M.S. and M.O. Schapiro
1991 *Keeping College Affordable.* Washington, D. C.: The Brookings Institution.

Muller, M.
1984 Report on Review of Research on Errors in the Pell Grant Program. Unpublished paper. World Bank, Washington, D.C.

National Association of Student Financial Aid Administrators
1990 FACTS - Financial Aid Concepts for Training Staff. National Association of Student Financial Aid Administrators, Washington, D.C.

National Center on Education and the Economy
1990 *America's Choice: High Skills or Low Wages!* The Report of The Commission on the Skills of the American Workforce. Rochester, New York: National Center on Education and the Economy.

National Computer Systems

1988-89 1988-89 End of Year Management Information Reports. Vol. 1. Submitted to the U.S. Department of Education, Federal Student Aid Processing System. Pell Grant Application Processing System Contract No. 300-87-0012. Information Technology, National Computer Systems, Iowa City, Iowa.

1989-90 1989-90 End of Year Management Information Reports. Vol. 1. Submitted to the U.S. Department of Education, Federal Student Aid Processing System. Pell Grant Application Processing System Contract No. 300-87-0012. Information Technology, National Computer Systems, Iowa City, Iowa.

1990-91a 1990-91 End of Year Management Information Reports. Vol. I. Submitted to the U.S. Department of Education, Federal Student Aid Processing System. Central Processing System Contract No. PM89002001. Information Technology, National Computer Systems, Iowa City, Iowa.

1990-91b 1990-91 End of Year Management Information Reports. Vol. II. Submitted to the U.S. Department of Education, Federal Student Aid Processing System. Central Processing System Contract No. PM89002001. Information Technology, National Computer Systems, Iowa City, Iowa.

National Computer Systems and Macro Systems, Inc.

1992a Central Processing System - Phase II Product CP/2/1. Management Information System (MIS) Plan (Phase I Product CP/1/7) - 1991-92 Cycle. Vol. I. Contract No. PM89002001. Presented to the U.S. Department of Education, Office of Student Financial Assistance. National Computer Systems, Iowa City, Iowa.

1992b Central Processing System - Phase II Product CP/2/1. Management Information System (MIS) Plan (Phase I Product CP/1/7) - 1991-92 Cycle. Vol. II. Contract No. PM89002001. Submitted to the U.S. Department of Education, Office of Student Financial Assistance. National Computer Systems, Iowa City, Iowa.

Pelavin Associates, Inc.

1989 Institutional Quality Control Pilot Project, 1987-1988 Project Year Evaluation Report. Contract No. 300-87-0110. Prepared for the U.S. Department of Education. Pelavin Associates, Inc., Washington, D.C.

1991a Institutional Quality Control Project, Flash Report: Comparative Analysis of the Institutional Data for 1987-88 to 1989-90. Contract No. PC90002001. Prepared for the U.S. Department of Education. Pelavin Associates, Inc., Washington, D.C.

1991b Institutional Quality Control Project, Institutional Data Analysis Report, 1989-90. Contract No. PC90002001. Prepared for the U.S. Department of Education. Pelavin Associates, Inc., Washington, D.C.

1992 Institutional Quality Control Project, Flash Report: Trend Analysis of the Institutional Data for 1988-89 to 1990-91. Contract No. PC90002001. Prepared for the U.S. Department of Education. Pelavin Associates, Inc., Washington, D.C.

Price Waterhouse

1989 Sampling Plan for the Integrated Quality Control Measurement Project. Prepared in association with Pelavin Associates, Inc. and The Gallup Organization. Submitted to the U.S. Department of Education, March 20, 1989. Price Waterhouse, Washington, D.C.

1990a Integrated Quality Control Measurement Project, IQC Pilot Analysis. Prepared in association with Pelavin Associates, Inc. and The Gallup Organization. Submitted to the U.S. Department of Education, August 21, 1990. Price Waterhouse, Washington, D.C.

1990b Integrated Quality Control Measurement Project, Findings and Corrective Actions. Prepared in association with Pelavin Associates, Inc. and The Gallup Organization. Submitted to the U.S. Department of Education, September 28, 1990. Price Waterhouse, Washington, D.C.

1991 Regulatory Burden and Institutional Compliance in Federal Postsecondary Student Financial Aid Programs. Final Report. Prepared for U.S. Department of Education. Price Waterhouse, Washington, D.C.

Rehab Group, Inc. and Macro Systems, Inc.

1981 *Field Testing of 1982-1983 BEOG Application Forms, Final Report.* Submitted to the U.S. Department of Education, Office of Student Financial Assistance. Contract No. 300-81-0014. Falls Church, Va.: Rehab Group, Inc.

Ryan, D.

1988 Why you can't do it all. *Student Aid Transcript* Summer:16-18. California State University.

Schenet, M.A.

1990 *Proprietary Schools: The Regulatory Structure.* CRS Report for Congress. Washington, D.C.: Library of Congress.

Shewhart, W.A.

1980 *Economic Control of Quality of Manufactured Products.* Milwaukee, Wisc.: American Society for Quality Control.

Siers, H. and J. Blyskal

1987 Risk management of the internal audit function. *Management Accounting* 68(February):29-35.

Thompson, L.H.

1991a Service to the Public: How Effective and Responsive Is the Government? Statement before the Committee on Ways and Means, U.S. House of Representatives, Washington, D.C., May 8.

1991b Vulnerabilities in the Stafford Student Loan Program. Statement before the Subcommittee on Postsecondary Education, Committee on Education and Labor, U.S. House of Representatives, Washington, D.C., May 29.

U.S. Congress, House

1992 *Report of the House of Representatives Committee on Education and Labor on the Higher Education Amendments of 1992.* House document 102-447. 102nd Congress, 2nd session. Washington, D.C.: U.S. Government Printing Office.

U.S. Department of Education

1990a *Audit Guide: Audits of Student Financial Assistance Programs.* Office of Inspector General, Office of Audit. Washington, D.C.: U.S. Department of Education.

1990b *FY 1990 Guaranteed Student Loan Programs Data Book.* Office of Postsecondary Education, Office of Student Financial Aid Programs. Washington, D.C.: U.S. Department of Education.

1991a *Institutional Quality Control Workbook.* Office of Postsecondary Education, Division of Quality Assurance. Washington, D.C.: U.S. Department of Education.

1991b *Program Review Guide.* Institutional Review Branch, Division of Audit and Program Review. Washington, D.C.: U.S. Department of Education.

1992 *The Office of Student Financial Assistance Did Not Assure That All Institutions Submitted Audit Reports or That It Recovered All Misspent Funds.* Office of Inspector General, Audit Control Number 11-00010. Washington, D.C.: U.S. Department of Education.

1992-93 *The Student Guide: Financial Aid from the U.S. Department of Education, 1992-93.* Washington, D.C.: U.S. Department of Education.

Winkler, N.

1991 Improving Guaranteed Student Loan Management: A Blueprint for Action. Paper presented at a meeting of the Panel on Quality Improvement in Student Financial Aid Programs, Washington, D.C.

APPENDIXES

APPENDIX

A

A Review of the Methodology Used in the Integrated Quality Control Measurement Project

Mark Reiser
Arizona State University

This paper is a review of the methodology used in the Integrated Quality Control Measurement Project (IQCMP), a project conducted to evaluate the quality of financial awards made in the 1988-89 award year under three Title IV financial aid programs: the Pell Grant Program, Campus-Based Programs, and the Stafford Loan Program (see Price Waterhouse, 1990). In addition to comments on the methodology that was used in the IQCMP, possible alternative methodologies are suggested.

ERROR

The IQCMP used the following definition of *error*: "Error is the difference between the award actually distributed and the award that would be calculated based on the best available data." Data that were considered to be the best available were obtained from the source of highest reliability (e.g., income tax returns and interviewers). One source was defined to be the most reliable, and it was then used as though it contained no error. When one source of information is treated as though it contains no error, it is sometimes referred to as the *gold standard*. The difference in awards as defined above had to exceed $50.00 before it was considered to be an error.

In the IQCMP, the student and the academic institution were examined as sources of error in each of the Title IV programs studied. Overall and composite error were also examined. *Overall error* was error resulting from either student or institutional error. Student error and institutional error do not necessarily add to overall error, however, because they do not necessarily have an additive effect.

Composite error is error in the financial award from all programs combined. For this type of error, two main types of analysis were performed. First, the magnitude and percentage of errors were examined. Then, in error-profile analyses, the presence or absence of error was modeled using several independent variables simultaneously.

As noted above, error calculations were performed using one or another source of information as an error-free gold standard. Since these sources used as standards almost certainly contain error themselves, the calculation of errors itself contains error. This feature constitutes a source of nonsampling error in the IQCMP. When no single source of information can be completely free of error, adopting a statistical model for measurement error is a better approach, because the *true value* is considered to be a latent (unobservable) variable and the different sources of measurement, called *indicator* or *manifest* variables, are all acknowledged as being subject to error. In many areas of social science, the *reliability* (or reliability ratio) is used as an indicator of the degree to which a variable is free from measurement error. In a technical definition, the reliability is expressed as the ratio of true variance to total variance, where total variance is equal to true variance plus measurement-error variance. Since no single source of information for determining financial aid eligibility is absolutely error free, it would have been very useful if the IQCMP had analyzed and reported the reliability of the different data sources. If more than one indicator is available, the reliabilities may be calculated in a straightforward way. The true value can also be estimated from a measurement-error model for multiple indicators. In future studies of quality control in student financial aid programs, the estimated true value for variables, such as wealth, could be calculated and used to determine the error in the amount of the financial award.

Generally, variables with low reliability are not very useful for calculating eligibility for financial awards. In the past, it appears that variables with large measurement error (low reliability) were either dropped from use on the student financial aid application or were the focus of regulations intended to decrease error during data collection. To the extent that error can be reduced with reasonable efforts, it is a good strategy to try to do so. But for some variables, such as wealth, it is very difficult to measure the true value directly, and an alternative to dropping such variables would be to estimate the latent true value from multiple sources of information, each of which may not be very reliable by itself.

Measurement-error methodology should be investigated in any future studies of quality control in student financial aid programs. It is an approach that is more efficient and justifiable than declaring one of the indicators to be the gold standard.

SAMPLING

The IQCMP was based on a sample of 3,310 students from 350 postsecondary institutions. Because data were not available for some students, 2,653 students were in the final data base. Details of the sampling procedure are not given in the IQCMP report, but they are provided in a separate sampling plan document (Price Waterhouse, 1989). A two-stage cluster sample was used in which postsecondary institutions were sampled in clusters of size 1, 2, 3, or 4. Because observations within each cluster are correlated to an unknown extent, methods of analysis that assume simple random samples are not appropriate. For proper analysis, each element of the sample must be assigned a weight based on the probability of selection for that element. In the sampling plan, expressions for the probability of selection are given on pages IV-8 and IV-9. The expressions appear to be incorrect, however, because they give the probability of selection as a sum of sampling rates across programs. The probability of selection calculated from this expression could be greater than 1.0, although the sampling rates actually used in the study are probably not high enough for that to happen. The correct expression for the probability of selection for an element, given the sampling plan, should be

1.0 – (probability not selected for Pell sample) ×
(probability not selected for Campus-Based sample) ×
(probability not selected for Stafford sample).

The probability calculated from this expression applies to the selection for the sample of all financial aid recipients. It is not the probability of selection for an element in any combined sample (i.e., a direct sample plus elements obtained as a by-product of sampling other programs). Moreover, it is not clear how the probability of selection for an element in a combined sample should be calculated, because it would require knowing the probability that a recipient is in one program given that he or she is in another program.

If probabilities of selection were calculated by the expressions given on pages IV-8 and IV-9 of the sampling plan, the weights used for calculating errors would have been incorrect, and estimates of error would be biased. It is not possible to say how large the bias would be: It could be trivial or it could be substantial.

In addition to sampling clusters of schools, the efficiency of the sampling design could have been increased through stratification by a number of variables, such as financial dependence versus independence. Since stratification was not used, post-stratification could be used to increase the precision of some estimates.

As stated in the IQCMP report (p. I-2), the sample of students was designed to be large enough to permit statistical inferences about the percentage of awards in error for each Title IV program with ± 5 percent accuracy at a 90 percent confidence level. This statement was apparently made with complex sampling in mind, since a simple random sample of 2,653 would allow statistical inference with ± 1.6 percent accuracy at a 90 percent confidence level. However, as discussed next, standard errors are not used consistently in the IQCMP report.

The exhibits in Section II ("Error in the Title IV Financial Aid Programs") of the IQCMP report present standard errors for many estimates. The basis for the standard errors is not clear, however. The standard errors given in the Section II exhibits have magnitudes (0.4 to 2.5) that appear to be based on an assumption of a simple random sample rather than the complex sample that was actually used. Although discussion in the sampling plan indicates that some standard errors were calculated by a bootstrap method, some may have been calculated by assuming a stratified random sample and ignoring clustering. It is not clear why standard errors would be calculated that way if bootstrap methods were available. Moreover, estimators for standard errors under two-stage cluster sampling are known (Cochran, 1977), and computer programs are widely available to perform the calculations (e.g., Super Carp). The description of the bootstrap method proposed in the sampling plan is very brief, and it is not clear how the bootstrap was implemented, particularly with regard to the selection of primary sampling units.

Only Section II of the IQCMP report gives standard errors. Other sections of the report give a large number of statistics, but standard errors are not given.

A footnote to Exhibit II-1 states that the percentage of recipients with error is based on 6.0 million students awarded Title IV aid during the 1988-89 award year. Similar footnotes can be found in other Section II exhibits. The purpose of the footnotes appears to be to emphasize that the errors were examined only among the recipients of Title IV financial aid, and not among students who applied for but were denied financial aid. Nevertheless, the footnotes are confusing and should be reworded, because they can be interpreted to mean that the percentages are based on the entire population of 6 million recipients rather than a sample.

Many sections of the IQCMP report compare percentages across variables and across domains. Financially dependent versus independent students and proprietary versus nonproprietary schools are frequently mentioned domains. The statement in Section II regarding ± 5 percent accuracy has very limited applicability for comparisons across variables or domains, and generally the appropriate interval would be larger than ± 5 percent. For comparisons across domains, one would probably be willing to assume independent samples for the different domains, although that would not necessarily be true, since both financially dependent and independent students would be selected from each school, and the clustering effect would induce a correlation among the students from the same school. However, assuming samples are independent across domains and that the domains split the sample into roughly equal-sized groups, the variance for the difference between two percentages would be roughly double the variance for a single percentage based on the whole sample. Therefore, confidence intervals would be about 40 percent larger and a difference between two domains is probably not significant unless it is at least as large as 7 percentage points. Interpretations of differences that are less than 7 percentage points are unwarranted, and the IQCMP report contains many such instances.

When percentages are compared across variables, the standard error for the difference may also be larger than the standard error for a single percentage based on the whole sample. However, since the statistics on each variable are calculated from the same observations, the variables have a nonzero covariance, and the standard error for the difference requires the inclusion of that covariance. There is not enough information in the IQCMP report to obtain the covariances between the variables, and so it is not possible to say, based on the report, how large the standard error for differences across variables might be. A statement such as the following from page II-1, "absolute student error was higher than absolute institutional error (6.6 percent of dollars and 5.1 percent of dollars, respectively)," is probably not warranted because the difference is probably not significant. Similar statements appear on pages II-6 and II-15.

MARGINAL ANALYSIS

The marginal analysis was conducted by comparing an award as actually distributed with the award calculated by substituting the value from the most reliable source for the variable under study. As discussed above, reliability ratios would be a very useful statistic for comparing variables and sources of information. Also, it would be much more preferable to use an estimated true value based on a measurement-error model than to declare one source of information to be the most reliable. The marginal analysis found that the variables for students' (and spouses') cash, savings, and checking, as well as various measures of income, household size, and number in college, were sources of a large amount of error.

ERROR PROFILE ANALYSIS

In addition to the marginal analyses discussed above, an error-profile analysis was conducted to examine the joint effects of predictor variables, such as income, assets, and year in college. Since the dependent variable in this analysis was presence or absence of error (either student error or institutional error), a preliminary analysis was performed using chi-square tests of association in contingency tables. All continuous variables were categorized for this analysis. Note that an analysis performed with contingency tables is still a marginal approach. The joint analysis was performed essentially by multiple regression, but an unusual series of steps were taken for the joint approach.

The preliminary analysis using chi-square tests is very close in purpose to the marginal analyses described in an earlier section of the IQCMP report, except now the dependent variable is the presence or absence of an error rather than the magnitude of the error. Hence, one would expect to find essentially the same results here as in the marginal analyses. It is not clear from the IQCMP report why continuous variables were categorized. With a categorical dependent variable and continuous independent variables, a logistic regression, which does not require the independent variables to be categorical, can be used for the same purpose as the contingency tables described above. Since the logistic regression does not throw away information by categorizing the variables, it would have been a more efficient approach for the continuous variables than the contingency table approach that was used. The loss of information due to categorizing the variables would generally be no more than 5 percent, so it should not be expected that there would be extensive differences if logistic regression had been used instead. (Logistic regression can be performed with PROC LOGISTIC in SAS.)

Since the categorization of continuous variables was based on percentile ranking, one possible benefit of the procedure would be to reduce skewness in the independent variables. If skewness was present (it is not possible to tell if it is from the IQCMP report) it could be reduced to an acceptable level by a more straightforward transformation. With variables such as income, the use of the log transformation effectively reduces skewness. Although loss of information due to categorizing continuous variables is probably not large, future studies of quality control in student financial aid programs should use logistic regression when appropriate.

It is also not clear from the IQCMP report whether the statistical methods used for the contingency table analyses were appropriate for a complex sample involving clustering. Standard computer packages (e.g., SAS and SPSS) operate on the assumption of a simple random sample; packages that are based on methods for cluster samples are widely available (e.g., Super Carp). The erroneous use of simple random sample methods will tend to produce p values that are too small; hence, some variables that are not related to error in financial awards will appear to be related. Logistic regression methods for cluster samples are also available (e.g., PC Carp) and would be the more appropriate tool.

Results from the contingency table analyses showed that various measures of income, various measures of assets, household size, and marital status were all strongly associated with student error. Among other variables, institution type and the method used by an institution to recheck data and calculations were strongly associated with institutional error.

To assess the effects of independent variables jointly on error, the IQCMP used a multiple regression approach. The multiple regression was based on some unusual methodology, few details of which are given in the IQCMP report. From the description, it appears that the dependent variable in these regressions was the presence or absence of error, that is, still a discrete variable. If the dependent variable is discrete, logistic regression, not ordinary multiple regression, should be used. The IQCMP report should clarify the method of estimation used here.

In preparation for the multiple regressions, continuous independent variables were created by a transformation of dubious merit. The transformation consisted of assigning a value to the categorical variables based on the proportion of students with error for the relevant category from the contingency table analysis. It is not clear why this transformation was used, since the transformation does not make the variables continuous. It changes the distance between the categories, but it does not produce a continuous variable. Moreover, it is not clear why continuous variables were thought to be necessary. For a discrete dependent variable and for discrete independent variables, a logit analysis can be performed to accomplish the same purpose that a multiple regression accomplishes for continuous variables. (PROC CATMOD in SAS can be used to perform a logit analysis.)

It is also not clear whether the method of assigning a value to categorical variables based on the proportion of students with error for the relevant category from the contingency table analysis was used on only the variables that were originally categorical or also on the variables that were originally continuous. For variables that were originally continuous, it would be pointless to categorize them by percentile rankings (as done for the contingency table analysis) and then transform them back to continuous variables by using the contingency table proportions for the multiple regression analysis. For the multiple regressions, the variables that were originally continuous should be used in that form, and not categorized first. The continuous variables could be log-transformed to stabilize the variance, and/or normalized, but transforming them from continuous to categorical and then back to continuous would be difficult to justify.

The effects of cluster sampling should also be recognized in the regression analyses used for the error-profile analyses. Ordinary least squares (OLS) regression is based on the assumption that observations are independent. Since cluster sampling was used for the IQCMP, observations within schools are correlated, and OLS should not be used to estimate parameters. In this situation, a nested-error regression model could be used to estimate model parameters by generalized least squares. The nested-error model has been well developed, and the effect of using it instead of an OLS model would be to widen confidence intervals around estimated values. That is, a variable is less likely to appear to be significantly related to error, because recognizing the correlation among observations within a school has the effect of reducing the sample size. (The nested-error regression model has been used with cluster sample data by Battese et al., 1988.) Estimation for the nested-error regression model can be carried out with the Super Carp computer program. Linear regression using weights to reflect the complex sampling could also be used, but there are advantages to the variance components approach used in the nested-error model.

Another useful approach to the joint analyses would have been to estimate a covariance matrix for the (marginal) errors calculated in dollars. This covariance matrix could have been used with exploratory multivariate techniques, such as a principal component analysis and a canonical correlation analysis. The latter analysis would have been particularly useful for finding clusters of independent variables that relate to key dependent variables. (The Super Carp computer package can be used to calculate the covariance matrix based on a two-stage cluster sample.)

The results of the error-profile analyses based on multiple regressions showed that errors in reported income accounted for a large portion of the student-based errors in financial aid awards. Whether or not a tax form was filed, use of estimated income, and indicator variables for type of award sought were also significant variables. Institutional variables strongly associated with error included type of institution control, institution type, method used to recheck files, and indicators for type of award.

SUMMARY

Some of the statistical methods used for the IQCMP were inefficient, especially in the joint analyses for deriving error profiles. Some alternative methodologies, such as including the reliability of variables and using estimated true values, are recommended strongly for any future studies of quality control in student financial aid programs.

Despite the inefficiencies of some of the methods, there is a consistency to the findings given in the IQCMP report. The marginal analyses, the contingency table analyses, and the joint error-profile analyses all found that reported income was an important source of error in the awards made under the Title IV programs. Reported household size was also found to be a source of error in many analyses.

The IQCMP report also addresses simplification of the financial aid formula and potential corrective actions. It is natural to consider whether the simplifications and corrective actions reflect the findings from the statistical analysis of errors. Several of the suggested corrective actions do reflect findings from the statistical analysis. In particular, the suggestion that awards not be based on tax information estimated by the applicant and the suggestions to require specific information on household size, number in college, and home value and debt are actions that address some of the consistently found sources of error. However, error in reported income, the variable most strongly associated with error over the different analyses, may not be reduced significantly by these suggested corrective actions. Perhaps other corrective actions should be considered for reported income.

REFERENCES

Battese, G. E., R. M. Harter, W. A. Fuller

1988 An error components model for prediction of county crop areas using survey and satellite data. *Journal of the American Statistical Association* 83(401):28-36.

Cochran, W. G.

1977 *Sampling Techniques*. New York: John Wiley & Sons.

Price Waterhouse

1989 Sampling Plan for the Integrated Quality Control Measurement Project. Prepared in association with Pelavin Associates, Inc. and The Gallup Organization. Washington, D.C.: Price Waterhouse.

1990 Integrated Quality Control Measurement Project, Findings and Corrective Actions. Prepared in association with Pelavin Associates, Inc. and The Gallup Organization. Washington, D.C.: Price Waterhouse.

APPENDIX

B

The Taxpayer as Customer

Mary Batcher, Statistics of Income Division
Paulette Sewell, Taxpayer Service Division
Internal Revenue Service

Many federal agencies have turned to total quality management as a means to improve the quality of their products and services and to make better use of their resources. The identification of customers and development of service standards for customer interactions are key components of total quality management. Unfortunately, the notion of having accountability to customers is somewhat novel in government. Funding is appropriated for agency activities as part of the overall governmental budget process, and there is little direct link to the customers each agency serves. Hence, with rare exceptions, there has historically been very little market pressure to build a customer focus into governmental operations. However, as agencies come under tighter fiscal constraints and closer scrutiny by Congress and the media, there is increasing interest in the quality movement (with its potential productivity gains) and, as a corollary, increased attention to the identification of customers and their needs.

The question of how to develop a sense of the taxpayer as customer should be preceded by some assessment of who the customers are. Although in some sense taxpayers are the customers of all federal agencies, in reality the number of agencies that provide a direct service to taxpayers is probably limited. Some exploration of who the primary and secondary customers are would certainly be beneficial. The needs of the primary customers must be met, and taxpayers may enter the loop only indirectly through one of the primary customers, such as Congress. While the public is always there as a consideration, in some cases a primary focus on taxpayers may not improve service at all.

For those cases in which the taxpayer is a direct customer, the experience of the Taxpayer Service Division of the Internal Revenue Service (IRS) may be of interest. Within the IRS, the Taxpayer Service Division was created with the sole purpose of providing customer service to the taxpayer. It is the unit of the IRS that is responsible for answering taxpayers' questions about filing their income tax returns and their account and payment status, providing assistance in filling out tax returns, distributing tax forms, operating outreach programs to the taxpayer, and so on. For most taxpayers, Taxpayer Service is the point of first contact with the IRS.

The organization of taxpayer services into a separate division contributes to building a sense of the taxpayer as customer into the culture. The message that customer service merits its own separate structure is not lost on employees of the Taxpayer Service Division. This message is first imparted during the personnel selection process, and it is reinforced through training, the performance review system, and the reward and recognition system.

Employees who will have contact with customers are selected with customer interaction skills in mind. Not everyone is able to perform well in a customer-service role and selection factors reflect that. The training that customer assistance staff receive includes a heavy emphasis on the importance of the taxpayer as the customer and customer-contact standards and skills, in addition to basic training in tax law, as needed. Customer-contact standards are considered a critical element in effective job performance, and employees are monitored against the standards by managers as part of performance assessments and by quality reviewers to identify areas where additional training or job aids may be needed. If training and managerial intervention fail, employees who cannot provide courteous and effective service are removed from customer-contact positions. By contrast, employees who provide exceptional customer service are recognized in a variety of ways, ranging from cash awards to small items of recognition, like certificates for correctly responding to a test question.

The above are areas of strength for the Taxpayer Service Division that might well be emulated in other environments. Additional steps can be taken, as well, to strengthen the sense of customer focus and the quality of customer service. They include the following:

- Develop a market segmentation approach whereby the various customers, internal and external, are identified, their needs are assessed, and strategies for addressing those needs are developed.
- Create a career path for customer contact staff. In most governmental applications, customer-contact personnel are relatively low graded and must move into other areas to advance.
- Involve customer-contact personnel in the development and communication of standards for customer contacts. These standards should be

continuously revised as the quality of service increases. Customer-contact staff should play a role in the revision of standards and should be as aware of the importance of the standards to the agency as are the top executives.

All of the above are factors that contribute to the development of a culture that values the taxpayer as a customer.

The related question we were asked to address in this paper is: How can an awareness of the taxpayer as customer be managed statistically? Before anything can be managed statistically, it must be managed operationally. This means that customer-contact standards must be developed and communicated to the employees, and managers must do their job of observing behaviors and coaching.

Given effective operational management practices, statistical management becomes a matter of measuring the system's performance. However, there are measurements that are designed to provide feedback at the work-unit level and measurements for the broader resource allocation and policy levels. At the work-unit level, measurement should be frequent, timely, specific, and detailed, and perhaps, it should only address key areas. Estimation procedures should be simple enough that staff in the work unit or local support staff can perform the calculations. There should be enough flexibility in the measurement system to allow the emphasis to change quickly based on operational needs or information from other indicators.

To be most useful at the policy level, measurement should be frequent enough to assess trends and should sample across the universe, rather than addressing only key areas. Measurement at this level requires more stringent confidence and precision in the estimates. There is also greater tolerance for statistical elegance in the estimation procedures.

The test-call program for measuring the accuracy of the IRS telephone assistance service is an example of a measurement system designed to meet upper management's need for data to inform resource allocation and large-scale system management. Data are generated weekly at a level of detail adequate to provide overall accuracy rates by call site and by area of tax law nationally. Results are available to IRS executives by Wednesday morning for the immediately preceding week. This allows monitoring of overall accuracy and an assessment of call-site accuracy trends, but it does not provide the kind of detailed information that is useful in local management practices and decisions or that can be used to address a downward trend. That kind of detail is provided by local test-call and call-monitoring programs. Local call-site managers are held accountable for achieving a specified accuracy rate. They, therefore, support these local measurement efforts and use the results to guide improvement efforts. The merit of improvement efforts is determined by the national accuracy rates. Taken together, this combination of measurements, one at the national level and the other locally controlled, has proven to be an effective statistical management tool for the telephone assistance service.

APPENDIX

C

Applying for Federal Student Financial Aid for 1992–93

Margaret Weidenhamer
Consultant

Students who wish to receive federal student financial aid must complete either the Application for Federal Student Aid (AFSA) produced by the U.S. Department of Education or one of the forms developed for states or geographic regions by multiple data entry (MDE) processors. For the 1992-93 school year, applications supplied by MDEs were required to incorporate verbatim all the instructions and data items from the federal version; they were permitted to append additional items needed to administer financial aid programs, including nonfederal programs, at the schools they served.

For 1992-93, the AFSA was the appropriate form for the following federal programs:

- Pell Grants
- Stafford Loans
- Supplemental Educational Opportunity Grants
- College Work-Study
- Perkins Loans

THE 1992-93 AFSA: PAPER VERSION

The paper version of the AFSA for the 1992-93 school year became available to applicants late in 1991. English and Spanish versions were printed. An electronic version, in English, was available at some school locations. The electronic version, known as Stage Zero, is discussed later in this paper.

The English AFSA for 1992-93 consists of a 4-page form and preaddressed mailing envelope stapled in the middle of a 12-page booklet. The AFSA booklet, as distinguished from the application form itself, consists mainly of instructions, definitions, and work sheets needed to fill out the application form. A limited amount of information on the five programs is provided, some on the first page and a little on pages 10 and 11. The following information appears on page 11:

> This booklet gives you only a brief summary of the student financial aid programs offered by the U.S. Department of Education. Each student financial aid program has its own special features and procedures. You can get more information from the booklet: The Student Guide: Financial Aid from the U.S. Department of Education Grants, Loans, and Work-Study 1992-93. To get a free copy, write to....

The 1992-93 *Student Guide* (U.S. Department of Education, 1992-93) is a 60-page booklet that describes the five programs listed above, as well as Supplemental Loans for Students and Parental Loans for Undergraduate Students. It discusses key topics, such as eligibility requirements and borrower responsibilities and rights, and provides Federal Student Aid Information Center telephone numbers. The telephone numbers are not given or referred to on the AFSA, however, where the need is probably much greater. On the other hand, the student guide does not provide definitions of *dislocated worker* and *displaced homemaker*, special circumstances that it states can trigger some flexibility in eligibility requirements. Instead, it directs readers to the financial aid application for those definitions. The student guide also gives advice on finding out about nonfederal sources of student aid.

A cursory reading of the 1992-93 AFSA when it first became available revealed some quirks one would not expect in such a document. For example, the first question on the form asks for last name, first name, and M.I.; those who don't know what M.I. stands for find no explanation anywhere in the booklet. And the Jacquelines, Christophers, Marguerites, and other applicants whose first name contains 10 or more letters also have a decision to make on their own, because they are not told how to squeeze their name into the 9 spaces allotted on the form.

Only one copy of the form is included in the AFSA booklet. There is no working copy for the applicant to use as a draft and keep as a record for reference if verification or correction of any of the information is required. Yet, the instructions state "Use a pen with black or dark ink; don't use a pencil." A black-and-white photocopy of the form does not adequately reflect the color coding that is used. Many applicants apparently get an extra copy of the complete application to get another copy of the form, wasting 12 pages to get 4.

The application form itself gives the overall impression that a decision was made to stay within a four-page limit without sufficient regard for other form design considerations (e.g., accuracy of item wording and clarity of directions). Perhaps because of a determination to save space, the form also uses a potpourri of formats. For example, the first two items in Section A cover the full width of the page—the answer spaces are next to the questions asked. Items 3 through 10 are in triple columns and the answer spaces are below the questions. Section B starts with items 11a-d, which span half the page; the answer boxes are to the right, and directions about what to do next are on the far right. Item 12 follows that style, but for item 13, the response categories are below the item, and each response is followed horizontally by two more questions and the answer boxes.

The directions at the bottom of the first page state that everyone is to answer the items in the white areas of the form. Students whose answers to the preceding items indicate they are "dependent" also answer items in the areas shaded red; those considered "independent" also answer items in the areas shaded gray. The mixture of formats, complicated by the addition of the white, red, and gray areas, continues for the remaining three pages. Further, item numbers are duplicated when identical, or nearly identical, questions are asked of parents and students. These design variations might present challenges for data entry personnel as well as applicants.

Panel members were concerned that the current design of the AFSA could cause inadvertent response errors that would complicate the processes of advising applicants, checking the accuracy of responses, and correcting erroneous data. They were also concerned because inadvertent response error, if undetected, can result in award error. The panel therefore requested help from selected federal agencies and other organizations thought to have experience in collecting and processing data similar to the information required for the 1992-93 AFSA. Reasons for including specific data items on the form were not mentioned in the letter.

The panel's request was mailed in mid-March of 1992. It stated in part:

> The panel is especially interested in expert advice concerning the complexity of the form and instructions especially for typical applicants (lower income, high school graduates and their parents). The panel would also like information on response errors measured for similar data. Comments or suggestions based on your organization's experience with the collection and study of similar data would be helpful to determine whether errors made by applicants or data processors might be reduced through revisions in wording, sequence, instructions, format, or other aspects of the application and related tasks. References to or copies of reports from relevant qualitative studies or statistical research that your organization has conducted would be appreciated.

None of the replies cited statistical research conducted by the organizations. One reviewer did mention that in "SIPP" (the Survey of Income and Program Participation conducted by the Census Bureau) substantial response error was measured on some similar income/asset items. However, that reviewer mentioned the possibility that, in the AFSA, the warning about penalties for supplying false or misleading information may improve the accuracy of responses. Some reviewers indicated they had not had any recent experience collecting similar data items, and a few declined to comment for that reason.[1]

Panel staff and consultants also commented on the AFSA based on their experience and an examination of material provided by the Department of Education, such as Office of Management and Budget (OMB) clearance documents for the 1992-93 AFSA and comments submitted by MDEs in reports to the Department of Education for the two previous years.

The opinions of reviewers from 13 organizations are reflected in this discussion. The excerpts listed below indicate the range of responses. The comments merit thoughtful consideration by those with responsibility for the AFSA.

Reviewers were generally critical of the AFSA:

- "The aid application forms and process are much more complex and onerous on applicants than they need be, more onerous than a 1040 tax form. Ironically, most of the students seeking aid come from low-income families which either file no tax return or file a 1040EZ. The student aid application form is probably the most complicated financial form they have ever seen."
- "We agree that this form and accompanying instructions are exacting and complex due to the myriad of financial requirements which must be documented by law. As a result, student-level applicants and low-income parents are likely to encounter much difficulty in both understanding and completing the AFSA."
- "I found the form to be difficult to follow. Part of the difficulty is due to the amount and complexity of the information required, but the overly complicated appearance and structure of the form also contribute to confusion."
- "Looking at the form, I don't think any of the questions are very difficult. But it has the appearance of being overpowering. The first page is cluttered and the rest is red and gray. From the face of it, my guess is that it is confusing."

[1]The panel and staff are very grateful to those who did respond; their comments and suggestions were extremely helpful. Regrettably, it was not feasible to include all their comments in this paper.

- "I think the similarity to income tax forms might underline the importance of completing the form correctly, but many people are intimidated by tax forms. I am concerned that this general similarity and the overall lack of "white space" make the task appear more formidable than it is."
- "Needed improvements would require a total redesign of all features mentioned in the letter—wording, sequence, instructions, format, and so on."
- "The form itself appears manageable for typical applicants.... The instructions that accompany the application form are quite difficult and complex. We would expect significant confusion and incorrect responses if the instructions are not modified."

Reviewers gave a wide range of specific comments and suggestions for improving the AFSA. For example, Section B, "Student Status," was singled out by several reviewers as difficult to understand. The crowded format took a lot of the blame. (A brief explanation in the instructions of the overall logic might help somewhat.) Some reviewers thought the sole purpose of this section might be to get the applicant to determine whether he or she should answer the questions in the red-shaded areas or gray-shaded areas. If the information is not used in determining eligibility for aid, they thought the section should become a work sheet in the instructions.

Marital status plays an important part in some key decisions applicants must make about which questions on the application form they are supposed to answer. It figures in the determination of whether the student's status is "dependent" or "independent" in Section B. It also figures in the definition of the term *parents* which applies in Section C, "Household Information," and the remainder of the questionnaire. The answer categories for marital status differ in each of the items on the form in which it is used; definitions are not provided anywhere. Four versions of marital status categories are found in the 1992-93 AFSA:

- Marital status of the student, Section A, item 8.
  - — I am not married. (I am single, divorced, or widowed.)
  - — I am married.
  - — I am separated from my spouse.
- Use of student's marital status in part of the directions that follow questions 11a-d in Section B. "Separated" is no longer a category.
  - — Unmarried now (single, divorced, separated, or widowed)
  - — Married now
- In the instructions for "Parents' Information - red areas," the unmarried grouping is broken into two pairs.
  - — Married to each other
  - — Divorced or separated
  - — Widowed or single

• In Section C, item 16, the categories for current marital status of "parents," as defined in the instructions for this section, are not grouped. They appear in this order:

— single	— separated
— married	— divorced
	— widowed

The marital status categories, as worded, are not mutually exclusive. "Separated" is not clear: couples may be separated legally or the arrangement may be informal, but in either case they are still married. "Divorced" and "widowed" are ambiguous for applicants who have remarried. The lack of precision in terminology and the variety of groupings used are a potential source of confusion that could lead to errors throughout much of the application. The errors might not be detected in routine edit checks.

The instructions for Section B state, " 'Parents' in questions 12, 14a-14f, and 15 means your mother and/or father, or your adoptive parents, or legal guardian. 'Parents' does not mean foster parents, and for this section, it does not mean stepparent. Later the instructions will tell you if you should supply information about your stepparent."

Information about stepparents is wanted in Section C, "Household Information," under certain circumstances, which are described in the instructions labeled "Parents' Information - red areas." For some applicants, the term "parents," as used in questions in the remainder of the form, is thereby redefined. The use of different definitions in different parts of the form may cause misreporting.

The labels for questions 18 and 19 in Section C do not correspond to what the instructions say is meant. A reviewer suggested that the following wording would be closer to the intent: (for 18) "How many people will your parents support in 1992-93?" and (for 19) "Of the number in 18, how many will be in college at least half-time in 1992-93?".

Section E, "Stafford Loan Information," provides an example of puzzling instructions. The first paragraph in the explanation on page 6 states: "Answering the questions in this section does not commit you to accept a Stafford loan nor does it guarantee that you are eligible for a Stafford Loan. For most schools you will have to complete additional forms. Check with your financial aid administrator." This statement has no apparent relationship to the questions in that section, all of which deal with loans received in the past. The instruction to enter "0" if the applicant has not received a Stafford Loan contradicts the direction given on the questionnaire. The statement about what loans should and should not be included would be easier to follow in a list format. Other aspects of the instructions were also scrutinized. Reviewers cited such concerns as excessive cross-references from one part to another, unclear definitions, duplication of information, and illogical sequencing.

Several reviewers thought the color-coding system currently in use was not helpful to applicants. Suggestions included clarifying the student's task by splitting the application into two forms, one for students who are dependents and the other for those considered independent. The determination of which form the applicant should use would be made through screening questions on a separate one-page form. (Split forms were used for two years during the 1980s. The panel was told the reasons for abandoning this approach were not documented.) Another idea for simplifying the process was consolidating the items to be filled out by all applicants, by parents, and by independent students, so that all white sections are together, followed by red areas, then gray areas. Both approaches should reduce confusion about which instructions apply and which items should be answered.

Another option that might be useful for this complex form is to convert the AFSA instructions into a working copy of the application. The questions and the answer categories would be interspersed with the complete instructions, examples, definitions, and work sheets, if any, needed for each data item. The student would retain the working copy for his or her records and copy the answers to a recording form containing question numbers, brief descriptions (e.g., name, address, title) for each, and answer boxes. The recording form, which would fit easily on four pages or fewer, would be the application the student submitted.

More of the reviewers' ideas are summarized in the box on the next page. Many are linked to comments reported elsewhere in the text.

It is possible that informal testing or formal research would indicate that some of the "faults" discussed here do not in fact create problems for applicants. It is also possible that testing and research would reveal that aspects of the form that were not criticized by reviewers *do* cause problems for applicants.

The following suggestions for review and testing were offered by the reviewers:

- A careful review should be conducted to determine minimum data requirements; then extensive questionnaire design work should be undertaken to develop a form that collects these data in a way that is simplest for applicants to provide. The questionnaire design work should address not only wording of questions but also form layout and general instructions provided. Cognitive psychology techniques could be very useful.
- It would be desirable to do some small scale testing to see how well people follow the form, and to identify questions which are not understood or for which people have difficulty providing information.
- We believe it would be helpful . . . to convene a focus group or panel of actual AFSA users (students and parents). ...[the Department of Education] would then be better able to identify those structural changes in format and content that are needed to improve the AFSA.

Why don't they —

- list the Federal Student Aid Information Center telephone numbers on the AFSA
- combine some AFSA sections (A and B, for example)
- number *every* question
- define terms, such as *spouse*, *rollover*, *exemption*
- refer to IRS forms precisely (e.g., year, line number) whenever they are cited
- restrict the AFSA to an application form and instructions; place all program information in the student guide
- move the AFSA reference to the student guide from page 11 to page 1
- expand the form to more than four pages
- document the reasons major format changes were made in the AFSA
- give each question a unique number
- explain how to get IRS forms rather than supplying work sheet #1 "to answer question 24 if you cannot get a 1991 tax form, but will be filing one"
- replace "big" words (such as *self-explanatory*, *optional*, *pertaining*, *determination*)
- explain all abbreviations, acronyms (apt., M.I., VEAP, FDC, and so on)
- put work sheets on the same page as the instructions for them or put all work sheets in one place
- number the pages of the form
- delete the chart on page 1 of the AFSA
- move the supplemental information sections ahead of certification signatures (item 38)
- reduce the clutter on the form
- supply two copies of the form in each booklet
- list consistency checks students can do themselves
- use the same terminology and definitions the IRS uses wherever possible
- tell if AFSA definitions are *not* the same as IRS definitions in items such as 11d and 18
- designate each item in every form consistently
- give the "completed" tax return and "estimated" tax return in item 22 more accurate names and define them
- warn students not to apply too early (e.g., before January 1, 1992) in the "deadline box" on page 1 of the AFSA and at the bottom of the third and fourth pages of the form
- delete duplication and overlap in the instructions

• Pretest with respondents typical of those who would use the form. If you can observe them completing the forms, and probe where they appear to be having difficulty or are making errors, it may help to explain *why* errors are made and how to correct or avoid them.

As Yogi Berra reportedly once said, "You can observe a lot by watching."

The informal testing methods suggested by the reviewers are not necessarily expensive to conduct, and they have been employed by many federal agencies. The use of such techniques is discussed in *Approaches to Developing Questionnaires* (DeMaio, 1983). Some examples of research are described, including qualitative group interviews (focus groups) conducted for the Social Security Administration among teenagers and adults to evaluate a proposed revision of the application form for a Social Security Number (SSN). Research on a larger, more scientific scale would be indicated for evaluation of any major design revisions under consideration.

The AFSA has never been field-tested among students. A predecessor form, the basic grant form, was field-tested under contract in 1981. Far fewer data elements were required by the legislation in effect at that time. The prototype used in the test was an uncrowded, two-page form color coded with shading for dependent and independent applicants. Two alternatives were also tested, including a version with separate forms for dependent and independent applicants. Much helpful information was gathered during this project and used to improve the form. The following quotation is from the contractor's report on the field test (Rehab Group and Macro Systems, 1981:6-7):

> There are certain ways in which OSFA [Office of Student Financial Assistance] would save money in future years and other ways in which it could improve its forms research projects. OSFA should consider actions in the following areas:
>
> (1) OSFA should better utilize existing routine activities that could provide information about problems applicants are having with the form; such activities include receipt of and response to calls and letters from applicants with problems and analyses of applications received at the processing site;
>
> (2) OSFA should consider utilizing formal testing procedures as a method of establishing the best terms, definitions, and data collection formats;
>
> (3) OSFA should explore major variations in the application form structure, including additional forms for special populations;
>
> (4) OSFA should provide for methodological improvements to be made in future field tests, including, for example, use of longer data collection periods, use of experimental application forms in the *actual application process*, use of sampling schemes that more directly identify specific subpopulations, employment of probability sampling techniques, and use of larger samples; and

(5) OSFA should consider making a comprehensive review of other comparable benefit application forms as a means of developing standards against which to measure performance of the Pell Grant form.

Over a decade later, those recommendations are still sound. The reviewers' suggestions outlined above for testing the 1992-93 AFSA are clearly in accord with them and should be implemented. Utilization of data from routine activities, as mentioned in research area (1) above, should include

- examining AFSA answers item-by-item separately for first-time applicants and renewers to identify those items that cause problems (not necessarily errors) for students and/or processors, and
- analyzing the apparent impact, if any, on answers to core data items of variations among application forms used by various states, such as font size, layout, and specific additional questions.

THE 1992-93 STUDENT AID REPORT

Applicants who submitted the paper version of the 1992-93 AFSA should have received a Student Aid Report (SAR) within about four weeks unless the AFSA was rejected. Rejections may occur because the form is unreadable, the application was dated or filed too early, or the signatures from all those who must sign the certification-of-accuracy statement were not provided.

The SAR contains the data given by the student on the AFSA, information from the Department of Education about the student's eligibility for federal student aid, and instructions on what to do next. It also includes a form (either an Information Review or an Information Request) on which to provide additional information, make necessary corrections, and verify any "assumption edits" that may have been inserted during processing for selected blank or inconsistent data elements. For example, if the question about whether parents' assets include a farm was not answered, the editing system assumes the answer is no; if the item about whether either parent is a displaced homemaker was not answered, the edit again assumes the answer is no.

Applicants who appear to qualify for a Pell grant (on the basis of the information they provided and the assumed values, if any, inserted by the editing system) also receive a payment voucher to submit to the school of choice. If the student submits corrections or additions, a revised SAR is prepared and sent to the student in about two or three weeks, according to the student guide.

The Information Review Form is of concern in the context of improving the forms used in the application process. The panel's interest was sparked by the comments of over 600 applicants who wrote to the Department of Education during 1991. They did so in response to the invitation in the SAR to voice their comments or ideas for improvement to either the department or OMB. OMB also received many public comments on the SAR which were forwarded to the Department of Education for review and appropriate action.

The response was "ED [the Department of Education] has also reviewed each of the letters provided in OMB's package to determine if further revisions to the SAR . . . are needed. Based on our review of those letters, no changes are required . . . " (U.S. Department of Education, 1991:5). According to a statement in the clearance file, the SAR design has been essentially the same each year since it was completely reformatted for the 1984-85 processing year. As noted earlier, the AFSA has become longer and more complex since then because of added data items.

One of the applicant letters the OMB forwarded to the Department of Education stated that the line item identification on the SAR should conform to the identification on the original submission to make it easier to review or correct and, therefore, more accurate. Three-fourths of the comments received by the department referred to confusion in reviewing or correcting data because of the lack of correspondence between the item sequence on the SAR and the item sequence on the AFSA. Table C-1 illustrates the back-and-forth movement required in the AFSA to locate items cited on the SAR and the attention students must pay to the color coding for some items; it makes the criticisms of the SAR very understandable.

It is not necessary to burden applicants with deciphering the relationship between the SAR items and the AFSA items. Two simple labeling changes on the SAR would make the task much easier:

- Delete the letters in the section headings shown in the "We asked for" column of the Information Review or, for sections E through O, substitute the letters that identify those sections in the AFSA.
- In the "You told us" column, identify the information source by AFSA section letter and item number.

If, despite these changes, applicants still find the form is more difficult than it need be, several other possibilities are obvious:

- Renumber the SAR and the AFSA so the item numbers match.
- Revise the SAR to conform to the sequence and item numbering in the AFSA.
- Revise the sequence of the AFSA to conform to the SAR.

The third solution would be in line with the suggestions made earlier in this paper, that is, that AFSA items be grouped according to who should answer them or split into two forms on the same basis.

TABLE C-1 Comparison of Data Item Locations on 1992-93 SAR Information Review Form and AFSA

SAR Information Review Form		AFSA	
Section title	Item No.	Section title	Item No.
A. Student's information	1-15	A. Yourself	1-10
B. Student's status	16-25	B. Student status	11-15
C. Student's (spouse's) household information	26-27	C. Household information [gray items]	20-21
D. Student's 1991 income and benefits	28-37	D. 1991 Income, earnings and benefits [white items]	22-28
E. Student's 1991 expenses	38-40	G. 1991 Expenses [gray items]	39-40
F. Student's asset information	41-49	H. Asset information [white items]	41-47
G. Student's veterans benefits	50-53	I. Your veterans educational benefits per month	48-49
H. Student's expected 1992 income and benefits	54-59	J. Expected 1992 taxable and nontaxable income and benefits [white items]	50-55
I. Stafford loan (GSL) information	60-64	E. Stafford loan information (formerly Guaranteed Student Loan [GSL])	29-33
J. College release and certification	65-78	F. College release and certification	34-38
K. Parents' household information	79-82	C. Household information [red items]	16-19
L. Parents' 1991 income and benefits	83-92	D. 1991 income, earnings and benefits [red items]	22-28
M. Parents' 1991 expenses	93-95	G. 1991 expenses [red items]	39-40
N. Parents' asset information	96-105	H. Asset information [red items]	41-47
O. Parents' expected 1992 income and benefits	106-111	J. Expected 1992 taxable and nontaxable income and benefits [red items]	50-55

THE 1992-93 AFSA: ELECTRONIC VERSION

The Department of Education's Electronic Data Exchange application process was introduced during the 1990-91 award year and has been expanding steadily since then. At participating schools, federal student aid application data can be entered and reviewed on a personal computer or an IBM-compatible mainframe system.

Many financial aid administration and security features are provided in the electronic application form (Stage Zero) for 1992-93 (version 3.0.0, released in December 1991), some of which are discussed in this section. The comments in this section are based on information in the Stage Zero user's guide (National Computer System, 1992-93), a demonstration of the system held at the Department of Education, OMB clearance materials, and experimenting with the software by entering answers for imaginary applicants.

In Stage Zero's Electronic Needs Analysis System, financial aid personnel can perform the following functions on student data already keyed:

- calculate the expected family contribution (to the student's financial needs), using the Congressional Methodology, as well as alternate family contribution amounts,
- calculate the estimated Pell Grant Index for determining Pell eligibility and an estimated Pell award amount, and
- apply verification selection criteria.

Electronic filing of renewal applications was introduced for the 1992-93 school year. It is available to returning students at participating institutions. (Renewals for other students require filling out the entire paper AFSA, no matter how much of the data filed previously is still correct.) Renewal records for students who meet certain criteria, such as having a calculated Pell Grant Index and not being in default on a student loan, are loaded into the software at the institution. Renewal applications are then printed; they resemble the Information Review Form in the paper SAR, but the section sequence and item numbers on the two forms do not match. The renewal application lists the data previously reported for many of the AFSA data elements; only changes to the data that must be updated each year need be entered. The updated data are edited, and a copy of the completed form is generated by computer. Signatures for release and certification are required solely on this form.

An "expert" application entry mode enables financial aid personnel to enter data from initial paper applications submitted by students. Three rather crowded screens are used; answer categories and the codes for them are omitted, but help messages are available. Eight user fields defined by the institution are available in the expert entry mode. Edit and review functions can also be performed.

According to the user's guide, the electronic AFSA "is intended for student use in the financial aid office environment, with monitoring and counseling done as needed by the financial aid staff. Some institutions may want to have aid administrator staff walk through the questions as the student enters his/her information. Others may have staff members use this entry mode while interviewing applicants" (p. 15-1).

Learning to use Stage Zero was easy. Experience with the keyboard was helpful, but almost any applicant should be able to adapt quickly. Even hunt-and-peck typists would not have serious problems. Answers to most of the questions are precoded, and those that are not, such as name, address, and SSN, do not generally require lengthy answers.

The first screen contains some simple instructions on using the system. It is in white letters on a blue background, the basic color scheme throughout the electronic application. Additional information about the questions mentioned in the instructions is available for every data item, even those for which no instructions appear in the paper AFSA. These help messages usually contain the information from the paper AFSA and information specific to Stage Zero, such as which characters are permitted (no commas in the address, for example), and what address abbreviations to use if the answer space is insufficient. However, no solution is offered for the problem of a name that does not fit in the allotted space and, obviously, writing in the margin is not an option.

The help messages pop up mid-screen. However, they cover less than half the screen and often the message is too long for the space available. Continuations are brought to the screen by pressing the "page down" key. That is not explained, and it isn't obvious there are continuations unless the first part ends in mid-sentence. Since it often is not possible to see the questions when the help messages are displayed, the help messages could be enlarged to the full size of the screen, as the work sheets discussed below are, to reduce the number of continuations needed. Adding "more," "continued," or an arrow when appropriate would be helpful.

The screen that follows the instructions contains a warning about purposely giving false or misleading information, a reminder that "you" and "your" refer to the student, and a place to enter the student's SSN. The SSN becomes the identifier for the record.

The wording, sequence, and numbering of the items throughout the electronic application match the contents of the paper version. A limited number of questions appear on each screen; none of the screens is crowded. Answer cells are consistently located on the right-hand side, except those for the longer items, such as name and address.

The person keying in the data can proofread entries on the screen and correct errors by backing up and rekeying. Edit or query messages appear on the screen during data entry, when appropriate, to alert the typist to incorrect, incomplete, inconsistent, or suspect data. The typist can stop at any point, but if the application is not completed, the entries made cannot be saved.

In some data fields, "wild" characters, as defined by the program, cannot be keyed (such as the letter o instead of a zero in a numeric field). But the software is tolerant of some unlikely answers, such as one-letter first and last names and numbers only for a street address.

Section A of the electronic AFSA is divided into three screens containing questions 1-4, 5-7, and 8-10, respectively, and the answer categories for them. The student's SSN is inserted automatically in item 5. (In later items, such as whether the student was born before 1969, previously reported data are also inserted automatically.)

Section B contains the items that determine whether, in the remainder of the application, the questions meant only for "independent" applicants or those meant only for "dependent" students should be answered. However, only the questions and the answer categories are shown; the complex skip directions on the paper version are omitted. Instead, the skips are decided by the software. Comparing the screens with the cluttered appearance of the same items on the paper AFSA makes one appreciate a key advantage of a computerized application system.

If the applicant is deemed dependent in Section B, a pop-up message on a red background states: "The remaining questions will ask you for information about your, (your spouse's), and your parents' finances." The help message for the definition of *parents* that applies in the remainder of the application does not include all the information in the instructions for the paper AFSA: the contents of the red box labeled "Parents' information - red areas," which explain the complex rules governing parents who have divorced, separated, and perhaps remarried, are not included in the electronic AFSA. (Stage Zero could be even more helpful if such crucial instructions popped up unbidden.)

In the remainder of the application, the section identification in a box at the top of screens on which information about parents or the household is requested appears in black letters on a white background, rather than the white-on-blue scheme used for student information. Some distinction is essential. In sections D, G, H, and J, the questions do not specify whether they are for the student or the parents. They are verbatim from the paper version, where the questions are printed just once, followed by two sets of answer boxes. Duplication of some item numbers, again because they are that way on the paper version, adds to the opportunities for confusion. (It took this author a while to notice the color coding; it should be made more dramatic where the items about parents start and where the subject switches to the applicant. The color coding also should be mentioned in the pop-up message that precedes these items.)

For the income, earnings, and benefits portion of the form, a pop-up message informs the student that the two work sheets in the paper AFSA are available. The Stage Zero work sheets do the mathematical calculations called for on the data entries and then automatically insert the totals into the proper answer fields on the application. (Even the programmers were misled in this section: The query about whether the work sheet for parents is needed says "your" instead of referring to "parents.")

In Section F, items 34a-c and 35b on the paper version were omitted from the computerized version. The user's guide explains that: "students are not asked for the name of their school or for permission to release their data to the school. It is assumed, by the choice to apply for aid at a particular school, that the student is interested in attending that school" (p. 13-14).

The calculations in work sheets A (for dependents) and B (for independents) are used in the paper AFSA to determine whether the supplemental information in Sections G through J is required. In Stage Zero those work sheets are not needed; the software makes the calculations automatically. The on-screen notice to those who have a choice is worded more clearly than the equivalent information on the paper work sheets.

Finally, the typist is asked if he or she wants to review the application, and choosing "yes" causes the display to return to the beginning of the application. Corrections can be made easily. When the data are okayed by the typist, "your application is now being validated" appears on the screen. Corrections can be made during validation if inconsistencies are flagged.

If the application passes the validation stage, the program automatically saves the file and prints a summary of the data entered. The two-page printout includes a section for office use only and a certification statement ["I have reviewed the information on this document and agree with its contents"] for the student to sign.

The Quality Control Guidelines in the user's guide say the student should compare the responses on the printout with the responses on the paper form, one item at a time. The specific instructions say the student should "match the item numbers and names to make sure you are comparing the same items" (p. H-4). It is not possible to do so, however, because item numbers are not shown on the printout, the section names do not match those on the paper AFSA, and the item sequence differs. If the student finds errors on the printout, the student is to circle the incorrect response and "write the correct response in the space immediately to the right of the incorrect response" (p. H-4). That can't always be done either; for some items, very little space is available on the printout.

It is surprising that the software does not provide for recording who has keyed the data for the electronic application. For quality control analysis, it

The following equipment is required for operation of the Electronic App software:

• IBM or IBM compatible PC with approximately 2.5 megabytes of available space on the hard disk to accommodate the software and data records and 512K of free RAM (Use the DOS CHKDSK command to verify that you have at least 512,000 bytes free)

• a disk drive that accepts 5.25 or 3.5 inch, double-sided diskettes in DOS format (note that double or high density drives are acceptable)

• MS-DOS operating system 3.0 or greater for non-LAN users or 3.3 or greater for LAN users

• A printer that is capable of printing standard 8.5 × 11 reports.

Installation of the Electronic App software requires approximately 2.0 megabytes of available space on the hard disk. Your additional data storage needs will depend on the size of your database, with each application record requiring about 600 bytes of storage space. A 360K floppy (or 360K on your hard disk) can hold about 600 application records.

Note to network users: The Electronic App software now supports LAN capabilities. Please refer to . . ..

SOURCE: National Computer System (1991:14-1).

would be valuable to know whether the information was entered by the applicant or by a specific member of the financial aid office.

Applications can be sent to the Central Processing System electronically, or data files can be mailed in on a floppy diskette. According to the user's guide, applications are processed and an Electronic Student Aid Report (ESAR) is sent to the institution within 72 hours. Even for applications submitted on floppy diskettes, the processed data are returned to the institution in the form of ESAR records in regular Electronic Data Exchange transmissions.

At present, the student completes the paper form, gets the necessary signatures, and then enters the data in Stage Zero—or someone else does the keying. This sequence is backwards. It does not take advantage "up front" of the many Stage Zero features that make it easier to understand what information is required on the application and to provide it accurately. If applicants could start with Stage Zero, working from notes, and fill out the paper form concurrently or subsequently (perhaps after more than one session on the computer), errors and burden would be reduced. In addition, a slightly modified version of the software would be appropriate for use off campus. Adding the capability to save and print incomplete applications is another change that would be helpful.

Personal computers in many homes and most offices would meet the requirements for installation of the 1992-93 electronic AFSA. The description in the user's guide of the equipment required to use Stage Zero appears in the box on the previous page. If they could use a tailored version of Stage Zero, high schools, churches, community organizations, civic groups, and mentors with access to a computer could aid applicants in filling out the form.

REFERENCES

DeMaio, Theresa, ed.

1983 *Approaches to Developing Questionnaires.* Statistical Policy Paper 10. Prepared by Subcommittee on Questionnaire Design, Federal Committee on Statistical Methodology. Available through NTIS Document Sales, PB-84-105005. Washington, D.C.: U.S. Office of Management and Budget.

National Computer Systems

1992-93 *U.S. Department of Education, General Electronic Support, Electronic App User's Guide, 1992-93 Cycle, Vol. II.* Presented to the U.S. Department of Education. National Computer Systems, Iowa City, Iowa.

Rehab Group, Inc. and Macro Systems, Inc.

1981 *Field Testing of 1982-1983 BEOG Application Forms, Executive Summary.* Submitted to the U.S. Department of Education, Office of Student Financial Assistance. Contract No. 300-81-0014. Rehab Group, Inc., Falls Church, Virginia.

U.S. Department of Education

1991 OMB Number 1840-0132: The 1992-93 Student Aid Report (SAR) Clearance Package. Memorandum from Director, Operations Improvement Section, Division of Program Operations and Systems, to Ira Mills, Federal Information Review Branch, IMCD, Office of Management and Budget. Washington, D.C. October 31.

1992-93 *The Student Guide: Financial Aid from the U.S. Department of Education, 1992-93.* Washington, D.C.: U.S. Department of Education.

APPENDIX

D

Laboratory Methods and Document Redesign

Leda Kydoniefs and Marie van Melis-Wright
Office of Survey Methods Research
Bureau of Labor Statistics

BACKGROUND

In response to the 1983 Advanced Seminar on Cognitive Aspects of Survey Methodology (CASM), interdisciplinary survey research centers and laboratories have been established at a number of governmental organizations (Jabine et al., 1984). In keeping with the CASM mission, such centers actively promote collaboration among behavioral scientists from various fields, statisticians, and survey researchers in order to improve data quality and the data collection process (Dippo and Norwood, 1992).

One such research center is the Behavioral Science Research Center (BSRC) at the Bureau of Labor Statistics (BLS). Founded in 1988, its professional staff includes psychologists from various specialties (e.g., social, cognitive, educational psychology, artificial intelligence), statisticians, sociologists, a psychological anthropologist, and research assistants. Currently, primary areas of investigation include questionnaire development and design, form redesign, interviewer training, interviewer participant interactions, interview administration methodologies, and basic research in the areas of memory, proxy reporting, confidentiality, and privacy.

Since 1989, BSRC has undertaken two major form redesign studies: an effort sponsored by the Internal Revenue Service (IRS) to redesign selected tax forms and the redesign of the BLS Survey of Occupational Illnesses and Injuries. Among the goals of the redesign efforts are to reduce respondent burden, improve data quality, reduce cost and processing time, and develop formats suited for use with different technologies (e.g., optical scanners, administration by computer).

A distinct feature of the BLS form-redesign project is the application of behavioral science methods to increase understanding of the cognitive, social, and organizational factors in the information-gathering process. Researchers have many data collection methods from which to choose, for example, expert analysis, interactional behavior coding, laboratory and field observational techniques, focus groups, vignette classifications, rating techniques, free and dimensional sorting, ethnographic and cognitive interviews, and concurrent and retrospective think-alouds (Forsythe and Lessler, 1990). This paper illustrates the utility of some of these methods using examples from the two redesign projects mentioned above.

IRS SCHEDULE C STUDY

Schedule C (Profit or Loss from Business) is an attachment to IRS Form 1040. It is used by taxpayers who classify themselves as "sole proprietorships." In 1987, taxpayers filed 14.5 million Schedule C forms. The data collected from Schedule C are used in aggregate form by the IRS and other governmental agencies to, for example, help determine estimates of personal income at the local level.

One of the goals of the redesign effort was to simplify the taxpayer's task, which included locating the description of his or her business or professional activity in the listing on the back of the form, finding the corresponding 4-digit code, and writing the description and the 4-digit code on the front of the form. To meet this goal, an interdisciplinary research team was created, which consisted of IRS representatives and behavioral scientists from the American Institutes for Research (AIR) and the BSRC laboratory. The research team used a variety of behavioral science methods to obtain different perspectives on taxpayers' problems with the form and the potential solutions. The methods they used included in-depth telephone interviews with IRS editors of Schedule C, observations and in-depth debriefings of taxpayers, concurrent and retrospective think-alouds with taxpayers, and an experiment evaluating taxpayers' performance under the old and revised versions of Schedule C.

Rather than focus only on the taxpayer, the research team decided to collect input from other users of Schedule C, specifically IRS editors of Schedule C and primary and secondary data users (e.g., Statistics of Income Division, IRS; and Bureau of the Census and Bureau of Economic Analysis, U.S. Department of Commerce). These groups regularly handle the completed forms, analyze or disseminate the data, or serve as gatekeepers and trackers/monitors of the flow of forms. Thus, they are in an excellent position to identify typical errors made by the taxpayer.

The BSRC team conducted a number of in-depth, semistructured telephone interviews with a subsample of editors of Schedule C from among the 26 national IRS Service Centers; the AIR team conducted observations and used concurrent think-alouds with a small sample of taxpayers; and IRS representatives used an open-ended written questionnaire to interview end users from the Census Bureau and the Bureau of Economic Analysis. All the methods combined yielded a wealth of qualitative and quantitative data pinpointing problems and errors, including lack of or unclear instructions, errors occurring during transfer of information from one side of the form to the other, small print and cluttered physical layout, missing or hard-to-understand principle business and professional code descriptions, use of invalid or outdated codes, and a tendency of taxpayers to favor the "Other" or "Unable to Classify" categories over more specific descriptions. Before making revisions, the research team also collected information from IRS representatives to make sure the revisions would not interfere with important organizational constraints (e.g., policies with regard to mandated statements, paper size, number of pages, format of instructions, and so on).

Based on the information gathered during the first stage of the research, the AIR and IRS focus of the revisions crystallized into:

- alphabetizing the main- and subcategories of the principal business codes on the back of Schedule C,
- increasing the size of the print,
- improving the clarity of and completeness of instructions printed on the form,
- moving the four-digit codes originally located to the left of the category description to the right, and
- removing visual "clutter."

The rationale for these changes was to facilitate searching, reduce scanning time and errors, and facilitate the taxpayer's task.

The final phase of the project involved two experiments. The first compared the existing Schedule C with a revised version on which the 4-digit code was listed to the right of the description of the activity. In experiment 2, three revised versions were compared. In both experiments, subjects in each condition were given a list of 48 scenarios (business or professional activities) and asked to complete a Schedule C for each of them. The majority of scenarios were descriptions of activities taken directly from the current form, synonyms of descriptions listed on the form, and ambiguous descriptions. The last group were descriptions for which several reasonable responses, including "Other" and "Unable to Classify," were options each subject might consider. Outcome measures included accuracy, response time, and a measure of preference by taxpayers for the various versions. In addition, behavioral observations, concurrent and retrospective think-alouds, and in-depth debriefings were conducted to investigate taxpayers' rationale for their performance.

The scope of this paper does not allow for an in-depth discussion of the results. Briefly, however, the findings from experiment 1 did not reveal any significant differences. In experiment 2, alphabetization and format changes yielded higher accuracy and shorter completion times than for the old version. Findings also showed that respondents did not read the directions, even when they were printed directly above the activity codes, and moving the 4-digit codes from the left to the right of the description caused more, not fewer, errors.[1] Not surprisingly, the accuracy levels for the various scenarios varied—from 85 percent correct for exact descriptions, 78 percent for synonyms, and 42 percent for ambiguous descriptions. An in-depth error analysis was conducted to determine the type of errors made by the taxpayer.

On the basis of the results of the experiments, a set of recommendations for the redesign of Schedule C codes was developed, as well as for large-scale testing on a representative sample of taxpayers.

Feedback from key participants in the research was very favorable regarding the methods and techniques used. In addition to the information necessary for the development of revised forms, the close collaboration between key players resulted in a firm commitment to the task at hand and future form development.

SURVEY OF OCCUPATIONAL ILLNESSES AND INJURIES

A major redesign of the Occupational Safety and Health Statistics (OSHS) system, the nation's source of information on job-related illnesses and injuries, was begun in 1987. The OSHS Survey of Occupational Illnesses and Injuries is a mandatory survey and is conducted by mail. The redesign effort included a review of all aspects of the survey: content, sampling, forms design, collection, and processing.

The forms redesign portion of the OSHS project was begun in 1989 and consisted of several pilot/feasibility studies investigating alternative survey formats. Once the decision was made in 1991 to pursue the design of a booklet format, the forms redesign efforts intensified. The goal was fourfold:

- Develop a booklet survey form with accompanying instructions that was "user friendly."
- Design a questionnaire format with a built-in flexibility that would permit certain minor variations in item content. (These variations are required in order to maximize the survey's utility across the nation.)

[1] This likely happened because the description of some activities took up two lines of text, in which case, the 4-digit code was put at the end of the second line. However, as it turned out, participants did not take that code, but rather selected the one below it (i.e., the code for the next category).

- Test and evaluate old (i.e., rephrased) questionnaire content as well as new survey items.
- Test and evaluate the redesigned OSHS survey that was developed.

To achieve these goals, a variety of behavioral science and test development methods were used, each of which added a different perspective to the knowledge base and forms redesign efforts. Focus groups, consisting of volunteers from nearby establishments, were used to test the newly developed items and instructions for clarity, comprehension, and respondent burden. Some respondents were videotaped in their establishments while completing the questionnaire, and retrospective think-aloud interviews were later conducted with them; others were videotaped using the concurrent think-aloud technique.[2] These "think alouds" permitted the researchers to view the respondent's interaction with the questionnaire and the respondent within the respondent's working environment.

After the focus group data were analyzed and the appropriate changes were made in the survey booklet, it was decided to evaluate the data collection and processing aspect of this newly developed survey format. The questionnaire was mailed to approximately 1,500 respondents located in four states. The data were then processed and analyzed within each state, using the state's "standard operating procedures." This method revealed certain deficiencies in the sampling portion of the survey document that were not evident when each respondent was observed individually. Once again, the test results were analyzed and the survey was revised accordingly.

Once the focus groups, concurrent and retrospective think-alouds, and test mailings were completed and all appropriate changes implemented, the forms redesign process was approaching completion. To ensure that the changes reflected "true" improvement and had not caused or created other errors or difficulties, the survey was mailed to approximately 200 respondents located in five states. The focus was again on evaluating the survey contents (i.e., comprehension of items and response options, clarity of instructions, and respondent burden). Establishments were sampled in such a way as to permit assessment of differences in data quality between large and small establishments and rural and urban establishments. In addition to the OSHS questionnaire, respondents were asked to answer a number of questions designed to collect information on certain complex items (e.g., employment average, total hours worked by all employees in a year), time required to complete the OSHS survey, and the "readability" of the survey booklet.

As the completed forms were received, debriefing interviews were conducted by telephone with approximately 50 percent of the respondents. The

---

[2] For further information on this and other techniques, see Mullin et al (1991).

focus of the interviews was to investigate the respondents' feelings regarding the new survey format and the additional items, achieve a better understanding of respondent burden, and obtain an estimate of the validity of the data received. The data obtained were analyzed and the survey item content and/or the design of the booklet was revised accordingly.

SUMMARY

The BSRC laboratory used behavioral science methods to investigate errors and to test revisions of the IRS Schedule C and the BLS OSHS survey. The methods used included focus groups, behavioral observations, concurrent and retrospective think-alouds, in-depth debriefings, semistructured telephone interviews, open-ended written interviews, and expert analysis. All of the methods yielded important information and enhanced the overall redesign efforts. While each has its own strengths and weaknesses in terms of psychometric properties, cost and time requirements, and so on, they all share the characteristic of providing information from perspectives that have often been ignored in the past.

REFERENCES

Dippo, C. and J. Norwood
1992 A review of research at the Bureau of Labor Statistics. Pp. 271-290 in *Questions about Questions: Inquiries into the Cognitive Bases of Surveys.* New York: Russell Sage.

Forsythe, B. H. and J. T. Lessler
1990 Cognitive Laboratory Methods: A Taxonomy. Paper presented at the International Conference on Measurement Errors in Surveys, Tucson, Arizona.

Jabine, T. B., M. L. Straf, J. M. Tanur, and R. Tourangeau, eds.
1984 *Cognitive Aspects of Survey Methodology: Building a Bridge Between Disciplines.* Washington, D.C.: National Academy Press.

Mullin, P. A., L. A. Miller, M. van Melis-Wright, D. B. Stone
1991 Laboratory Research Methods for Improving Surveys. Paper presented at the GAO Technical Conference, University of Maryland, College Park. Available from the Behavioral Science Research Center, Bureau of Labor Statistics.

APPENDIX

E

The IRS Experience with Cognitive Labs and Forms Design

Mary Batcher
Statistics of Income Division
Internal Revenue Service

The problems with income tax forms are legendary. Not only are they very complex, but they come complete with difficult instructions. In addition, very few people can totally avoid interacting with the forms.

The content and format of tax forms are of interest to many parts of the Internal Revenue Service (IRS), outside agencies, the practitioner community, and taxpayers. Despite what may be impressions to the contrary, the IRS pays a great deal of attention to improving the design of the more common forms, especially the 1040 family of forms. Many other less familiar IRS forms and schedules are extremely important to users of tax data. They contribute key components to the data bases used in tax policy and statistical analyses. Consequently, the Statistics of Income (SOI) Division of the IRS, which has primary responsibility for those data bases, has been supporting work by the Bureau of Labor Statistics (BLS) cognitive lab, the Behavioral Science Research Center, to improve some of the less well known forms.

Specific details and reports on the forms redesign work are available from the author upon request, but the focus of this paper is the effective use of cognitive lab technology to improve complex forms and instructions and the implementation of suggested improvements in an environment that is simultaneously bureaucratic and hands-on operational.

USE OF THE LAB

In general, the SOI Division is still working out the best way to use the resources of the BLS cognitive lab. Some areas that make a difference in the effective use of the cognitive lab for forms design are specification of the problem; communication among the processing staff, data users, and the lab researchers; and availability of resources, in terms of time and funding, to allow for proper problem formulation, exploratory work, and testing of alternatives.

Problem Specification

The importance of having a well-defined problem is clearly not unique to forms design. However, problem specification has been particularly troublesome in the division's use of the BLS cognitive lab to improve forms. The lab's SOI customers are often not very knowledgeable about the lab's capabilities and methodology. Forms improvement can appear deceptively simple; many in the SOI Division, for example, have their own commonsense rules about how to clarify instructions or make forms more user friendly. This lack of familiarity with the lab's methodology, coupled with a sense that the task is relatively straightforward, contributes to a misconception that the only problem specification needed is to ask the lab to "fix" a particular form.

It is important that specific goals and limitations are communicated to the lab researchers as part of problem definition. Forms can be improved with a number of goals in mind: error reduction, appearance, ease of processing, and so on. The primary objectives should be agreed upon by the customers and specified for the lab. The limitations should also be well defined. These include the usual cost and time constraints but may also include specification of untouchable portions of the form, page or line limits, and limits on how many of the feeder items, forms, and instructions are to be addressed. Defining limitations has been a difficult task on occasion because of the interrelated nature of the IRS forms and the many uses for them beyond simple determination of taxes owed.

Finally, part of problem specification should be the identification of any known problems with the form under consideration, including high-error items. This seems obvious, but in a large bureaucratic environment with multiple users of forms, researchers may have to make contact with several areas of the agency, including both field and headquarters staff, to locate all the relevant information.

Communication

Even under the best of circumstances, it is not likely that the cognitive lab staff and the customer will have a completely clear mutual understanding of the problem and desired outcome. It is, therefore, essential that there be frequent communication between the lab and its customers throughout the conduct of the study. This is especially critical given the lack of familiarity of the customers with the lab's capabilities and limitations. Expectations must be established and continually reestablished as each of the participants learns more about the problem and the others' capabilities.

Resources

The IRS is a production-oriented agency. As a result, there is not a general appreciation of the difference between data collection for exploratory purposes and for testing of alternatives. Often exploratory work is viewed as testing, and thus, time and resources are not allocated for a testing stage. For example, focus group testing using forms to identify problem areas is frequently viewed by the IRS customers as adequate testing to support recommendations. They do not see the need to continue to a second stage and test the performance of alternative versions of the form according to defined criteria using larger groups of respondents. Frequently, despite suggestions by the lab, no provision is made for actually testing the focus group recommendations.

General Observations on Use of the Lab

In general, from the perspective of the SOI Division, researchers in the cognitive lab must learn to understand and deal with results-oriented, operational customers, who will probably never fully appreciate the complexity of the forms design task. However, the operational customers do know what they want, although they may need some persistent prompting to specify it. In identifying customer wants and needs, it is important that the cognitive lab researchers avoid imposing their definition of what the customer needs and ignore what the customer wants. The relationship will not succeed if the customer does not receive some version of what he or she wants. As the lab and the customer learn more about each other's skills and unique needs, the customer's wants should come into closer alignment with his or her needs as seen by the forms design and cognitive experts.

IMPLEMENTATION ISSUES

Some factors affecting the successful IRS implementation of the recommendations of the cognitive lab are the multiplicity of IRS customers and elements of the IRS culture itself. As noted, there are multiple users of each of the tax forms throughout the IRS. Although the request for forms design work generally comes from only one of the many IRS users, each of the other stakeholders has an opinion about proposed forms changes and, often, the potential to block proposed changes. The titular IRS owner of the tax forms is the Tax Forms and Publications Division. The SOI Division is supporting cognitive lab work on the forms that are important in the SOI data bases. The division has kept the Tax Forms and Publications Division involved with SOI on this research. This has been an important element in securing support for the recommendations of the lab. In addition to controlling forms changes, the Tax Forms and Publications Division is the only part of the IRS that is fully aware of the complexity of the task and the importance of conducting research on forms and basing decisions on the results of appropriate testing.

Although the SOI Division has been able to involve its primary external customers and the major IRS owner of the tax forms in the forms improvement effort, it has depended on the Tax Forms and Publications Division to coordinate the involvement of the other stakeholders. The traditional vehicle for this coordination is a meeting at which stakeholders are given an opportunity to comment on proposed forms changes. There are organizational and cost limitations that support this approach, but less formal contact with the major stakeholders at an earlier stage in the process might reduce resistance to proposed changes and ensure that their perspectives are considered.

The IRS is not a research or statistical agency; it has a specific operational mission—to administer the tax laws. Hence, the broad IRS culture is very strong and strongly operational. On the positive side, regarding ease of implementation, the IRS has the ability to move more quickly than other governmental agencies once an objective is determined. On the other hand, there is often a tendency within the IRS to listen to advice, understand it, and choose to follow it or not depending on how well it fits conventional operational wisdom. Advice linked to operational considerations, like error or cost reduction, is more appealing to most in the IRS than advice linked to cognitive theory. Results based on any kind of testing are valued; however, there is little critical assessment of the testing methodology or differentiation among types and purposes of testing.

In general, in any application of cognitive lab technology to forms design, attention to the organizational culture should pay off in identifying the best techniques to aid implementation. A standard tactic that has worked well for the SOI Division has been to begin with a few small projects whose results can be seen quickly and publicized. Once users within the IRS see some of the improvements, they tend to become enthusiastic about using the lab to improve forms and instructions.

APPENDIX

F

Alternative Approaches to Audit and Program Review for Student Financial Aid Programs

Urton Anderson
C. Aubrey Smith Center for Auditing Education and Research
The University of Texas at Austin

The Department of Education has used two types of "audit" to control student financial aid programs at participating educational institutions: program review and independent audit.[1] With the 1992 reauthorization of the Higher Education Act (P.L. 102-325), a third type, the state postsecondary review, has been added. Because there is yet considerable uncertainty about how this third "audit" mechanism will be implemented, it is discussed here only in terms of the 1992 amendments' intent and how such a mechanism might affect program review and, particularly, independent audit. After a brief treatment of program reviews, the remainder of the paper focuses on the independent audit.

PROGRAM REVIEWS

Program reviews are conducted by Department of Education personnel with the objectives of determining compliance with program regulations, evaluating financial and administrative capabilities, and providing technical assistance. The limited resources the department has for these reviews are allocated using a risk model consisting of seven components. The risk components given the greatest weight (20 percent each) are absence of a

[1] The department also has responsibility for controlling student loan programs at some 12,000 participating lenders and 47 guaranty agencies. Control of the student financial aid programs at these types of institutions also involves audits, but such audits are beyond the scope of this paper.

program review in the past four years, default rates (two prior years) greater than 30 percent, and the number of overdue audit reports. The other four components of the model (given a weight of approximately 10 percent each) are significant increases in the number of guaranteed student loans (GSLs) or Pell grants over the prior three years, change of institution ownership in the prior three years, whether the institution is being monitored for financial capability, and a subjective assessment based on impressions from student complaints or other negative publicity regarding the institution.

The department, until recently, conducted approximately 1,000 program reviews each year out of a potential 8,500 institutions, an average annual coverage of about 12 percent of the universe of postsecondary institutions. Current plans call for 600 to 700 reviews per year. The risk model appears to be appropriately targeting program review resources. Even using a conservative measure of review benefit, average liabilities assessed per review appear to more than cover their cost. Further, the reviews seem to be increasingly effective; average liabilities assessed per review have increased from $37,000 in fiscal year 1989, to $86,000 in fiscal 1990, to an estimated $150,000 for fiscal 1991.

INDEPENDENT AUDITS

In addition to being subject to program review, the Higher Education Act of 1965, as amended by P.L. 99-498, required educational institutions participating in student financial aid programs to have an independent audit at least every two years.[2] The purpose of the independent audits is to help program managers in the Department of Education meet their stewardship responsibilities. In particular, the audits are designed to help departmental managers determine whether institutions participating in the programs

- provide reliable financial data,
- have an adequate system of internal control for the institution's financial aid operations, and
- comply with program regulations.

The audits are performed, under contract to the institution, by state and local governmental auditors and by independent certified public accountants (CPAs). The cost of the audits may be recovered by the participating institution as either a direct or indirect administrative expense. However, no special appropriations are made for audit costs. The cost must be built into the institution's specific grant document or overhead proposal. To the ex-

[2] The 1992 bill reauthorizing and amending the Higher Education Act of 1965 requires that independent audits be conducted annually (Section 487(c)(1)(A)(i) of the act, as amended).

tent that administrative costs exceed the program maximum, additional costs for the audit are not recoverable.

Independent audits may be conducted in one of three ways. The particular approach taken depends on the type of institution (public, private nonprofit, for-profit).[3] Public and private nonprofit institutions have some degree of latitude in selecting an approach; for-profit institutions are limited to one approach. Each of the approaches addresses the three audit objectives listed above, but the audit resources required varies considerably across the approaches.

Approach One—Audit Guide

Under this approach (also called a "program audit"), the auditor follows the *Audit Guide: Audits of Student Financial Assistance Programs*, issued by the U.S. Department of Education (1990). The guide allows two alternative methods of conducting the audit. Using the first method the auditor integrates the auditing procedures with the audit of the financial statement of the institution and provides an opinion on the financial statements and a report on supplemental data (i.e., the schedule of expenditures for each student financial aid program). Using the second method the auditor renders an opinion only on the Modified Statement of Cash Receipts and Disbursements for student financial aid programs. The approach taken to assessing the adequacy of internal controls and compliance is the same under either method. Reporting on compliance requires identification of all material instances of noncompliance discovered during the audit.

The "audit guide" approach can be selected by public and private nonprofit institutions.[4] It appears to be required of for-profit institutions. During the 12 months ending March 31, 1992, the Department of Education processed 3,040 independent audits that used this approach (51 percent of the audits processed during the period).[5]

Approach Two—A-128

Public institutions of state and local governmental entities may satisfy the independent audit requirement through audits conducted in accordance

[3] The type of audit does not depend upon the auditor. State and local governmental auditors as well as independent auditors (CPAs) can perform any of the three types of audit.

[4] There appears to be some restrictions on adoption of the "audit guide" approach for some private nonprofit institutions. According to Statement No. 6, Question 5, of the President's Council on Integrity and Efficiency (1992), nonprofit institutions with total awards of $100,000 and more than one student aid program must use the A-133 approach (discussed below).

[5] This information is from the Department of Education's semiannual reports to the President's Commission on Integrity and Efficiency concerning the quality of non-federal audits. At the time of this writing, I had not been able to determine how many of the audits were of student financial aid programs versus other Department of Education programs.

with Circular A-128 of the Office of Management and Budget (1985).[6] Single audits are required of state and local governments receiving more than $100,000 per year in federal assistance. However, a state or local government can elect to exclude institutions of higher education from its A-128 audits. If the college or university is excluded, it would be subject to the audit requirements of A-133 (see below). With few exceptions the audits are required annually.[7]

The objectives of the single audit are the same as those set out in the Higher Education Act for independent audits of student financial aid programs. However, in the single audit the objectives apply to a much larger entity, namely, the complete governmental unit. The extent to which student financial aid programs are covered by the single audit depends on whether the program is characterized as major or nonmajor. For governmental units receiving between $100,000 and $100 million in federal assistance per year, a "major" program is any program receiving the larger of $300,000 or 3 percent of total federal assistance to the unit.[8] It appears that determination is made on the basis of each type of student financial aid program.

If a student financial aid program has been determined to be a major program, audit procedures would be similar to those under a "guide" audit. Although the *Audit Guide* is recommended for use in determining compliance when major student financial aid programs are involved in an A-128 audit, the guide is used primarily to identify specific compliance requirements to be tested. The minimum sample size requirements and mandatory audit areas in the guide need not be followed. However, selection and testing must include a sufficient number of transactions from each major program to support the audit opinion on each program.

If the student financial aid program is determined to be a "nonmajor" federal program, limited testing of the internal control structure and compliance is required. For nonmajor programs it is required only that the auditor obtain an understanding of the internal control structure's policies and procedures that are relevant to preventing or detecting material noncompliance. Testing of specific federal compliance requirements is performed only if a nonmajor program transaction occurs in some other audit test.

---

[6] The Office of Management and Budget (OMB) issued Circular A-128 in conjunction with the Single Audit Act of 1984. Circular A-128 provided more specifics as to how the Single Audit Act was to be implemented.

[7] The 1992 reauthorization of the Higher Education Act requires annual audits of all student financial aid programs.

[8] Units receiving more than $100 million in assistance apply a schedule going from $100 million to greater than $7 billion. For example, a "major" program would be one with federal expenditures greater than $3 million for a unit with federal assistance of between $100 million and $1 billion. The criterion is $20 million for units with assistance of over $7 billion.

Unlike reporting on compliance in the "audit guide" approach (in which only material instances of noncompliance must be reported), under the Single Audit Act the auditor is required to report *any* noncompliance event found during testing, regardless of its materiality.

In the 12-month period ending March 31, 1992, the Department of Education processed 2,576 independent audits conducted under the A-128 approach (43 percent of the audits processed during the period). Quality control for A-128 audits is divided among various federal agencies. The Department of Education was the cognizant agency (i.e., had responsibility for overseeing the implementation and the quality control of the audit) for 91 of the A-128 audits. The department also had general oversight responsibility for 1,758 of the A-128 audits.[9] Other federal agencies had cognizance or general oversight responsibility for 727 of the audits.[10]

To illustrate the variation in coverage of student financial aid programs in A-128 audits, coverage of public institutions in the A-128 audit of the state of Texas is presented in a subsequent section of this report.

Approach Three—A-133

In 1990 the Office of Management and Budget issued Circular A-133 to implement the single audit concept for nonprofit organizations, particularly institutions of higher education (Office of Management and Budget, 1990a). This approach applies to nonprofit institutions receiving $100,000 or more a year in federal awards, unless the institution receives all the award in a single program.[11] When the federal award is only in one program, the institution has the option of using the A-133 approach or the "audit guide" approach.

Under A-133, the individual student financial aid programs are combined and treated as a single program in determining whether the A-133 approach is required and also in determining whether the combined program is a major program. A program is considered to be a major program under A-133 if the total across all student aid programs is greater than $100,000 or 3 percent of total federal funds received (whichever is greater). Thus,

---

[9] General oversight involves less responsibility. Usually it consists of working through direct recipients to ensure that subrecipients meet their audit requirements and providing technical assistance when requested.

[10] This information is from the Department of Education's semiannual reports to the President's Commission on Integrity and Efficiency concerning the quality of non-federal audits. At the time of this writing, I had not been able to determine how many of the audits were of student financial aid programs versus other Department of Education programs.

[11] State and local governmental institutions of higher education excluded from the governmental unit's A-128 audit can elect to be audited under the A-133 or the "audit guide" approach.

under most applications of A-133 to educational institutions, student aid programs will receive greater audit coverage than under the A-128 approach because each program will be reviewed for the adequacy of the institution's internal controls and tested for compliance.

The A-133 audit of student financial aid programs differs from the "audit guide" and A-128 approaches in that it takes an integrative approach to the institution's administration of the individual aid programs. Guidance for audit procedures under this approach is provided in the *Compliance Supplement for Single Audits of Educational Institutions and Other Non-profit Organizations* (Office of Management and Budget, 1991). Procedures for determining whether the institution meets the objectives of reliable financial information and adequacy of internal controls are similar to those in the "audit guide" and A-128 approaches because integrative approaches are most likely taken for these parts of the audit under those approaches.[12] The greatest difference is in the compliance portion of the audit, where compliance is considered across individual programs with respect to (1) types of services allowed or not allowed, (2) eligibility, (3) matching, level of effort, and/or earmarking, (4) special reporting requirements, and (5) special tests. In addition, for A-133 audits the specific testing procedures and sample sizes in the *Audit Guide* do not have to be followed. Nor are any individual programs in which the institution participates excluded from compliance testing because they are nonmajor programs.

Reporting requirements for A-133 audits are similar to those for A-128 audits. However, unlike A-128, in the A-133 approach the auditor is not required to report instances of immaterial noncompliance found during testing. Instances of immaterial noncompliance are required to be reported in a separate written report to the institution. The institution is then required to submit this list to the appropriate federal agencies, which for instances found in student aid programs would be the Department of Education.

During the 12 months ending March 31, 1992, the Department of Education processed 371 A-133 audits (6 percent of the independent audits processed by the department).[13]

---

[12] The possible exception might be in the audit of the financial information. Sampling of transactions for testing under A-133 would define the population as all student aid transactions; whereas under A-128 audits, transactions for individual programs determined to be nonmajor would be excluded from the population, and under the "audit guide," transactions might be excluded because the individual program is considered immaterial. However, even under A-133 it may be more efficient to stratify the population by individual program.

[13] This information is from the Department of Education's semiannual reports to the President's Commission on Integrity and Efficiency concerning the quality of non-federal audits. At the time of this writing, I had not been able to determine how many of the audits were of student financial aid programs versus other Department of Education programs.

ATTESTATION VERSUS COMPLIANCE OBJECTIVES

The model underlying the approach taken in the independent audit requirements for student financial aid programs is that of the attestation audit. The attestation model developed from the need for users of organizations' financial statements to have assurance about the reliability of the information in the statements. In this model the management of the organization makes assertions about the financial condition and activity of the organization (i.e., prepares the financial statements for the period). An auditor independent of the organization then collects evidence regarding those assertions. The evidence collection must be sufficient for the auditor to come to an opinion regarding the appropriateness of the accounting methods used in constructing the statements and the presence or absence of significant error in recording and compiling the period's financial transactions and in applying these accounting methods. Over the years this basic attestation model has been extended to go beyond the financial statement assertions to other areas, such as software, student enrollments, market shares of radio and television audiences, and rates of return of investments.

The basic attestation model is an output-based quality control mechanism. That is, the model views the financial statement assertions as the outputs of a process (i.e., the accounting system) that produces a product (i.e., the financial statements), the components of which (the individual assertions) are then tested after completion (i.e., when the financial statements have been prepared by the organization). Because of the cost of taking this approach with large and complex organizations, the approach has been gradually modified to allow consideration of quality control mechanisms in the production process (i.e., internal controls). However, the emphasis of the model remains on output. Only in the past few years, with the issuance of Statement on Auditing Standards No. 55 (American Institute of Certified Public Accountants, 1988), have the standards for financial attestation audits required the auditor to give explicit consideration to internal controls.

A risk-based framework (Statement on Auditing Standards No. 47) for allocating audit resources within the financial attestation audit has also evolved (American Institute of Certified Public Accountants, 1983). In this framework, *audit risk* is defined as the risk that the financial statement will contain a material misstatement after the completion of the audit. This risk is set to be relatively low (5 percent or less). Three component risks are considered to determine audit risk: inherent risk, control risk, and detection risk. *Inherent risk* is the likelihood that the financial statement innately will contain a material error, assuming there are no related internal control structure policies or procedures. *Control risk* is the likelihood that the internal control structure policies and procedures would not prevent or detect a material error. *Detection risk* is the likelihood that the auditor's procedures would not find a material error present in the financial statements. In using this risk framework to allocate audit resources, the framework is applied at the individual assertion level as well. Resources are allocated over assertions such that overall audit risk is equal to, or less than, the acceptable (set) level. Inherent risk and control risk are assessments made by the auditor rather than a decision variable. However, since assessment of control risk at less than 100 percent requires testing of control procedures, the decision whether to consider controls for a specific assertion influences the resource allocation. Detection risk is a function of the auditing procedures (i.e., the effectiveness of the test, the sample size, and so on).

The attestation model appears to work well in determining whether the institution has met the objective of reliable financial information, but it is not clear whether it is an appropriate model for testing the achievement of the compliance objective. Unlike reliability of financial information, the ultimate goal of the compliance portion of the independent audit is not the verification of the implied assertion that the student financial aid program is in compliance or that the noncompliance rate is less than "x" percent, but actual minimizing of noncompliance. Certainly an annual, or biannual, audit can influence the extent of compliance through the effect the expectation of an audit has on auditees. However, random audit, or risk-based audits with a random component, can accomplish the same objectives with significantly fewer resources.[14]

Even keeping within the current attestation framework, a risk-based approach to the compliance objective could improve the efficient and effective use of audit resources. Currently, under all three approaches to independent audit of institutional compliance, effort is allocated on the basis of dollar coverage rather than risk of noncompliance. In the "audit guide" approach, resource allocations for auditing program compliance is determined by mandatory procedures and minimum sample sizes. Under A-128 and A-133 audits, various coverage rules apply to testing of institutional controls and compliance. Some indication that the independent audits expend audit resources with less efficiency and effectiveness than possible is found in a comparison of average liabilities assessed per audit and average liabilities assessed per program review (which takes a risk-based approach). For fiscal year 1989, average assessments per audit were $10,300 compared with average assessments per review of $36,675. For fiscal 1990, average assessments per audit were $23,827 compared with $86,243 per program review.

Movement toward a risk-based approach for A-128 audits is being advocated by the National State Auditors Association (1992). The American Institute of Certified Public Accountants (1992c) has also adopted a risk-

[14] See Baron and Besanko (1984) and Anderson and Young (1988a,b) for demonstrations of the optimality of randomized strategies.

based approach to compliance auditing in SAS 68, *Compliance Auditing Applicable to Governmental Entities and Other Recipients of Governmental Financial Assistance.* This standard was issued in April 1992 and is effective for audits of fiscal periods ending after June 15, 1992; hence, details of its implementation were not complete at this writing. However, the risk approach is analogous to that in SAS 47 for financial attestation audits (discussed above); it focuses allocation of resources on attestation of compliance rather than achieving compliance.

ILLUSTRATION OF A RISK-BASED APPROACH

To illustrate the coverage of a risked-based audit approach and to provide an indication of the variability that exists in the coverage of student financial aid programs across the three audit types, a description of the audit plan for the 1992 audit of financial aid programs in Texas public higher educational institutions is presented.

The audit of student financial aid programs in public colleges and universities in Texas is conducted by the Office of the State Auditor under a single audit conducted on a statewide basis (i.e., the A-128 approach). This audit covers not only the state-supported colleges and universities, but all state agencies. The objectives of the audit are an opinion on the statewide financial statements and statewide schedule of federal financial assistance, a report on internal controls, and an opinion on compliance with specific requirements applicable to each major federal financial assistance program.

In terms of the compliance objectives, 43 major federal programs must be audited; 2 student financial aid programs (Guaranteed Student Loans and Pell Grant programs) are designated as "major" programs.[15] A top-down approach is used to plan the auditing on all major programs. Under this approach, audited prior-year federal expenditures are analyzed. Then, audit work is scheduled at state entities where at least 85 percent of the respective major program expenditures occurred. However, because of the highly decentralized nature of the student financial aid programs (44 locations administer these programs), the 2 major student aid programs are audited on a three-year cycle. In each year of the cycle, an analysis of prior-year expenditures is made in order to schedule an audit for at least half of related expenditures.[16] Thus, in any given year of the cycle, approximately 43

[15] "Major" programs are determined according to size criteria in OMB Circular A-128. In the state of Texas application of the criteria, any program with federal expenditures of $20 million or greater is a major program.

[16] The "related expenditures" are the 85 percent of the total for each program. Note that for the GSL program this does not include expenditures for the Texas GSL Corporation of the State Higher Education Coordinating Board, which are audited every year because of different compliance requirements.

percent of the expenditures in the GSL and Pell Grant programs are audited. Applying these procedures for the GSL program, 23 of the 44 administrative locations are audited over the three years of the cycle, and 9 to 12 locations are audited in any given year. For the Pell Grant Programs, 20 of the 44 locations are covered over the cycle, and 9 are covered in any given year (Office of the State Auditor, 1992b).

Within each location selected, a risk-based approach is used to determine the amount of audit work to be done on each compliance requirement for major programs. This represents a departure from the "safe harbor" approach suggested by *Compliance Supplement for Single Audits of State and Local Governments* (Office of Management and Budget, 1990b); it follows instead the risk approach suggested in SAS 68 (paragraphs 63-73).[17] The model used to make this determination consists of two main components: (1) impact and (2) risk analysis of federal compliance requirements.[18] The procedures for implementing the model are as follows:

1. Determine compliance requirements.
2. Determine impact of requirements.
3. Assess inherent risk.
4. Gain an understanding of the policies and procedures of the control structure that are relevant to preventing or detecting material noncompliance.
5. Assess control risk based on preliminary understanding.
6. Determine level of compliance testing based on impact and risk (both inherent and control risk).
7. Test control structures and perform compliance testing of individual transactions.
8. Reassess level of compliance testing (i.e., determine whether an adequate level of audit evidence is obtained) and expand testing, if necessary.

In this model the auditor makes an assessment of impact (materiality) for each general and specific compliance requirement by considering (1) relative effect of the individual requirement on total program expenditures at the location, (2) significance of the individual requirement to the program's meeting its primary objective, and (3) the size of the program in absolute dollars. The three factors are scored on a nine-point scale, the scores are

[17] "Safe harbor" refers to the practice of following all requirements and procedures recommended in the OMB's compliance supplements. If all recommendations are followed, the federal agencies agree not to question the procedural aspects of the audit.

[18] The impact component is analogous to the notion of materiality in the audit of financial statements.

combined, and the aggregate score is mapped to a category of low, medium, or high impact.

Assessment of risk involves assessment of two basic components, control risk and inherent risk. Control risk is assessed based on the auditor's knowledge of the various control structures affecting each compliance requirement. Assessment of inherent risk consists of an evaluation of the individual compliance requirement on six factors:

1. Structure of transactions—number, size, and complexity of the transactions for which the compliance requirement applies.
2. Newness of the program—for example, a program that has been operating three years or longer without significant change is considered a low risk with respect to this factor.
3. Program carried out through subrecipients—the greater the percentage of expenditures carried out through subrecipients the greater the risk.
4. Program contracts for goods and services—the greater the percentage of expenditures carried out through contractors the greater the risk.
5. Program subject to federal program review—for programs that receive routine program reviews by a federal agency, the risk is low; if the program review occurs every two to three years, the risk is moderate; and the risk is high if the program has never received a program review.
6. Expectation of noncompliance—if the program has not been cited for an instance of noncompliance in previous audits, the risk is low; if material noncompliance was found in audits in the past three years, the risk is high.

The risk evaluation score on each of the six factors is combined to obtain an overall inherent-risk score. The inherent-risk score and the control-risk score are then averaged to obtain an overall risk score, which is then mapped to a category of low, moderate, and high risk.

A table is then used to map the nine possible impact/risk combinations to a level of test work for nontransaction-based requirement and sample sizes for transaction-based requirements. For example, a requirement assessed as low impact and low risk is tested with a sample size of 5 transactions; a requirement assessed as high impact and high risk is tested with a sample of 75 transactions (Office of the State Auditor, 1992a). Further, when major programs are tested at more than one location, auditors at each location make the risk assessments. They then modify the recommended sample size given by the model for the respective locations by the location's proportional share of total program expenditures.

Other Title IV programs, such as the Perkins loan and Supplemental Educational Opportunity Grants programs, are treated in the Texas single audit as nonmajor programs. For these programs the A-128 audit requires that the auditor obtain an understanding of the policies and procedures of the internal control structure that are relevant to preventing or detecting noncompliance. Specific federal compliance requirements are also tested when transactions involving these programs are selected as part of some other audit test.[19] Because of the diverse internal control structures and the large number of nonmajor federal programs in the Texas statewide audit (183 program locations), a three-year cycle is used to meet the requirements of obtaining an understanding of the internal control structure. One team of auditors is assigned to audit the nonmajor programs across all locations. This team gains an understanding of internal control structures by reviewing federal "control" questionnaires completed by selected agencies and higher educational institutions. The nonmajor audit team reviews the questionnaires for adequacy, determines if follow-up is required, and performs any additional work.

As this description of the Texas A-128 audit plan illustrates, the extent of audit coverage any location with a student financial aid program would receive varies greatly depending on the type of audit approach taken and the way in which the audit unit is defined (e.g., the GSL program in all public universities within a state versus the GSL program at a particular institution). If, for example, the state of Texas elected to exclude its institutions of higher education from the statewide audit and cover them under the A-133 or audit-guide approach, significant additional audit resources would be required because of the change in what constitutes a major program and the loss of economies of scale in moving from verifying a single set of assertions about one large population to verifying multiple assertion sets.[20] For example, under an A-133 audit, all student financial aid programs at each location would be covered, because under this approach the individual programs are combined and covered as a whole. In the A-128 audit as implemented in the state of Texas, however, even those programs considered to be major do not receive coverage in approximately 50 percent of the locations.

Such differences in coverage matter only in terms of resource requirements if one takes as the objective of the independent audit to attest to the institution's financial statement and compliance rates. However, if the objective of the independent audit is to improve compliance rates, one might

[19] These are generally only those compliance requirements related to allowability and eligibility.

[20] The reason such large economies of scale are realized by moving to assertions about a larger population is the desire to keep constant audit quality, as defined by the precision of the assertion in terms of percentage of the assertion quantity and not absolute quantities. Thus, one wants the assertion to between ±10 percent of the dollar value of the annual program expenditures rather than the assertion to be accurate with a range of ±\$20,000.

question whether the A-128 audit achieves this objective. Discussion with internal audit directors at several public universities in Texas (two at institutions selected for coverage in the statewide audit plan and one at an institution that is not covered) revealed that they regard the student financial aid programs as very high risk in their own audit plans and intend to devote considerable resources to auditing compliance despite the coverage in the statewide audit. Further, even though the Texas single audit incorporated a risk-based approach, it did so only within location. As in all three approaches, the emphasis remains on dollar coverage rather than directing resources to those areas with the weakest compliance.

ALTERNATIVES TO CURRENT APPROACHES TO AUDITING COMPLIANCE

In this section three alternative approaches to the compliance audit requirement are briefly described and the advantages and disadvantages of each are discussed. The alternatives are (1) a risk-based approach to the audit-guide, A-128, and A-133 approaches, (2) a certification model, and (3) a centralized risk-based approach.

A Risk-Based Approach to the Audit Guide, A-128, and A-133 Audits

In this alternative the current approach of combining the audit of the financial statement with the compliance audit is continued. However, the extent of compliance testing that is done for a particular compliance requirement is determined using the compliance risk model presented in SAS 68 (paragraphs 63-73). The approach used in the Texas audit plan described above is an example of this approach. Such an approach could be directly applied to the audit guide and A-133 approaches in cases in which student financial aid is considered a major program, but it does not solve the problem of the A-128 audit in allocating resources across multiple locations.

A risk-based approach can be taken even a step further, however, if one relaxes the current A-128 requirement that a "representative number" of transactions be selected from each major federal program for compliance testing. As a recent draft of a position paper by the National State Auditors Association (1992:12-13) points out:

> In complying with requirements of the Single Audit Act and Circular A-128 we have learned that many of the same federal programs are audited as major programs in all states. In addition, certain specific programs meet the requirement for classification as major within particular states year after year. These programs have been thoroughly audited, and generally

> state program staff have corrected the major problems from early audits. Thus, we are experiencing a decline in questioned or disallowed cost.

The position paper goes on to note that while major programs are given thorough and consistent audit coverage, nonmajor programs are not. In fact, there is no assurance that they will be given any audit coverage. Yet, at the same time, the nonmajor programs constitute the vast majority of federal programs in each state.

To correct this weakness, the position paper proposes a departure from the current notion of major and nonmajor federal programs. The auditor would test for material noncompliance in the full population of federal programs using a combination of stratified sampling and analytic procedures. A sample of transactions from all federal programs would be stratified so as to obtain a significant portion of the sample from the largest programs. A second group of transactions would be drawn from the smaller programs. And a third group of sample transactions would be selected from among those programs perceived by the auditor to have an unusually high risk of noncompliance. In addition, analytic procedures would be applied to the full population of federal assistance programs. These procedures might indicate areas or programs with increased or decreased levels of risk from those assumed during the planning phase of the audit.

A Certification Model

This alternative is based on the model for ensuring compliance in the European Economic Communities "Eco-audit" scheme and by internal auditors in organizations implementing total quality management programs. The approach consists of relying on those people actually involved in the process to take more responsibility for the quality assurance of the process. Critical points in the process are "audited" or certified by people who are independent of the process, but not necessarily independent of the organization. For example, in the "Eco-audit" scheme, management at each site participating in the scheme prepares an environmental statement that includes a description of significant environmental issues, a summary of the figures on pollutant emissions and the like, a presentation of the organization's environmental policies and specific objectives for the particular site, and an evaluation of the environmental performance of the protection system implemented at the site. This statement is then verified by an accredited environmental auditor (i.e., one who meets specifically outlined standards of training). This auditor can be an employee of the organization (if the organization has set up an appropriate system to give independence from the activity audited, such as an internal audit function) or external auditor (Council of the European Communities, 1992).

The important modification in this approach is that the emphasis on the "auditor" is on being qualified to conduct the audit rather than organizational independence. One of the problems frequently encountered with the independent audit of student financial aid programs is that the independent auditors do not understand the program compliance requirements or financial aid operations. By requiring more specific accreditation of the auditor, the quality of the audit process is improved. Allowing the audit to be conducted by auditors who are direct employees of the organization, yet independent of the activity, can increase the quality of the audit because the auditor has knowledge of the institution and the industry.

This type of approach is already in use at some institutions with student financial aid programs. Under the "sample certification" requirement in the Department of Education's Institutional Quality Control Pilot Project, a "third party," such as an institutional auditor external to the financial aid office, certifies that the sample has been drawn according to procedure (U.S. Department of Education, 1991:3-4 to 3-7). Extensions of this technique to other compliance areas would seem productive.

A Centralized Risk-Based Approach

Consideration should also be given to centralizing the compliance audit activity either at the federal level (in the Department of Education) or at the state level (such as with a state postsecondary review entity, as Part H of the 1992 reauthorization of the Higher Education Act proposes).[21] By centralizing the responsibility for the audit of compliance, audit resources could be targeted most effectively to those areas where audit would provide the most benefit in identifying compliance problems and proposing corrective action. Further, by including a random component in the selection of program locations for audit,[22] the benefit of increased compliance due to the anticipatory effects of audit can still be realized.

During the 1980s, organizations began to develop risk models to improve the allocation of internal audit resources across the organization. The objectives of internal audits are considerably broader than those of the financial attestation audit (i.e., audits of financial statements). They include not only reliability of information, but also efficient use of resources, effectiveness in achieving goals and objectives, safeguarding of organizational assets, and compliance with regulations and procedures. Rather than defin-

[21] The state postsecondary review as proposed in Part H of the 1992 reauthorization legislation is not intended to centralize the performance of the audits of compliance requirements but to centralize eligibility review.

[22] Here "location" means an audit unit, that is, a unit responsible for the administration of a program. There could be two or more geographical sites to a location, and there could be multiple locations at one geographical site.

ing risk in terms of the likelihood of material error in financial statements (as risk is defined in SAS 47) or of material noncompliance (as compliance risk is defined in SAS 68), risk is defined as the uncertainty or vulnerability that an event could adversely affect the organization (Institute of Internal Auditors, 1992). In terms of compliance, the goal is to identify areas of greatest exposure so that the risk of noncompliance can be minimized or managed. Thus, in the internal audit setting the focus is less on maximizing coverage than on targeting areas of greatest exposure so as to minimize risk. Such an approach is similar to that employed by the Department of Education in allocating its program review resources.

The goal of such risk models is to provide an assessment of the risk at each audit location (i.e., program administrative unit). For example, in applying this to student financial aid programs, the risk of noncompliance of each program at each administrative site would be assessed using a model such as the one developed for the Texas single audit.[23] Audit resources are then assigned to locations with the highest risk.

This procedure can also be modified to include a strategic component by stratifying the locations into risk classes. For the highest risk class, all locations are audited that year. In the next highest risk class, 60 percent are randomly selected for audit. The process continues with random selection of 15 percent in the next highest risk class and 5 percent of those in the lowest risk class.[24] Thus, coverage of a particular location is always possible, thereby providing the anticipatory effect on auditees' behavior (see Anderson and Young, 1988a; Siers and Blyskal, 1987).

CONCLUSIONS AND RECOMMENDATIONS

Study of the auditing literature, the guidance given for performing the compliance portion of the independent audit, and discussion with various individuals in the student financial aid and audit communities indicate that there is some question as to the consistency of audit coverage and the effectiveness of the compliance portion of the independent audit.

Based on the foregoing analysis, several recommendations can be made for improving the effectiveness of audits for achieving compliance.

1. Implementation of a risk-based approach to individual compliance

---

[23] Models with greater sophistication have been developed in industry, but that sophistication comes in techniques used to identify the factors to be included in the model rather than the sophistication of the procedures used by the individual auditor for assessing each factor at a location. See Siers and Blyskal (1987) for the model used by E.I. Du Pont.

[24] Coverage over time is also assured because one of the factors in most risk models is the amount of time since the last audit. Thus, even those locations initially assessed as low risk will receive coverage as the time since their last audit increases.

requirements, such as suggested in SAS 68, would improve the effectiveness and efficiency of the compliance portion of the independent audit.

2. Extension of a risk-based approach across audit locations would further improve the use of audit resources in meeting the objectives of compliance audits. To maximize the benefits of this approach, consideration might be given to centralizing the compliance audit at the state or national level.

3. Increasing use of "certification" would reduce the need for third-party audits to meet compliance objectives. Such an approach places more responsibility for quality assurance on those actually involved in the process. Critical aspects of the quality assurance program can be "certified" by people independent of the student financial aid office but not necessarily from outside the institution.

REFERENCES

American Institute of Certified Public Accountants

1983 *Audit Risk and Materiality in Conducting an Audit.* Statement on Auditing Standards No. 47. New York: American Institute of Certified Public Accountants.

1988 *Consideration of the Internal Control Structure in a Financial Statement Audit.* Statement on Auditing Standards No. 55. New York: American Institute of Certified Public Accountants.

1992a *Audits of State and Local Governmental Entities Receiving Federal Financial Assistance.* Statement of Position 92-7—Supplement of AICPA Audit and Accounting Guide, *Audits of State and Local Governmental Units.* New York: American Institute of Certified Public Accountants.

1992b *Compliance and Internal Control Reporting for Student Financial Assistance Programs Using Service Organizations.* Proposed Statement of Position—Proposed Amendment to AICPA Audit and Accounting Guide, *Audits of Colleges and Universities.* New York: American Institute of Certified Public Accountants.

1992c *Compliance Auditing Applicable to Governmental Entities and Other Recipients of Governmental Financial Assistance.* Statement on Auditing Standards No. 68. New York: American Institute of Certified Public Accountants.

Anderson, U. and R. Young

1988a Internal audit planning in an interactive environment. *Auditing: A Journal of Practice & Theory* 8(Fall):23-42.

1988b Strategic auditing: A different game. *Internal Auditing* 4(Fall):14-24.

Baron, D. and D. Besanko

1984 Regulation, Asymmetric Information, and Auditing. *Rand Journal of Economics* 15(Winter):447-470.

Council of the European Communities

1992 Eco-audit scheme. Proposal for Council Regulation (EEC). COM(91)459. *Official Journal of the European Communities* No. C 76:2-13.

Institute of Internal Auditors

1992 *Risk Assessment.* Statement on Internal Auditing Standards No. 9. Altamonte Springs, Fl.: Institute of Internal Auditors.

National State Auditors Association

1992 *Position Paper - Single Audit Act.* Draft, March 1992, National State Auditors Association, Lexington, Ky.

Office of Management and Budget

1985 *Circular A-128, Audits of State and Local Governments.* Washington, D.C.: Office of Management and Budget.

1990a *Circular A-133, Audits of Institutions of Higher Education and Other Nonprofit Institutions.* Washington, D.C.: Office of Management and Budget.

1990b *Compliance Supplement for Single Audits of State and Local Governments.* Washington, D.C.: Office of Management and Budget.

1991 *Compliance Supplement for Single Audits of Educational Institutions and Other Nonprofit Organizations.* Washington, D.C.: Office of Management and Budget.

Office of the State Auditor

1992a *Impact and Risk Analysis of Federal Compliance Requirements.* Austin, Tex.: Office of the State Auditor.

1992b *1992 Statewide Audit Plan.* Austin, Tex.: Office of the State Auditor.

President's Council on Integrity and Efficiency

1992 *Questions and Answers on OMB Circular A-133.* Statement No. 6. Standards Subcommittee. Washington, D.C.: President's Council on Integrity and Efficiency.

Siers, H. and J. Blyskal

1987 Risk management of the internal audit function. *Management Accounting* 68(February):29-35.

U.S. Department of Education

1990 *Audit Guide: Audits of Student Financial Assistance Programs.* Office of Inspector General, Office of Audit. Washington, D.C.: U.S. Department of Education.

1991 *Institutional Quality Control Workbook.* Division of Quality Assurance. Washington, D.C.: U.S. Department of Education.

APPENDIX

G

Biographical Sketches of Panel Members and Staff

BENJAMIN F. KING (*Chair*) is professor of decision sciences in the College of Business at Florida Atlantic University. Previously, he has held tenured faculty positions in the Graduate School of Business of the University of Chicago and the School of Business Administration and the Department of Statistics at the University of Washington. He was the director of survey methods at the Educational Testing Service. His research interests include survey sampling, Bayesian methods, and general applications of statistics to problems of business, public policy, and the law. He has been an associate editor of applications and of reviews for the *Journal of the American Statistical Association* and has served on two previous panels of the Committee on National Statistics. He is a fellow of the American Statistical Association and the American Association for the Advancement of Science and an elected member of the International Statistical Institute. He has A.B., M.B.A., and Ph.D. degrees from the University of Chicago.

THOMAS J. BOARDMAN is on leave from Colorado State University, where he is professor of statistics. He joined the university as an assistant professor in 1968 and served as the professor-in-charge of its statistical laboratory for over 10 years. He is co-director of its Center for Quality and Productivity Improvement. His research interests have centered around applying statistical thinking and methods to help people make better decisions. Author of more than 80 technical papers, Boardman is a fellow of both the American Society for Quality Control and the American Statistical Association. In addition, he is an elected member of the International

Statistical Institute. He currently serves on the board of directors of the American Statistical Association. He was a reviewer for the Baldrige National Quality Award, the U.S. counterpart of Japan's Deming Prize. He is a member of a task force appointed by the governor of Colorado to create a Colorado Quality Award. With Eileen Boardman, he is the author of the *Workbook for Quality Improvement and Statistical Thinking* and several other publications designed to be helpful to quality improvement teams. Boardman holds Ph.D. and M.S. degrees in statistics from Rutgers University and a B.A. in mathematics from Bucknell University.

*JERRY S. DAVIS is vice president for research and policy analysis of the Pennsylvania Higher Education Assistance Agency, a post he has held since 1981. He has an Ed.D. in higher education from the University of Georgia. Davis has been doing research on student financial aid and related topics since 1968 and has published extensively from positions with the College Board, the Southern Regional Education Board, Brookdale Associates, the National Task Force on Student Aid Problems (the Keppel Commission), and other organizations. Since 1981, he has written the report on an annual survey of state financial aid policies and practices for the National Association of State Scholarship and Grant Programs. He currently chairs its research committee and has chaired similar committees for the National Council on Higher Education Loan Programs and the National Association of Student Financial Aid Administrators.

RONALD S. FECSO serves as study director of the Panel on Quality Improvement in Student Financial Aid Programs. He received a B.A. in mathematics from Rider College and an M.A. in mathematical statistics from the University of Rochester. He serves at the National Research Council through an Intergovernmental Personnel Act assignment from his position as senior research statistician at the National Agricultural Statistics Service of the U.S. Department of Agriculture. Survey design and research and the development of quality improvement methodology are his major research interests. He enjoys teaching and serves on advisory committees for several higher education institutions. Currently he is the program chair elect for the Section on Survey Research Methods of the American Statistical Association and chair of the Quantitative Literacy Group and member of the organizing committee of the annual Quality Assurance in the Government Symposium of the Washington Statistical Society.

NATALA K. HART is director of the Office of Scholarships and Financial Aid at Indiana University-Purdue University at Indianapolis. Previously,

* Served until May 1992

she was executive director of the State Student Assistance Commission of Indiana (1989-91); director of the division of financial aid at Purdue University (1985-89); and vice president for student assistance services of the College Board (1982-85). She worked at the College Scholarship Service from 1978 through 1981. She has B.A. and M.Ed. degrees from Ohio University. Hart has been coordinator of a statewide effort since 1990 to encourage access to higher education for disadvantaged students through the College Goal Sunday project. She is currently a member of the Student Loan Marketing Association Student Financial Aid Administrators Advisory Panel and sits on the selection committee for Coca-Cola Scholars. She served as governmental affairs commissioner for the National Association of Student Financial Aid Administrators in 1990-91 and on the board of directors of the National Association of Higher Education Loan Programs in 1989-91. She has been the recipient of a number of awards, among them the President's Award (1985) and the Committee of the Year Award (1989, 1991) of the National Association of Student Financial Aid Administrators, and the Distinguished Service Award from the Indiana Student Financial Aid Administrators (1989).

WILLIAM J. HILL is director of research and technology at Allied-Signal, Buffalo, New York. He is the research and technology quality officer. He is on Allied-Signal's Corporate Quality Council. During 1991-92, he was the first Emerson Professor of Quality and Productivity Improvement at the University of Wisconsin-Madison and the director of its Center for Quality and Productivity Improvement. He is a past recipient of the organization's Shewhart Medal (1990) and the inaugural William G. Hunter award for his contributions to quality technology and its transfer into practice. He is a fellow of the American Statistical Association and the American Association for the Advancement of Science. He received a B.S.E. in chemical engineering from Princeton University and a Ph.D. in statistics from the University of Wisconsin-Madison.

LINDA INGRAM is a research associate with the Committee on National Statistics. She received her M.A. from the University of Maryland and has done doctoral work at American University in political science. She has worked on several projects of the Committee on National Statistics in such areas as poverty, disability, and the census.

SUBRAMANYAM KASALA (Consultant) is associate professor of statistics at the University of North Carolina at Wilmington. He received B.S. and M.S. degrees in statistics from S.V. University, Tirupati, India, and a Ph.D in statistics from the Indian Statistical Institute, Calcutta, India. He previously taught at the University of Pittsburgh. His research interests have centered on asymptotic theory, multivariate analysis, nonlinear time series analysis, and multivariate calibration theory.

FREDRICA D. KRAMER (Consultant) is a consultant in social welfare policy in Washington, D.C., and works generally with government, public policy, and research institutes. She served as the study director of the National Research Council's Panel on Quality Control of Family Assistance Programs. She has served as staff and consultant to the Research Council on a range of issues, including persistent poverty, children at risk, deregulation, and law enforcement and criminal justice. She received a B.A. in political science from the University of California at Berkeley, an M.U.P from Hunter College, City University of New York, and an M.P.A. from the University of Southern California. She also has completed all but the dissertation in public administration from the University of Southern California. She has worked in social welfare policy in state, local, and federal governments and in Congress, specializing in welfare and employment policy, service delivery and service integration issues, and persistent poverty.

GARY A. LORDEN is professor of mathematics and vice president for student affairs at the California Institute of Technology. He received a B.S. from Cal Tech and a Ph.D. in mathematics from Cornell University. Previously he taught at Northwestern University and, as visiting professor of statistics, at the University of California, Berkeley. His research interests are in statistics and probability, especially sequential analysis, multistage testing, and decision theory. He is a fellow of the Institute for Mathematical Statistics.

REBECCA A. MAYNARD is trustee professor of education and policy at the University of Pennsylvania. She has a Ph.D. in economics from the University of Wisconsin. Her current research includes two major federally sponsored demonstration programs aimed at preparing youth for the work force in 2000: the National Dropout Demonstration Assistance Programs, sponsored by the U.S. Department of Education, and a Demonstration of Innovative Services for Teenage Parents sponsored by the U.S. Department of Health and Human Services. Previous research has included evaluations of major social welfare demonstrations and field experiments, including supported work programs for welfare mothers, income maintenance programs for low-income families, and employment-training programs for poor adults. Among her early research was a pathbreaking study of the effects of income on the school performance and educational achievement of children in low-income families. More recently she has conducted methodological research on use of experimental and nonexperimental study designs as well as demonstration and policy research on children's issues. Formerly, she was senior vice president of Mathematica Policy Research, Inc., and directed the research activities in its Princeton office. She has served on numerous national advisory panels, including the National Research Council's Panel on Child Care Policy.

ROBERT E. PARILLA has been president of Montgomery Community College in Rockville, Maryland, since 1979. Previously he taught chemistry and served as dean and college vice president with Cuyahoga Community College. His degrees have been awarded from Kent State University, the University of New Hampshire, and Florida State University. He is a member of the National Advisory Committee for the Education and Human Resources Directorate of the National Science Foundation. He is a commissioner with the Commission on Higher Education of the Middle States Association of Colleges and Schools and a board member and treasurer of the Council on Postsecondary Accreditation. He was a member of the Committee to Study the Role of Allied Health Personnel of the Institute of Medicine and the Committee on Mandatory Retirement in Higher Education of the National Research Council.

THOMAS D. PARKER is senior vice president for finance and administration at The Education Resources Institute, a private not-for-profit corporation in Boston, bringing financial institutions and educators together to assist students and parents nationwide in financing education. He has written and consulted widely on education administration and finance issues, on philanthropy, and on issues of access to higher education; he teaches the history of higher education and higher education administration at Boston University. He has worked as an administrator at Harvard University and Bennington College. He served in the Office of the Secretary of the U.S. Department of Education, at the National Endowment for the Humanities, and at the Fund for the Improvement of Postsecondary Education. He has an A.B. degree (magna cum laude) from Harvard College and an M.A. in teaching and an Ed.D. from the Harvard Graduate School of Education.

S. JAMES PRESS is professor of statistics at the University of California, Riverside, and was chair of the Department of Statistics from 1977 to 1984. He received a B.A. from New York University, an M.S. from the University of Southern California, and a Ph.D. in statistics from Stanford University. He previously taught at the University of Chicago, the University of British Columbia, the University of California, Los Angeles, and Yale University. His research interests have centered on multivariate statistical analysis, Bayesian statistics, econometrics, and applications of statistics to the physical and social sciences. He is a fellow of the Institute of Mathematical Statistics, the American Statistical Association, the Royal Statistical Society, and the

American Association for the Advancement of Science. He is a member of the International Statistical Institute, the Bernoulli Society, and the New York Academy of Sciences. He was a member of the Committee on National Statistics of the National Research Council for six years and has served on several other panels of the National Research Council.

BRIAN ROWAN is associate professor of education at the University of Michigan. He received a B.A. in sociology from Rutgers University and a Ph.D. in sociology from Stanford University. He was previously senior research director at Far West Laboratory for Educational Research and Development and chair of the Department of Educational Administration at Michigan State University. His research focuses on issues related to school organization and effectiveness, education policy, and applied social research. He is a member of the U.S. Department of Education's Program Effectiveness Panel, serves on the editorial boards of the *American Educational Research Journal*, *Educational Administration Quarterly*, and *Educational Evaluation and Policy Analysis* and is a frequent consultant to educational research and development organizations.

JUDITH M. TANUR is professor in the Department of Sociology of the State University of New York at Stony Brook. She received a B.S. in psychology and an M.A. in mathematical statistics from Columbia University and a Ph.D. in sociology from SUNY at Stony Brook. She is a fellow of the American Statistical Association and the American Association for the Advancement of Science and an elected member of the International Statistical Institute. She edited the *International Encyclopedia of Statistics*, *Statistics: A Guide to the Unknown*, and *Questions about Questions: Inquiries Into the Cognitive Bases of Surveys*. She was previously a member of the Committee on National Statistics of the National Research Council, serving on its Panels on Statistics for Family Assistance Programs and on Quality Control for Family Assistance Programs and chairing its Advanced Research Seminar on Cognitive Aspects of Survey Methodology. She was cochair of the Social Science Research Council's Committee on Cognition and Survey Research and book review editor of the *Journal of the American Statistical Association*. She has been an American Statistical Association/National Science Foundation/Bureau of Labor Statistics senior research fellow and currently serves as a co-editor of *Chance*.

SHARON L. THOMAS PARROTT is vice president for governmental relations at DeVRY Inc. in Oakbrook Terrace, Illinois. DeVRY Inc. is a North American degree-granting higher education system funded with private investment capital. Thomas Parrott received B.A. and M.A. degrees in history from the University of Illinois. She previously held faculty and administrative positions at George Williams College in Illinois. She also served with the U.S. Department of Education in the student aid area. She has served in numerous elected and appointed positions with the National Association of Student Financial Aid Administrators including two terms as a member of the board of directors. She is currently serving as vice president of the College Board/College Scholarship Service Committee on Standards of Ability to Pay.

MARGARET WEIDENHAMER (Consultant) is a consultant based in Arlington, Virginia. She majored in social psychology as an undergraduate and graduate student at the University of Maryland. While a federal government employee conducting a wide variety of surveys and providing technical advice on other agency projects, she had extensive experience in designing, testing, and evaluating data collection forms.